OTHER WORKS BY JANE AUGUSTINE

Editions, with introductions and annotations:

The Gift by H.D. : The Complete Text
The Mystery by H.D.

Poetry:

A Woman's Guide to Mountain Climbing
Arbor Vitae
Transitory
Night Lights
Krazy
High Desert

Chapbooks:

Lit by the Earth's Dark Blood (fine art edition)
Journeys
French Windows

Thomas Augustine Morley: *Untitled (Pharaoh's Dance),* 2019

TRAVERSE

TRAVERSE

Collected Poems 1969 to 2019

JANE AUGUSTINE

DOS MADRES

2021

DOS MADRES PRESS INC.
P.O. Box 294, Loveland, Ohio 45140
www.dosmadres.com editor@dosmadres.com

Dos Madres is dedicated to the belief that the small press is essential to the vitality of contemporary literature as a carrier of the new voice, as well as the older, sometimes forgotten voices of the past. And in an ever more virtual world, to the creation of fine books pleasing to the eye and hand.

Dos Madres is named in honor of Vera Murphy and Libbie Hughes, the "Dos Madres" whose contributions have made this press possible.

Dos Madres Press, Inc. is an Ohio Not For Profit Corporation and a 501 (c) (3) qualified public charity. Contributions are tax deductible.

Executive Editor: Robert J. Murphy

Illustration & Book Design: Elizabeth H. Murphy
www.illusionstudios.net

Typeset in Adobe Garamond Pro & Warnock Pro
ISBN 978-1-953252-01-2
Library of Congress Control Number: 2021938117

First Edition

Published by Dos Madres Press, Inc.

ACKNOWLEDGEMENTS

My deep thanks go to the original publishers of the volumes in this collection:

— to Marsh Hawk Press. its editors, designers and poets, for *A Woman's Guide to Mountain Climbing, Arbor Vitae, Night Lights* and *Krazy: Visual Poems and Performance Scripts;*

— to Spuyten Duyvil, editor/publisher Tod Thilleman, for *Transitory: A Poem Sequence;*

— to Dos Madres Press, editor Robert Murphy and designer Elizabeth Murphy, for *High Desert.*

— "Reunion," "Downsizing" and "Return" were originally published in *Reunion Poems*, a collection edited by Joanna Semel Rose, Bryn Mawr class of 1952, created as a gift to the class for its 65th reunion. My special thanks go to her for long friendship and encouragement, and for her generous overall support of contemporary literature.

— My gratitude also goes to the British painter Dame Paula Rego for the creative inspiration of her life, work and friendship.

— Deep ongoing thanks to Elizaeth Murphy for her design skills and solutions to the problems presented by this collection.

— Cover Painting by Thomas Augustine Morley: *Untitled (Pharaoh's Dance),* 2019

— Author photo by Star Black © 2021

In memory of my parents,
Marguerite and Waldemar Augustine

and

for my children and grandchildren,
Meg, Tom, Jeff and Pat Morley,

Felix and Daniel Grèzes,
Anthony, Diego, Philip, Leah and Ellen Morley,

my brother Rolf Augustine,
and the extended family, past, present, and future

and

for M.D.H.

as always

Traverse:

mountaineering: the act of traversing or making one's way across the face of a mountain or rock; also concr., a place where a traverse is made;

nautical usage: the zigzag track of a vessel sailing against the wind; each of the runs made by a ship in tacking is called a traverse.

—*Shorter OED, 2236*

The path is the goal and the goal is the path.

—*old saying in Vajrayana Buddhism*

TABLE OF CONTENTS

A WOMAN'S GUIDE TO MOUNTAIN CLIMBING

(2008)

poems of the 1970s

ARBOR VITAE

(2002)

IV: French Windows

V: On New York Time

TRANSITORY

(2002)

poetic sequence from a 1991 journal

I. At First

II. War

NIGHT LIGHTS

(2004)

V. Cities

KRAZY: VISUAL POEMS & PERFORMANCE SCRIPTS

(2015)

I. FORM/inForm

V. OR, a Poem of Choice

HIGH DESERT

(2019)

Prologue

I. High Desert

TRAVERSE

COLLECTED POEMS
1969 TO 2019

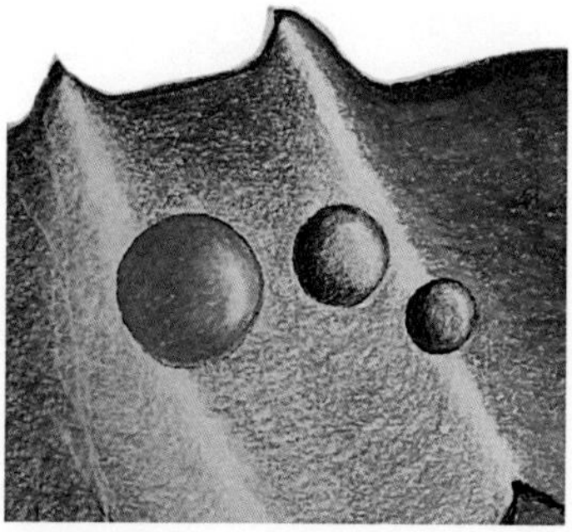

A WOMAN'S GUIDE TO MOUNTAIN CLIMBING

The high peak at night holds back the sun,
The deep vales are never bright by day.
Natural for mountain people to grow straight:
Where paths are steep, the mind levels.

—Meng Chiao (751-841)
Wandering on Mount Chung-nan
tr. A.C Graham

Part One

JOURNEY

The Passes: Hardscrabble, Independence

Pass: a way or opening by which one passes through a region otherwise obstructed or impassible, especially a narrow and difficult or dangerous passage through a mountainous region or over a mountain range.

— *Compact OED, II.* 2089

(i)

Beginnings
can't be seen
until an ending.

On the road out of town
bleak prairie blanches to dirt
split by arroyos—here the Arapahoe

drove back the Utes into Hardscrabble Pass,
road rising so slowly one doesn't
notice then steep narrow

tree-clotted, the sun cut off
by the overhang of Suicide Spire
named for a pair of teenaged lovers

—old tales perhaps have lost their power—

from Hardscrabble
first sight of the mountains:
snow-summits blur into cloud.

(ii)

Independence Pass closed in winter,
        but this is late spring—
                snow up higher maybe—

but risk the turnoff.
        Brute tractors
                swarm over mud-mountains   gears

clash   earth's gashed, mauled into
        a dam, power for the Arkansas
                Fryingpan. A lake's displaced.

        I detour round its draining.

(iii)

Independence Pass open in summer—
        snow plows have just broken through—

colder than I've ever been, and clear
        Free I say   not to need

        or be familial, generous.

A brink.

No end to wind's buffeting.

(iv)

Down the Divide by dark:
        waters of the Roaring Fork
                plunge downward with me

run both ways, some back
        to the Diversion Tunnel
                and the Fryingpan, some west

I don't know which:
        by moonlight pass the blackened
                bones of roofless shacks

where a deluded few still come
        gold-hunting—

Independence: a ghost town.

(v)
in eclipse

Lost Man Campground:
green firewood burns smoky and goes out.

The waning moon's malformed; darkness bites
into her left side. On rough grass at meadow's edge

I try to sleep. The larches rustle.
An anchorite might wake at 2 a.m. to say

an office, but I've no rule of life. Committed
by default to night and cold, my wakefulness

is mere disease. This road's not on the map
of "the highest state." The moon's a mirror

hung with a sable veil.
Someone is mourned. In darkness

something seems to bend over me,
a branch perhaps that dips and breathes

(amorphous as remembering,
which the self-exiled must not)—a warm breath...

shock then   that it grows solid,
a human head, gross body, some other camper

stumbling in wilderness,
some clumsy drunk who'll clutch at anything.

My suffering double begs my bed.
Why not, I think. The sky's a stranger too,

who's snuffed her lamp. I'm free

(vi)

I knew a woman, a Jew and refugee,
who until the war's end hid
in a Bavarian cave,

subsisted on roots and berries, then
married an angry man, but rich. She lived
better in America.

Here's hermitage – a cabin at road's end,
once ours, abandoned in midwinter
so the plumbing's shattered.

The solitary has to hike to the outhouse,
haul buckets from the pump—
a clean start over.

Mountain passes   not peaks
but straits   limiting, hard to get through.
Hard is what makes it possible.

One enters another country under
moon and sun, eyes of the world
that never close. Resources here:

the well goes down a hundred feet, powerline's
connected, stove takes wood.
Snow falls for three days, covers all.

The mind snowed in   not free
yet not in a prison camp
rests in its meditative cave.

Nothing is lost.

I don't know the end of that woman's
story, heard she'd become depressed
and left him.

Refuge is journey

—so to begin

Toward Break of Night, a Dream

The song was used for curing, and was given to the poet (Owl Woman, called Juana Manwell)...'
—*Technicians of the Sacred*

(i)

Fog. A man on the dock. Creak of hawsers. Spray
at the porthole a mouth twisted against glass
and falling away
 The stateroom door unfastens each time the deck
tips too steeply. I fasten it again and again.

(ii)

Airfield. Stumbling in shiny shocking-pink heels,
I run cross-country to catch the Alaska jet, taxiing
for takeoff
 The pilot opens the cockpit for me, but my leather
coat is missing and no mastercard to charge a new one.

(iii)

The full moon crashes toward me, a stone-shod brewery
horse to roll my skull over in the furrows. Because
I lost the saddlebags
 I fall under his hooves. My father's low wall and
my mother's pear trees do nothing to stop him.

(iv)

He stands among oleanders with a revolver. Weeping
I pick up my infant son unconscious and carry him in among
jukeboxes and whisky.
    The pay phone dial sticks. The line is dead.
I scream and scream. Men at the bar turn and stare.

(v)

and wake outside the house while inside shadows still
brush the curtains. Unarmed, must I move only to cold
country?

> *Owl woman, see for me in the dark what I hold and release.*
> *Free me to live by the body's sources.*

A Woman's Guide to Mountain Climbing

nine steps to start with

I. Gear

A woman can carry
on her back
everything needed to survive—

    tent, sweater, sleeping bag
    canteen, fly-rod, cheese
    cookpot, poncho, map
    tampons, bowie knife
    and book of stars

can't climb
without these essentials

almost can't climb
with them

II. Rationale

If someone asks
    why you're climbing
    say
    you have the moon
    in mind

    each night
    she meets
    these barrier peaks
    with her eye
    more fully open

and undersea
clenched in the shell's night
the pearl persists
in shaping her moon
around

a central irritant

III. Method

Must
start
slow   to stay strong

past the first switch-
back   take abnormally short steps
boot-toe to heel   no more lift

than barely clears the ground   hunch
forward to ease the pack-strain
of lone effort
watch

don't step onto any root or stone
that you can step around
a stubbed toe dislocates the whole

backbone   don't stop to rest—
to start again is harder
just

keep moving by
almost not
moving   but

don't resist:

no choice of method
nor to improvise   the path's external, practical
thus discover, not invent

technique is all:
less why than how
you climb

up   out   beyond tree-line
and the last wind-twisted cypress
past trail's end in scree and talus

to confront the mountain:
nothing

but rock:
earth's scooped-out skull   its juts
and fractures sharpened

in the over-bright and nearly non-sustaining air

IV Digression on Trail-bikers

Revving motors outroar the waterfall.
Trail-bikers in plastic bubble helmets

leap over the rise. Their goggles
protect them from the dangerous green

of aspen and alpine fir. They're teaching
their sons how to smash through underbrush

and wipe out silence. But now what
unnatural sight confronts them? A woman

carrying her misshapen world on her back.
They flex their nail-head gloves, pretend

to smile, say "You've got a long
walk ahead of you." She says "Longer than

you think: over the peak. Can't get there
except on foot. Takes days." They look

blankly at her madness, voom and leap away.
Of course there's nothing—is there?—

that those engines between their thighs
can't climb to and back from in half an hour

V. Continuing

Too far above trees. Too far above
    the last campsite. Nothing but steepness.
        No firewood, no wind-shelter.

The ridge hides the peak. Must rest
    every ten steps, fall to elbows and knees
        under the minimum needed to survive.

Only the smallest plants live here—
    too little air. My eye tries
        to magnify them, tiny bright blue hopes.

Lungs rasp. Shoulders collect knives.
    Not strong enough to go on.
        but what to do

    when it's as hard to climb down
    as up? Shove off the pack a while.
        Lie flat. Try to sleep. The moon

also sleeps at times. Hides out.
    Then begins to climb again, the night
        strapped to her spine. Climbs and keeps

        climbing

VI. On the Ridge

12,800 feet in the Sangre de Cristo mountains

At sunset your pumping heart
brings you to the ridge:

the point where you can
at least stand up

the mountain that threatened to fall
on you now under foot

the boot's fulcrum no razor's edge
but street-wide

paved with saxifrage whose threads
sunder the granite:

Standing you look west   down
to where night already gathers

in an unknown basin deep
among unnamed peaks

at eye-level still lit
by flaming day   more deserted

strange and lovely than the way
you came by:

Deer have carved a trail
to a glacial pool

where you follow   make camp
provisional facing moonrise

rest up for the next
riskier   more solitary climb

VII. Visitation

the moon in Sagittarius

Sleeping, tent-flap half-open,
moon on my forehead

a woman shrieks far away
and again—wildcat waking me.

Night breeds
creatures to encircle me.

I came from known dangers
into these:

ground tremor reaches me
before the sound

of hooves on rock
breath in frenzy, snorting

pawing outside
the tent's back corner—

I'm in his path—
too terrified to rise,

face what I fear—
shapeless threat, a beast

ruler of this place
where I'm intruder—

face old fears that grow
of violence, injury

who'll care for me?
how shall I get well?

Helplessness holds me
tight under cover.

When a bear attacks they say
play dead.

I hide until that animal rage
baffled moves off through the willows

and come awake fully then,
slowly regret the chance lost

to stand up living eye to eye
find it after all merely

a white-tailed deer
also terrified.

> *Here in the courtyard of the moon*
> *why did I fail to trust her?*

I push back the tent-flap
climb out:

There she rides
high on the mountain's saddle

helmeted, bow drawn
and quiver full of stars

VIII. Carrying One's Weight

(i)

Impossible
to carry a backpack
equal to one's body weight:

a woman should not carry
more than one-fifth
of what she weighs   a man one-third

I've put aside
the lady's light pack-frame
and silky nylon bag   choose a heftier

man's size with tough rucksack and shelf-bar
sling a walking stick under it
to lift this excessive

33 pounds to my 117

(ii)

Carrying one's weight:
not dumping shit, tears, chores, claims
on others:

nor foot-dragging—as if you imagined, sir,
your pith helmet guarantees you
a native carrier

(iii)

A woman often carries more
than her own weight—
the child's too

in the pit of her stomach
and balanced heavily upon
her watchful head: a long safari—

and think of those men who carry none
of their own weight,
who float asleep on the inner springs

of their mothers' curls,
whose bathtubs' crows-feet
are their secretaries' hands and knees,

that gray elephant of women's service
bearing up the weight
of the blue-jeweled globe

(iv)

Impossible to carry
all one's weight

    impossible to justify this life,
    earth I stand on, air I breathe
    clear water plunging
    of its own weight
    into my cup.

I can't carry much—
a full canteen's too heavy—
but a spring-fed stream in every canyon
meets my thirst

what is given   not solely limitation
but abundance:
more gifts than we can drink in.

Under these stony peaks
reservoirs go on collecting,
burst out most brightly
from the narrowest fissures

(v)

Rock under my foot
takes on that 33-pound pack
till my legs are extruded granite

I no longer carry this load
but the rock—
pillars that pass downward
inward through the earth's caves and rivers
to the molten center.

Now it is fire
that effortlessly bears the burden

(vi)

More technical advice:

in packing your knapsack
place the heaviest items on top.

Shoulder these, keep them
uppermost in your mind,

knottiest problems
where your greatest strength is.

Buckle the frame's web-strap
across your pelvis—
weight shifts to that point

but every woman knows this

(vii)

Burden of the body:
because of it
loitering street bums
hiss out their hatred

I am my body.
Impossible to say:
it is what
they hate

I am who they hate:
being alone
"resolved to call
no man master"

burden of the body's history:
    the man's blundering entry
    the birth-tearing
    submitted to

as if owed, and not a gift given.

I carry this weight
    whether I want to or not
    naked into the arms
    of my lover

who trembles the deeper he enters.

    He learns my body's power.
    It is not his.
    He cannot touch it.

I carry my self
    alone all night
    up a steep trail

among rocks
    the lair of the rattlesnake
    and the mauling bear

I carry my weight

    beyond delusions of support.
        No one else
        can smooth my path
        or clothe me in smiling weather.

No moon:
the air is cold.

The lean cheekbone meets it

IX. Mountain Death-Camas

hiking the Phantom Terrace trail

(i)

In marshy shade
masses of ivory bells

splinters of the moon
around a gold star-center

root, stem, leaf, flower
all fatal

(ii)

in sun mirrored
off a glacial lake

a young man

sleeps on grass
hair moon-pale

unprotected face
reddening to purple

I should wake him

warn against the sun—
at these cool heights

we forget
it burns

(iii)

Not my problem,
this man who doesn't
know the mountains.

He's brought a ten-speed bike
new, emerald and chrome
to 12,000 feet—

must have had to carry
what was meant
to carry him.

Bright technological sun
unquestioned,
we never look at you.

We say we see
by you
even when blinded

(iv)

Warrior sun—the winner!

cannon to blast the moon
out of the sky.

I protect myself

with hat, dark glasses,
long-sleeved shirt

rely on feet

to carry me past
the camas-laden meadow

and the sleeper

past tree-line
where the path disappears.

Rocks only now

and boots resisting

(v)

I walk into the moon's country.
Her fullness rises,
a cooled and softened sun.

Both eyes of the sky
have cleared, strip
down to essential body,

lose the flesh of thought.

My white bones float
out to meet that naked source

by which I see both dark and light,
            wildflower both beautiful
and lethal—
                        no illusion
therefore no consolation

(vi)

Daylight:

down again to the clouded lake,
the meadow ambiguously starry

to hear he'd killed himself
—the youth with moon-pale hair—

and boy scouts found
beside his shattered skull

a pistol new and silver
as his ten-speed racer.

Ah—

                        inexplicable loss, that life
consumed by its own terror

not mine.
    I have three sons

one dark, two fair

who ask which boots are best,

which pack-frame lifts the load.

They also need my words,
can only hear

their own

(vii)

Cortège of motorcycles
bears away
the messy body-remnant

leaving tire-tracks
in the crushed camas.

The web of death
hangs everywhere
not mine to weave

or to untangle.
In it that pale hair

is twined with mine.
Choiceless I choose
the moon

as two in one.
And deeper shadows form

under the edge illumined.

Climbing Uncompaghre

13,000 feet in the San Juan
Mountains with Patrick, age 15

A side trail down
as if to water
but the creek is dry—

no path beyond: we think
we'll find it later,
come instead to bones

a deer's bleached ribcage.
A sad place, my son says.
Bare rock-cliff facing us

we've missed our way:
we backtrack, climb
the ridge and see our path again

stamped into deep grasses.

Not our last sadness:
the winter I left, he came
to visit, wrote on my tenement desk

"I cried for my mom and me."
We ate Christmas dinner on the floor;
we had no table.

Now in our summer hiking
still we carry loads
on our backs, and trail-food.

My son says, look at the stream
running from the peak
and I say where? where?

He says, we'll make it.
Above, a thin scar of path
crosses the mountain's shoulder

to the base
of that gray rock-tower
where the last scaling starts.

Correspondences

September in the Colorado Rockies

When red stars glow ruddier—Antares a ruby

in the scorpion's armor, Arcturus a copper eye—

look along the ground for crimson leaves replying:

five-pointed wild geranium, grape holly, strawberry

leaf fruit and tendril. Look at your own hands

chapped in the first frost, and the campfire dying.

Rosita Cemetery

(i)

Graveyards
are stiller
than other hillsides

They hold
nothing
but the attempt to hold

Plastic wreaths
are sadder
in their lasting

than an obelisk
with a name.

(ii)

In stillness here
vitality

out of hard ground:
the mind leaps

invents these dead
as if their histories

seethe on
hidden under gravestones:

wind always stirs
this plot of pines

beyond them
walls of heat immobile,

boulder
in a dry creek-bed.

Even in that fixity
a lizard

darts into shadow.

Gentians

near the Sangre de Cristos,
after the accidental death
of Robert Secora, 17

A purple gash
in the oat-fields' wide green
spread out below still-snowy mountains—

Barbed wire blocks us:
gingerly I lower it
for the ranch foreman's wife to step over.

We wade across
to gaze down into the fringed cups
lit, it seems, by the earth's dark blood.

She tells me how
they had to send away the homeless boy
who later fell under the blade at Canda's sawmill—

the ranch's owner
wouldn't take him in
so how could they?   She says

"Did you ever see
so many gentians? I used to find just one
or two. We might as well pick plenty—

tomorrow they cut
these oats—see, the kernel's
just coming out of the splitting pod—"

Fireweed

In the charred clearing
fireweed

which won't seed
in undamaged turf

proliferates.

Pinkish-purple tongues
of flame leap into the air

where one midsummer night
the campground dump burned,

its glow the only light
on the mountain.

We rode up by jeep,
kept watch a long time

lest the blaze take
the whole forest—

covertly pleased by
danger and the finality

of that consumption.

Locoweed

When cattle eat it
they go mad and die—but we

find it *mille fleurs* in a meadow,
spikes of streaked white-lavender

or shading blue to purple,
tall candles in the grass

we gather by the armload
lovely as the mountain air

that also shades from blue
to purple, clouds in it mauve-white

scudding and billowing—
great space in motion,

dome of high lucidity
calm in its lunatic hues

over us. And beside us
locoweed stabs and glows

in a blue bowl on the windowsill.

Western Gothic Romantic Classic

Moonlight slips a white knife-blade
inside the tepee door.

The ground is hard and the man
whose lean hipbones hook with hers

is a stranger—mountain climber
he said, first ascent in the Andes,

cited *Jefe* he said, Peace Corps, strumming
guitar by the campfire where she stumbled in

after a lonely hitch in the badlands
and the black hills. She's thirsty.

Who asks where water comes from
after a long drought? She drinks all night

from his fountain and he from hers.
He ropes her to his piton and she falls free.

At 3 a.m. she dreams him as Orion
climbing the eastern sky with a sword of stars.

At dawn they wake and laugh; they're caked
with dirt they beat out of the old sleeping bag.

He asks her to stay, to ride and climb
with him, and she says yes.

Through desert sage and rock they walk
back to the ranch house. Dry country.

Rattlesnakes, she thinks. One thin trickle
piped into the horse corral.

Inside after stark sunlight
it's hard to see—

cougar and bearskin on the bed,
.44 magnum and ammunition belt

slung on the bedpost.
From a photo he is smiling

leaning on a rifle
wearing a green beret.

At Mid-month

Ripening in my darkness
every month

not a red moon to reduce me
to useful function

nor a wound to stopper
with bandages

—I say a woman is not a myth
not an emergency ward

not an empty cup to be filled
blest—

it thickens   one silk layer quilted
over another

a fine soft place   our warmth
the child-bed

every man wants to be brought to.
But you know

ripeness is not all   is stasis
binds

bursts   unable to ask
the next question:

time then to undo
throw away

bits of string   clips   bands
the lump of petrified wood

in the desk drawer   everything
we save

thinking someday it may save us,
slough off

with only a slight pang
all those prized sentiments

and start over. I'm glad to move
into another house

            carpeting   curtaining   —a chance
to "make it new."

Just as glad to say goodbye
to a lover,

pack a knapsack, move on

So at mid-month I pitch my tent
in a deep valley,

listen to its rivers
underground:

new blood rising
to feed

to shed.

After Yeats

(i)

Take care, he said, your poems are almost
too beautiful (he who often makes too much
of her "beauty"). Under lovely images pain is lost
or blunted—do you want that, he asked.
                                        She's tough,
she thinks, and unromantic, sworn to accost
her self-deception, but is re-reading Yeats and loves
his elegance. She wants to bypass pain and sing
a desert world in music golden and piercing.

(ii)

Under noon sun someone rides a white mare
down from the mountains, through boulders and pine.
She's wearing jeans and a green halter, with bare
brown back and shoulders, midriff lean
from pitching hay. Her hat falls back and frees her hair.
Her lover, who's dismounted, watches her. Two men
walk to her stirrup, offer up a coffee-can
of wild raspberries. She scoops a handful,

raises it red and dripping till the juice
runs down her arm. Slowly she licks
the fruit-blood off her skin. Her hair blows into
her mouth. Red smears her lips.
Throned in the saddle she sits sensuously
eating, and the men look down, abashed by this.
The horse stands and shakes the loose reins
while rubies splash onto her snowy mane.

A Bracelet of Turquoise from Aguilar

On my arm, three small oceans
anchored on two silver equators,

their green-blue brilliant as mountain noon,
ecstatic hue, the shimmer of a glacial lake

two thousand feet below the climber
who walks the highest ledge over sheer drop

not perfectly steady but facing
both heights and depths, luminous herself

in that blue luminosity.

Turquoise from Aguilar contains black matrix.
A heavy continent upthrust blots out the blue,

outlines it.
                I walk, in a nightmare, a tunnel
or half-blind street, searching how to

"clean up my act." A woman friend is angry:
you were rude, you were reading when you should

have been watching the actors—her eyes
are light blue.
                I wake to strange knowledge.

In waking life she likes me, especially for
not hiding how I build myself up, how I strive

for those heights and expansions. In this waking
the man who loves me holds me in his arms.

That dark weight I call my "self" heaves up
rough-edged into turquoise air, the opening day.

The dream-self fades, the day-self won't resume,
too tentative, yet both are lingering—

On my arm, the weight of this rock: blue
waters, black islands sand-polished to luster,

poise in the grip of bright metal that's hammered
and beaten and molded.
                                        The sky

opens endlessly outward but never
fails to encircle the planet.

Part Two

ON LOSS

Anti-Cycle for the New Year

(i)

Dark days,
  thin snow on the roofs.

Graying, he described me.

    Too long a mother:

      no cycle
of return to
  before that.

(ii)

Light snow on the airfield
  —take it lightly.

The great engines grind,

  lift my sons off
    our common ground

  in a long curve
      opening.

(iii)

Poets praise motherhood
  especially
  if they are fathers

and move on to
less burdened women.

No new start for me,
only the old

effort to juggle loss
against
the continual gift

wrapped in tissue
that gets thrown away

(iv)

I strip the tree whose little lights
the shivering tinsel multiplied—
hopes, joys—

When I was a child I thought I'd die
after Christmas. I thought rightly:
nothing ahead but comedown.

I lit a tree for my sons, who fly
east, who will wing back my way,
but it's not my symbol,

this cut convention drying in a corner,
seduction clung to—
now I lean
towards plain day. I stand

at its uncurtained window.

(v)

Pity these cycles
beginning again:

the woman betrayed by lovers
will once more encounter brutes;
connoisseurs who find little to suit
their tastes will find less;
the writer of radical protest
will find the middle class more obtuse;
the taciturn poet at parties
will find the girls mute—

all will come beg me to tell them
they're right because they are wronged

and my cycle starts. I'll be drawn
into murmuring sympathy—yes,
I support your plausible lie:
external forces exist
and are vicious—

Again I'll be drawn
into failing to say what I know,
what I constantly say to myself
as a charm against panic

The world's self-made.
Observe! Observe!

(vi)

The long curve of the year
empties.

We're out of bread:
must get more
somewhere

Supplies come through
on odd timetables.

We rotate on a bent
axle-tree
—thus the Sahara
once a polar icecap.

You can see the bend itself
on the non-stop jet
to California,

the mind in its long passage
over the winter Rockies

its momentary lights
a pattern
on the night airfield:

gray snow

going back to water.

Mayday and All

For Jeff, born in May

"Nothing is so beautiful
as spring,"
says Hopkins.

Elizabeth Bishop writes:
the cow takes
a long time

eating her calf's after-birth.
I'm not
as driven as before

this May morning—
don't get to
Inwood School till 9:20.

Children write poems
under my direction,
puzzle out

the ways of symbolizing.
I'm pleased   relaxed
lean back against the black-

board—
        suffering floods me
and last night's dream:

I was menstruating
huge clots—my liver
guts, spleen

came away and lay
thick in a basin where
my son (who'll be 18

tomorrow) looked and touched them.

Again
a downward pressure
in my body.

I woke thinking:

more
is coming away.

My Father's Death

in the Napa valley, California

(i)

Under the long lanai
I weed out parched ferns

from among the green.

The fern-bed grows in the humus
of a great oak's stump.

Years ago my father

left a space in the new roof
to frame that tree.

Now an empty square
lets in

the sky beyond it.

(ii)

Sun everywhere
hammers gold on every leaf-edge—

laurel, buckeye, jasmine.
Grapevines open a green fan

over the birdfeeder.
Jays fly down

find no seed   dry water-dish
binoculars in a closed case

on the redwood table.

(iii)

No body:
that unimaginable change—

to be in my own body
is painful

a pull on it
a tearing away

of the root.

Yet grass that bent under his foot
a few days ago

still bends to the wind,
rebounds.

The sun
on new-leafing oaks

must hold a part of him
burning in the air,

a body-house
for my intensest longing.

(iv)

Here droop roses, Paul Scarlets
my father trellised in the buckeye
purpling as they fade

last week as rich as blood,
as velvet—a touch of human art
in the random green

like the garnet pendants he bought
for my mother's ears,
or carnation stuck in his lapel.

In the lanai's vines once he hid
a clay owl-bell,
music to answer the linnets.

          Everywhere in this garden
my father's touch:
I can't bring myself

to prune the roses   must watch
every petal dry and fall
each rosehip shrivel

to a knobbed bone.

(v)

     Dream:

in a suit of cream-colored linen
he comes walking

I seize his white hand:

"I know you're dead
but how good to touch

even a vision"

(vi)

All that's left of my father's body:
my body

that speaks the book of the dead
to itself:

> Whatever you see, however terrifying,
> recognize
>
> as your own radiant mind—

my father's mind

living in me   windborne red-throated bird
that flies

between light and no-light.
                                        The space
is empty.

It is what I see. Pain radiates.
In its broken flame

he lives.

On Loss: Five Meditations

for A.J.M.

(i)
Meditation on the Void

"Gone, gone
gone beyond—"

mantra misunderstood
as deprivation

terror of losing
familiar pain

as if dying—
no heart, if no ache—

my loss!
my loss!

but my cry finds
no wave to carry it

(ii)
Dealing with Guilt

A false note
in this suffering:
as if

touching
the ark of the Lord
I'm killed for it,

the child in me
battered by stones
under the fathers' law:

in me
the mother wakes
and speaks gently

to that child:

you are not
bearer of the world
like God.

No blame.

(iii)

On Change

Remember the star
at the tip of summer's tent-pole

gone now
behind the white mountain?

We cannot remember
what is always here

•   •

But I remember you
as if unchanged.

The error hurts.
We're not selves

fixed in orbit
but elements decaying.

•   •

After that star explodes
its light
will reach us for a while.

Two truths in one—
it burns
and is burned out.

Change
is our only continuity.

(iv)

After the Winter Solstice

Out of a dark season
sun turns
imperceptibly towards us,

candle taller
the longer it's lit:
light in the mind

rising
earlier,
reaches deeper

into thickest
sharp-needled pine
this little

then
a little more—
the way

coming into the world

•   •

and coming into myself
that slowly—
not seeing

at first:
stung and tangled
in my own

dark branches
but
waking every morning

to look
out of a window
slightly less gray.

(v)

Meditation on Endings

In a German prison
the condemned man marvels
at a laurel leaf
floating in his soup

"its tracery of veins,
its perfect form."

Between us   bars after all,
the last visit made

Let it be executed.

Let me be
restored
to the branch in leaf.

Masque: Apparitions Out of the Life of Fiona Starker

huerfano, Sp., orphan
scene: southern Colorado

I Ante-masque

In the mountains, no mothers.
Huerfano's a desert county
and I live north of it

but I don't need to be held
or rocked. I stoke my own cabin stove
with pine, warm up enough

till Fiona Starker with her russet hair
rides by on her Texas palomino.
I follow and bow to her

on the stone doorstep of Phantom Ranch,
a woman my mother's age
who is alone

with husband, horses, money in oil
and souvenirs of travel. We talk
all night of journeys,

passages unseen and seen. I tell her:
the moon is my mother
who lights the mountain's tip.

She says: the night is mine,
            whose chill makes me build
            so big a fire.

I say: your hair itself is fiery.
            Listen, she says, to the tongues
            of flame:

II Masque: Apparitions

(i)
Limousine

I am driving too fast along a desert track
at shadowless noon
    in my scarlet sports car, a Triumph
    bought to blot out the death of my son—
        driving away from his ashes
        buried near Rosita, the ghost town,
driving west to the Sangre de Cristos
toward Phantom Ranch where I live alone
(my husband off in oilfields somewhere)

ahead of me I see a black Cadillac
limousine, in it
    two priests with grim faces fixed
    on the mountains and the abbot's
        retreat house, my only neighbor.
        I pass them, speeding.
Why don't they turn their heads to look at me?
My hair blows and blazes like copper;
my steering hand is ringed with tiger's-eye.

I glance in the rearview mirror. Dust billows
and clears. The road
    is empty. No priests, no limousine.
    I stop, get out. For fifty miles, clean
        to the Spanish Peaks—emptiness.

        Meeting the abbot next week
in town, I ask half-joking if he lost two priests
on the road to Phantom Ranch. He glares
and turns away.

At nightfall I sit at solitaire.
Lightning burns moon-white
    among the piñons. The cards speak
    of two black kings, messengers
        of forces that can bend a life
        to ashes and send a woman out
into desperate places.
                    But my speeding sports car
has conjured them away, my red Triumph
that sees these apparitions but will not give in.

(ii)

The Thimble

All day I hunt my new brass thimble
    in bureau drawers,
    jewel boxes,

    while maple leaves press their gold palms
    against the leaded
    windows—

cold wind through New Jersey woods
where Washington's men
executed

one of their own, a traitor.

Dry vines rattle on the grape arbor
where my eight-year-old son
sat in his wheelchair

before I had to leave him
in the hospital
too long ago

to think of—I traveled then,
Paris, Milan, Beirut . . .
Tonight, no button

on my winter coat, no way to sew it.

Alone in the house I sleep.
At dawn on the bedside table
a thimble,

fluted silver, such as one might
have used in 1775
speaks to me:

mend, mend. But vine leaves
have been embroidered
green on linen;
gold cannot be stitched to lawns.

The fabric of the past is seamless.
    Why do you bring a tool
    too late?

    I had no choice.

•   •

Now, alone in the western mountains
    I hang up larkspur,
    monkshood

    to dry, flowers for winter.
    The brittle stems
    whisper

    in the cellar. I sleep.
    And rise to find
    the thimble

    on the rose-pink rim
    of the washstand.

(iii)

A Winter's Night

Blizzard builds a wall
    against my storm doors.
Fire burns hotly
    behind its screen.
Snow falls again,
        the road
  to Phantom Ranch impassable.

Snowed in two miles away
    that catty woman telephones:
a mountain lion's down
    prowling her pasture,
our minister's wife is
        divorcing him,
  says he beats her.

I hang up. Silence
    outside silence.
I never spoke in court, for
    the child's sake
though I could have told
        the judge plenty.

      Diamonds

replaced tears. I bought expensive
    Paris silks, a blouse
richly crocheted, white
    to start over in,
bride to myself alone—
        Are the doors locked?
  The mountain lion

tracks down the loner or
    the winter-weakened,
travels fifty miles a night
    as fast as gossip.
Well, the altar silver's tarnished
        and the lode
  has petered out.

What then the worth of death
and silence?

This new husband that I can't
    live with nor
live without, who's gone
    again—
            but hush!
I rise, make tea, play
        solitaire.
  My sleep is hard

and blank. Pale morning finds
    snow over all untouched
but my bedroom closets open.
    The white silk blouse
is dangling from its cushioned hanger
        ripped to shreds
  as if by cat's claws.

Night Song for Two Voices

for C.

(i)

Song of the Brain-Damaged Girl

i am a rocking chair
down and up   down and up
air is blinking
sometimes i am a creek
loose over stones
splash comes back and back
my cold toes sing
to my cold fingers

some nights i am the cat
holding in secrets
i am her quiet corner
and orange slit eyes
dishes rattling   my mother's voice
makes things happen
cat weaves under the rocker
listening to air

when no one's talking i'm afraid
i'll disappear
i try to wake my ears
i try to stop it
water erasing
a blackboard—
shapes like sleep
pushing up
in my throat. . .

(ii)

Song of Her Mother In Reply

You are my midnight puzzle-piece.
Wakeful I turn
and turn you again to fit
into the green garden of my living.
But you obtrude.
The mower's blade flings up
a stone that blinds me.
My fingers cannot bring you to flower.

Yet this morning I watch you
rocking under the pines.
The sun is good to you;
cat sleeps in your hands.
You feel what we all feel
and your kindness draws out mine.
Now I root myself
beside you deep in human ground.

• •

But your eyes close before they close.
A tornado tears into the trees.
I look at you, mirror
of my mind edging blackness,
shapes pushing up—
Then I can only reach out, reach in
to whatever will hold us all,
my daughter, the terror,
insoluble love and pain.

Dry Season

visiting California

A long drought, but outside my mother's windows
green of oak, acacia, laurel
conceals the hardening soil

My bachelor brother stammers, comes home every
weekend. Old streetcars his one hobby,
on Saturdays he lays trolley-track

for a rail museum up the hot valley.
He is a perfect son, echoes the phrases
his late father spoke, unlike me never rages

or weeps. The lawn browns only in patches.
We look at the pines, don't notice withered
buckeyes. Radio says "perfect weather"

meaning: no rain, when rain is all that's needed.
Yet this week desert thunderstorms in Mexico
drowned hundreds. I watched my brother mow

what lawn is left. He said, "We used to vacuum
up the cuttings. Now we let the grass
grow through." Over the past

three days I've seen
that green absorb its dead.
And in woods behind it the brown spreads.

Cragmont Avenue Childhood

(i)
Windows

I looked north from my bedroom window
into thick pines and acacias.
I wanted to climb out by a rope,
become an explorer in that
tangled forest.

From my bedroom's west window
I saw the bay, a blue platter
on bright days. I wanted
white sails to skim out through
the Golden Gate

under my own power, like gull's wings,
like wind, irrepressible.
I wanted to cross illegally
into unkempt gardens adjoining mine
where goldfish slept

in the depths of a rocky pool
and surfaced, glittering.
I wanted my own garden,
hedged, in it narcissi and
thornless roses.

I sat in my own white bedroom
on my ruffled and spotless bed.

(ii)

Sandbox

Stepping out of the french doors
into the patio hot
under my barefoot sandals

stepping over the splintery high
blue sides of the sandbox
into the warm grainy

half-pleasant uncertain sand—
I might have been climbing
mountains, it was that

adventuresome. All morning
I staggered in that small sea
while bees whirred overhead

in honeysuckle. I staggered
and stood, bent, sat. Sand
grated everywhere, sticking

to my body. It was not nice
exactly—it was like dirt
maybe, but playful. I loaded

and unloaded buckets of sand
and nothing much was happening,
it seemed.

(iii)

The Basement

Possessions hoarded in orange crates:
nails and tools to patch, repair, align—

Down dark stairs to the "drying room":
my undershirts pinned on lines strung up

over trunks stuffed with my mother's
and grandmother's raiment:

I dressed up, pledged myself that someday
I'd wear velvet and bugle-beads

with no musty smell. I changed to jeans,
crawled under the foundations

on hands & knees through the black cave
around and down to the garage:

I opened every door in that basement—
paint-closet, furnace room, old victrola—

I inspected all the things we owned
believing that they held what I could know,

believed it after I left home
and my parents cleaned out the house for tenants;

I still go down those stairs
rifling through cans of missing & broken parts

trying to name their blind odors.

I Help My Mother Move Out
of her Old House in the Napa Valley

(i)

It is not my life
under these lichened oaks,
    these redwood eaves
but my mother's life—

I was ten and climbed
a young laurel where she couldn't
    see me, and laurel leaves
touched my hair with pungent fingers—

She called and I came
back, and didn't mess up
    paper with my writing.
I followed her housework

inside stone walls.
Outside the rich stink of sun
    on grass and poison oak—
Sleeping nights under an unfinished roof

I covered my head
as a bat's wing
    fanned me in the dark.

(ii)

The house is a body

from which we come;
now it is emptying out.

Is it her life only
that disappears as I am
packing, filing, discarding?

My mother sits in the bath
massaging cramped legs,
in place of her right breast

the skin pinned neat and flat
across, under it the heart
pulsing.

In the pale water,

slightly distorted,
her ankles, blue with burst veins

are slender as mine.

(iii)

Paintings done when I was eighteen,
twenty-two, mementos of talent—
no room for them in
my makeshift apartment,
nor for my father's book of Schubert's songs,

but I take these: *vom Wasser*
haben wir's gelernt

how to move on—
    maybe I'll sing yet.
Rain falls these nights

in dusty California. I sit up
    late and listen to the dripping.
Old papers in the garage await
    our junkman.
In the morning my mother

greets me in her green pants-suit.
    Buds tip the laurels.
I wrap and mail to myself
    her old evening gowns.

We will never leave this place.

The Stars

(i)

In the mind's midnight
the fixed stars ride

tonight I gaze at the space
between them

(ii)

A ruddy star invisible
until it falls –

and then for a moment
flaring

I long to see it stay
—a comet, a signal—

but only its exploding gave it
that luminous trail

of fire

(iii)

At midnight
two darknesses:

confusion
and illimitable space—

in the west
a star-sickle to slash through;

overhead the dipper
swings from Arcturus's peg

pours out what it
cannot contain

what does not
contain it

iv)

In the northeast burns
yellow-white Capella
star of the first magnitude

in the meadow grass
its slow imitator
ignites   goes out   goes on

(v)

The stars live in the dark
as I do

I lie down on the bony ground
to stare up

letting go—

O diamonds, fall into my eyes
become my seeing
clear and indestructible.

Part Three

RECLAMATIONS

By Night

(i)

Moon-sliver: darkness rises
to hone its edge.
Our love as soon as we spoke it
entered nightfall.
We hold hands on the road
and cold wind chills them.

A star fell, you tell me
but I wasn't looking.

I'm alone. The stars see nothing
but I stare back, design their meaning
as a jeweler sets diamonds:
the scorpion has stung me,
the archer draws his bow
to pierce me—

Last sun-trace gone, no road. We stumble
over rocks. Why
did you do that? What
did you mean? Words
into darkness, our hands clench.
Sky only slightly lighter than massed pines
is slashed by the moon's curved sword,
heart's weapon, crescent phase.

(ii)

Crowned by the deathless stars, imagining
one won't die, yet they speed outward, losing us—
Antares, "opposing Mars," that blood-soaked planet,
also is red, roils in its ruby gases, dying.

That jeweled wound throbs all night.

In empty dark death reddens,
swallows me. I burn to blackness,
crowned with bone.

Enter this open torture.

Take this charred hand and come.

A Self-Portrait Fails

(i)

A self-portrait fails
from intense effort not to beautify,
refusal to shy away
from any flaw.

    but black pen-line's too blunt
    for shadows' subtleties,
    hopeless to shape hair's mass
    filament by filament,
    though nothing less is truthful—

Five Matissean strokes might do it better
but cheat on the harder questions.
Anxious honesty
        ticks in each fine point
        ("you over-explain," says a friend)
        derange the whole.

    Low forehead can't be erased
    back to its plain height—
    the image over-pretty after all:

too much romantic blackening.

(ii)

But why a mirror anyway and self as subject?
Better the outward apples of Cézanne, objective eye,
the world
compassionately studied.

On the desk, cluttered with the world's requests,
Still in that mess, desire to see set the glass,
propped the artist's pad beside
that imaged face and tried

to build the infra-structure,
that illusory "very thing itself."

If hand can link to thought, then form externalized
in black on white cements belief.

What's wanted is
a stronger replica

to stare back from the page, immutable
and reassuring: yes, this is—
this is more
than vaporous assemblage

and moment of its failing.

Cold Flashes

Redwood Canyon, California

More cold than hot,
these irrelevant shivers of body-change—
a warning, the first frost.
One might

walk out in such an autumn dawn
under the leafless branch of the persimmon
gazing at that bright fruit, and say: now

it is ripe, frost-nipped; no fever here
and no distortion. But eating the persimmon
makes the mouth pucker from the tart edge

of the scraped skin. Pain without dignity:
don't mention it—a flush freezes under
my shirtsleeves. The monthly bleeding had

meant renewal. Now the moon is locked behind
low fog. I walk in a mist of silver,
shattered droplets of the moon. This back road

narrows past vineyards, past our stonewalled
country house, now sold, and dead-ends
up the hill somewhere. I wanted change

not to be so radical. Prune trees were uprooted
to plant these vines, an axe to white spring
blossoming. What ripens now? The grapevines too

are bare. I'm haunted. Nothing certain
in this travel, no road signs, yet everywhere
deep smells of leaf-mold under redwoods,

sequoia sempervirens, the after-perfume
of dissolving forms. Not much to count on.
Thought in its soft reflections echoes moonlight,

drifts and holds its own.

For Buddhist Friends on the Birth of their Twins

She is the treasure of the house.
Great good fortune.
—I Ching

(i)

A white bird rises over a mountain trail,
her wing star-pale
against dark pine branches.

In the grass a leaf-mottled
brown bird startles:
rustle of wings, a bright eye.

(ii)

Anna is grace and power,
beneficence of your broken heart.
Whenever you walk by moonlight
you will think: she, infinite pearl,
    mirror of the sun
but purer, as tears are purer than water.

(iii)

A third son is magic.
Disinherited in fairytales,

where the first son becomes king,
second son his general,

what left for the third but seeking?

He slips out alone by dark
penniless, homeless, to find

he can leap the river of poison
fly over the double ring of snow peaks
to the source—Michaël,
warrior-prince,
"who is like god?"

(iv)

Great good fortune, this birth-journey.
Cloud-moving wind
leads us to take the narrow road
to the deep north.

Bashō:
"in the utter silence of a temple,
a cicada's voice alone
penetrates the rocks."

Waking in Front of a Cracked Mirror

This jagged life
holds at the frame's edges

but the body fractures in the center
of the glass I salvaged

off the street,
hung over our loft-bed

to increase light in close quarters.
This body

disjointed at breast
and breast-bone, subject

to chills and sweats, matches
this mind caught

in bifurcations,
inconsistencies. Look, voyeur of self,

and laugh at this cubist nude,
a patchy image

the only possible reflection of fact.

Next to the cracked mirror
a branch of bittersweet

has stood
through two winters and still offers

its gnarled orange fruit. The background's
dark, the figure shifty.

A life torn apart under this dual
    emblem—the seed's

    endurance and the easy
    shatter of gleaming surfaces.

Before the mirror was hung, the wall
showed cracked as well,

and grimy. Can't
redecorate my life, its pain

    and spackle over every defect,
can't

choose what stays or leaves:
I sleep badly
            fragmented

• •

Dawn opens naturally behind the curtains.
Sun doubles

in the glass.
My thoughts, your thoughts, pale scraps split,

bodies float and re-assemble in the
morning light

rise

in that riven silver.

Autumn Meditation

for Meg on her 24th birthday

October dusk: we're walking east on 60th street.

As many years of my life have passed
since your birth as before it—
from now on I am clearly more mother than child.

Dry leaves blow from plane-trees onto stoops
of brownstones. You, my autumn daughter, in russet
blouse and fawn-beige skirt, stride beside me

firmly, as if I were in your charge, might go
astray. Apparently I've given you my strengths
and certainties, left myself with questions,

ruminations which seem to you too fragile,
remnants of oak and maple. Leaves swirl around us,
making the fall wind's power visible. Secretly

I still want to teach you, not how to master the world
any more, but how to trust it, let its beauty happen.
    Tomorrow you fly back to Paris. Now we stand

on this broken leaf-strewn curb, a balance-point,
your birthday, when I came to life as your mother,
and you, strong as now in your first push outward,

took on the burden of my courage which lets you go.

For Patrick, My Son

(i)

About the divorce
        my incomprehensible explanations
        over airport salad
                "it's certain that fine women eat/
        a crazy salad with their meat"
that I understood—but

didn't want
        to eat crazy   or be fine
        I think he thought . . . but you know
                it must be night
                for the moon to rise,
        that calm mind which sees itself
chopped to bits on the riffled lake.

        If I say I feared I wasn't sane
you'll be afraid   but
        if I was
then why—?   But night falls
every night: we sit
        to eat. In the chef's salad sliced cheese
                and ham, no stranger a mix
than any other. Bit by bit
                we take it in

(ii)

In the play the deaf girl's
        only speech is weeping:
                that we understood
        without a translator
but within limits: her sign language
        lucid
        to those who know it, gate to meaning

In a prickly barberry bush
        beside my office
                bird-whistles, chortlings,
        no visible sign of their source—
the deaf girl's hand
        gestures invisible thread
        from her heart to his

incomplete   need   help
        "This isn't the place to talk,
—we can't," you say
        my fork by your fork shredding the lettuce.

Reclamation: Aspen Stump and Willow

in the Colorado mountains

Hiked again to the old pond
on the way to the high lakes,
found new green beside the gray

half-sunken aspen stump—
this mountain's strewn with silvered logs
brought down by snow and beavers.

So what one remembers
lies cumbersome, tarnishing,
loses its sharp edges.

Around it spring new grass tufts,
aspens' lemon-green leaves, blue spruce
white violets and arrowleaf

altering that landscape. Old logs shape
a new lake. Old creek trickle
leaps in white waterfalls.

It's natural for these hikers
in high air looking up each day
to find noon skies clearer

and each night starrier than the night before.

Any Mother's Unsent Letters

(i)

to a son in the mid-west from back east

A clipped azalea twig un-watered since autumn
blooms a pink frill by the frost-rimmed window.

I teach poem-writing to squirmy tenth-grade boys.
Marginalia: "This poet sucks." It's Friday. Your

anger, too, lurks cheerfully. Nightmare of loss recurred
but my car, not my purse, was stolen. Hunting

for money to buy it back, I overslept, drove up island
to the high school, slow truck in front, red van tailgating.

Not so late after all. I pay big phone bills.
You say you'll go back to college at the vernal equinox.

(ii)

to a son down south from up north

In my study a whole wall bulges with books. Computer's
cursor swiftly ticks lines out of a bursting mind.

I write, you write: how does poetry make politics?
You are a political journal's El Salvador expert.

Salvator is masculine. A mother's mistakes comprise
many pages of X-ed out facts, insurrections,

American mayhem—divorce. Blood all over. The boy
tells the counselor "I know my mom will always love me."

For your wedding in May I'll buy the bouquets and corsages.
Outside, snow sinks between hummocks of half-green grass.

(iii)
to a son in the far west, more or less

Short takes: fear-flashbulbs explode in the dark. Booze.
Bars. Gay guy's taunt. Fight. In dirty snow his wallet tossed

(they said) by you. Blank. Jail. No memory, no defense.
Workhouse months in fear-safety. Out, out . . . these things pass.

Taxi driving. Fare after fare accrues merit. No drinks.
New girl deserts. Bills. Back at school graphics training

goes slow. Each hand-inked letter must perfectly stay
within bounds. How long since we walked in clear mountain air

among pines where a wild creek's water-leaps and pools
made us speak together of all things' ever-living goodness?

(iv)
to a daughter on her own

Slim in a fire-pink batik dress beside the pea-green parrot
of Sainte-Phalle's fountain, you never strive for impact.

You step onto the music-barge La Péniche at Pont St-Michel,
fumble for cigarettes. From below, African drums reverberate.

Your voice on Sunday radio *sur la mort d'un algérien*
tué dans les rues simply requests justice, an end to racism.

Rue Notre-Dame de Nazareth, birthplace of Otto Diesel,
with penthouse chandeliers and rose gardens—what's relevant?

Murmurs: oh mom, don't . . . Dusk on the Seine. Late sun gilds
cathedral towers. You look up, skeptical, elegant, standing aside.

(v)

to the stepson who comes on weekends

McDonald's, Adidas, Izod, Newcleus, Haagen Daz, Kiss,
Def Leppard, Police, The Terminator, VCR, Star Trek, Star Wars,

J.H.S. 184, M-15 bus up First, M-14 crosstown, Frank's
Pizzeria, Pepsi, M & Ms, anywhere after school but homework.

Quarters for PacMan, Alligators, Bombs Away—the brain beeps
digitally, chasing orange and green day-glo blobs all night.

Age of innocence. Your crammed skull makes Kolkata's streets
look like denuded prairie. I'm out of it, finding no way

to hawk what has no brand name. I hardly blame you.
Why shouldn't you have these airbags to cushion the crash?

Part Four

WHAT IS COMING

Dislocations

in memoriam Richard Borden
from East Hampton, New York

Yesterday a bobwhite dropped down on the corner deck rail,
Rust-stained feathers ruffled and bent by late wind.
Black and white stripes curved his head with surety.
My gaze steadied him. But fidgety I turned to tune
radio's jazz to softer classic – and he was gone.
Wood birds don't find enough seed here: my fault.

Again the lost purse nightmare, my San Andreas fault-
line, where deep earth-shifts begin. I wake and rail
against myself. I've lost my keys. No dream: they're gone,
as long ago my friend Anne lost the carpool-van keys. Wind
blows friends away. "Time like an everlasting—" Hymn tune
forgotten pricks green in winter-blanched lawn's surety.

NASA loses its Delta rocket. Red Chernobyl radiates surety
of vested loss and error. A bus today instead of train, no fault
of the system, naturally. Late, late—the wheels' rough tune
runs on the slow shore detour past gray shacks and split-rail
fences, where old cherry trees bloom thick into salt wind.
I'm wrong again: what's bypassed is not lost, not gone.

One composes in pencil to erase, replace words gone
awry in the moment of patching a semblance of surety.
My son had the courage to write you, an uncle dying, as wind
drops over the Annapolis River. Cowardice is my prime fault;
"too late" my excuse. From bus to train at Shirley, and the rail-
roadbed jolts on to the city. Now engine trouble—that old tune

we hate. I'll be late to work, but deeper guilts tune
out the trivial. . . . It's two weeks later, and you're gone
in that unknown going, and I again am carried by the sleek rail
as the train moans one long note through the futile surety
of spring's repeated greening. Certainly it's no human fault
that one stands outside another's life bucking its wind –

and won't won't won't admit into one's lungs that wind
of dark: for any, every one some version of the piped-in tune
of glucose, morphine. "O sing ye a new song" in default
of ancient psalm? Not yet possible. I'm going—nearly gone.
Turned over my well-swept house to tenants, without surety
of seed left for the lost bobwhite on his gray deck rail.

Around your garden, too, a rail fence, and ceaseless wind
lifting into surety of air the birds that twitter a tune
of one life gone, as all, a blameless ending, without fault.

Contexts

for H., the mother who gets phone calls

(i)

In rain held off by roof and window,
she, dry, still knows wet,
her mind the lowering gray sky

outside her son's mind. Now she knows
they are statistics, commonplace.
His hard grind has to be greased

by "stuff" but—
"not dealing,"
he says, "no needles—"
His phone-voice believes itself,

so free from referent is the self-
enclosed world of language.

(ii)

Enough hooey.

He is her son—yes, a sentiment. "He,"
deictic pronoun, floats meaningless. But "son"—
there's context for you.

Dreamt she bore him again, shoved him out
dripping with amnion
full grown, as gray-eyed mind

sprang adult from world-generator's
skull. No myth umbilical hooks
one to one
—so he from her in utterance's
severance of thought from body.

Not hooked, she knows hooked:
his thought-world skids on tracks
only apparently parallel.

"Son": if only a word could detox

(iii)

"Mother" is the overbearing word.

Literature mothers language, molds random
gene-words to the unique production

she grunts out between her legs, then names.
The noun is not to be confused with what is named.

It's him. Nothing to do with language.
Call these lines "the mother ghazal"

because one never shakes off the form
and role of somebody's mother, but in fact

the same independence exists. He is he.
Fixes travel in his blood that once

was made from hers, so words are circling
uselessly through her: oh—oh—oh

on a wet night dry labor
that won't deliver him again.

(iv)

        And heads get hooked on their own forms.
Nightfall means dank wet outside to one
        and to another, warmth of the inner hearth:

        It's a party. Her frizz-haired friend
smokes a joint and groans, "I couldn't stand
        the guilt. That's why I never had children.

        Too afraid. Knew I couldn't bear
the responsibility—"
                        Indicted. The listener

still believes in the declarative sentence,

brave or deluded says to herself again:
        better to have a son than not to have one

. . .

        But what if he o.d.'s?

(v)

Dark eases in. Eaves drip a little,
a few words drift from the TV—

so thoughts dance across the mind-screen,
breaking down fear and the tired need

to settle fear. Shouldn't she let him fade
from her brain, displaced by imitation swordplay

and British accents in jiggly TV color?
His phone's disconnected now, the night over-quiet.

She sits up till 4 or 5 a.m., as if
her sleeping might let him down, writes him

letters to go perhaps unread—
certainly unread, writes in the grip
of the horribly questionable mother-cycle:

    yeah, useless—

(vi)

Syzygy these days,
the weatherman announces moon and sun
aligned, and earth

in its ellipse
closest as it can be to the sun—still 93 million
miles away.

Murderous tides
along the coast, moon-pulled, tell us that close
is no better than far.

This storm follows from that near star.

This poem is no letter. It has
no end. Its moebius-strip
unending surface

slips back into unseen beginning
in circling water, wet still falling,
resumption *da capo al fine*

What Is Coming

(i)
Oblique

Piner's Nursing Home, California,
Bethesda Care Center, et al.

What approaches is imageless:
odor of deodorizer at the nursing station,
oxygen cylinder outside a closed door.

A door is closing. A voice
activates a telephone. Temporary
transmission of impulses connects

"Mother" " child" —false labels for
the long severed. Memory means severance.
That warning on the bottle

went unread. What approaches
is wordless, the one word too much.
Low slant winter sun shines blank

and blank mind speaks. What must
be known can't be. Do you imagine
pear-blossoms warm in the old orchard,

a cycle counted on as river-circle
underground? Don't. Return's not
endless. What approaches

is new. I dip a cup and bring up
silt to drink. I send words back
to a voice outliving words.

The neural circuitry clicks off.
It will come obliquely, like that. Seem
not to be happening.

After-pulsations image a net
that holds. Spaces between the knots
define the net; thus the void of "mother"

energizes a continent of wires.
Every mother's cord is cut. You forget.
One promises to phone again, not wholly

disbelieving in equipment. Oxygen
is odorless. What approaches isn't.

Isn't. Breathe it in.

(ii)
4 p.m. in New York

Snow's clarity which lit up morning windows now
turns faintly gray, reminds—but why do I object?

Lunchtime in California: chicken soup at Piner's.
My mother holds a saltine ladylike in her left hand,

thinks: that old gal over there's completely gone,
but I—why soup for breakfast? Who's this visitor,

my daughter or granddaughter?

My mother introduced me to her roommate.
Then my mother introduced me to her roommate.

Memory is form, holding a self like skin.
It goes, and the person goes, all but a haunted body.

More snowfalls, blue under darkening sky,
simplifying the landscape to gaps and blotches.

I dislike this night's way of looking in at me.
I go round and twist the wands that shut the blinds.

Part V

CLOUD, ROCK, SCROLL

Cloud, Rock, Scroll

from the Colorado mountains, meditating on H.D.,
myth-maker, in her sea garden, as dead priestess
and Helen in Egypt – "she herself is the writing"

(i)
Rock Rose

Wild roses among rocks
in sun-blanched grasses
twine the cabin's split steps.

Petals infold
concealing gold stamens.
Drought crumples them.
Night frost will surely
scatter them—

yet more at morning
bloom among boulders.

Your peony-pink
is stitched on green leaf-brocade
sprung from dust.
How has desert thrust you up?
You are foreigners
born here.

Your silk spins from a harsh worm.
You flare in high wind.
Do your roots reach

down to a hidden river?

At sundown mountains darken.
The sky fills with rose-fire clouds.

(ii)
Rock Lily

Lily of the rocks,
lily of aspen shadows,
rare mariposa, your ivory petal-cup

streaked with subtlest purple
bends to the meadow
on a single stalk

as a wise woman averts her eyes
not needing praise.

Delia of Miletus, priestess,
healer, speaks after death as one
who "stood apart,"
and "sang a secret song."

Lily of willow springs,
lily of mountain mist,
you are rooted far
from white sand
or temple column—

an offering
without shrine

(iii)
Wraiths

on a trail to tree-line

Fog hides the peaks.
Scarves of mist drift among pines.
The dark boughs drip.

No laurels in these woods,
no spirit's scented flower-breath.
The stream runs cold

and rough. It speaks
of nothing beyond itself. It eats away
the trail beside it.

Deeper woods.
An old mine-shaft
—human remnant—fills with dirt
under a fallen fir-trunk:

after that no trace
of construct or precursor.
                    Rain begins.

Wet trees stand
in the path, wraiths black but veiled.
I fade into their landscape, insubstantial,

an absence.
No deity, shrine nor scripture,
crucible nor angel
but her seeking mind remembered

and these shape-shifters, pale
behind cracked branches, draw me on—

Rock creates the fall of water,
air its dispersion,
earth its catch-basin.

Formless runnels
form cross-trails.
Mud hollows hold
a momentary silver,

sky-mirrors,
light-givers,

incessant
reformation of water.

(iv)
Sky

Blue sky of emptiness:
deepest blue   strongest
blue of amethyst, of lapis,

of turquoise buried
under most ancient rock   blue
of transient lupine,

drooping harebell at
lake's rim two miles high in blue
air where fossil shells

imprint the granite—

blue   over these peaks
once sea-bottom, your height

depth endless, "nothing
whatever yet everything
comes of it."   Water

in blue tarns above
tree line covers pearly stones
that sink from sight as

mountains rise to hide
in clouds that lie on those blue
mirrors. Sky, water,

rock self-existing,
enmeshed in utter difference,
open mystery

—"not why it is but
that it is" – that mind can see
as word and woman

in one hieroglyph:
she herself is the writing

—and light to read it.

(v)
Now

Light changes:
gray in the cabin window.
Thunder rumbles and the power goes off

a moment. Mountains make weather. Now
hail pummels stovepipe and roof,
then sun, blatant,

creates
leaf-shine in wet scrub oak.
This transience, this rough-walled one plain room

bind and drive one's thought. Rock roses' blooming
passed but left leaf and thorn,
grubstake
            for another season.

My heroines
work alone. "Mountain Charley"
put on men's clothes, shipped on a Mississippi river-

gambler's boat, went west, panned gold in Victor
and Cripple Creek, sent money
back to St. Louis nuns

for two daughters' convent schooling.
She was eighteen and widowed. She had no way to live
but crudely, in disguise.

No myth,
this history hacks itself out in unruly
shapes.

My west, how have you written me?

• • •

Now you, shape-shifter,
name-changer,
in Helen's white chiton
girdled with purple
of mountain gentian,
haunt my crude refuge.

No myth but you,
disguised by names,
initials, images of sea,
wind, sand, of poppy-flame
you meet my mind
with mind no place

but here on uneven
rock that rises
distant to the mountain
shrouded
in cloud.

No Fuji or Olympus.

Still,
eidolon, for you
an offering:
this effort,
watercolor
of the pale yellow
rippled under-edge of thunderhead,
sun held a moment in end-glow:

this scroll.

ARBOR VITAE

Heaven and earth are trapped in visible form:
all things emerge from the writing brush.

– *Wen Fu: The Art of Writing*
Lu Chi, 261-303 A.D.
(tr. Sam Hamill)

And he shewed me a pure river of water of life,
clear as crystal, . . . and on either side of the river,
was there the tree of life

– *Book of Revelation 22: 1-2*
King James version, 1611

Part One

ARBOR VITAE

Arbor Vitae

at the house of a friend, Helen Wildman,
on Lake Paradox in the Adirondacks

(i)

White apple blooms
outside the window
Below, a dark brook winds

White moon rises
above the pines—
window glass clean with rain

(ii)

Silent house, gray morning:
slow gaze wakes
silence of thought.

Wine-brown trillium,
triple-sepalled, sprung
from its three-leaf stalk

sends a long filament
curving into the depth
of a glass vase.

Order, beauty in repose,
invisible growth.
Downstairs, a woman's voice

engineers action:
to plumb, wire, fix, wake up,
make it happen

(iii)

Yesterday—death-day of a friend
two years ago. I forgot, busy

shopping with Helen's daughter,
half-blind, whose brain tumors recur.

That death: a suicide by pills.
The daughter cooks, mends, quilts

with her one good eye. Helen cut down
overgrown trees that blocked

the view. The blind girl looks across
the gray-blue length of Lake Paradox.

She's ready to swim five miles,
a friend in a boat beside her.

The suicide's ashes: where are they?
Her last note: what did it say?

(iv)

Seen from a side window

gray fog obscures
the greening oaks

beyond the gray house
of Helen's brother—

Close to the glass
a sharp slash of cypress branch.

(v)

In the farthest camp
under the pines
Helen's grandfather died.

East of its quiet,
a smaller camp looks over
a stilled silver cove.

Between them a meadow
of wild strawberry flowers.
Fruit to come, persisting ripeness.

(vi)

Arborvitae, thick cedar,
stands on the brook's bank,

branching leaf from twig
too multiple to sketch

one by one, too elusive
en masse—
Last night

on the lake a low mist.

Watercolor
couldn't render

such metamorphosis
of water.
                    Still, the brush dips

once more, for Lu Chi wrote
        When cutting an axe handle

        with an axe, surely the model
        is at hand.

PART TWO

METAPHYSICS OF THE INTERIOR

Snow on Horn Peak

in the Sangre de Cristo mountains, Colorado

Morning half cloudy, half clear.
Best pen lost.
          My oldest son, out of detox,

paints the pines in watercolor
from a palette long unused.
          Snow-melt feeds

blue fields of wild iris lower down.
Up here, one gold mustard-bloom
          in leafy green

A small brush puts yellow

          in almost
          the right

          place

Swallows

Swallows swan-dive
under the eaves: cry *your house*
is our house of air

• •

Where do I live?
          in Minnesota tomorrow
in the operating room
          with the infant grandson

          who almost died at birth

• •

A wren whistles while
          I write near her nest. Swallows'
white wing-stroke gone

                    into sky.

• •

Hearts of birds beat,
keep beating even without
          monitors' zigzag

          or watching eye.

Metaphysics

if any, repose in grass this June
dried wheat tufts suggest autumn.

Illusion of time: the view towards town
twenty years ago the same, one thinks,

the viewer changed but held, close
to hope, still doubting that green is only

made in the retina.
                                        My son paints Winsor's Green
(Light) on Strathmore paper because *it is*

that way, and the world less doubtful
than one's thought of it—without

which it isn't . . .
                                says who? Consciousness
is cellular, says Teilhard, in case

one should forget to bid the swatted cockroach
to become buddha.
                                        Aggression won't

supply green. And could photosynthesis
produce ink for the poet's randomness which

hardly frames art, that neurosis skewing
acceptance?
                                Getting old? Well, resist

that thought as a reflex fed by newsprint.
But the physical transfixes an internal

metaphysical fear: sooner to die
rather than later, as this cinquefoil's bright

yellow fades, and the chickadee
who sits on my boot-tip is surely not last year's.

Some fat chipmunk, however, steals
birdseed from the finches, and no intervening

helps. Five droplets out of an overhead
cloudpuff threaten this page unpreventably

as the helpless face of any woman
crossing 23rd street at Second Avenue

to think a boon might come from bodies
of students shot in Tiananmen Square.
Logic

won't de-corrupt governments, except
where a word properly lodges its depth

in the fluidity of things, which have a way
of constancy in greens of varying

grays—Payne's Light, for instance, for rocks
that stay mostly unseen, and yet crop out

holding landscape, or land-thought
resembling it, enough to wake you, caught out

in metaphysical blur—self-doubt, as if
good were invisible. Wake you to get up and walk.

Metaphysics II

Does a word hold a thing,
a bowl of water reflecting
the moon? Thought, like water, exists

but slips out of form continually.
This self too slips and falls
within its shadow body till the final

disassembling. Momentary brain-cells
hold sun, moon, a few chemicals—
what besides these holds all up-welling

history, memory? The brain-bowl
can contain more and more
without enlarging. When it goes

words stay, as on this page, and others.
One spider's body exudes its web
whose fine chain hangs and breaks, yet

these transient nets remain, the wish
that the son who tans himself in this
mountain air can hold his strength and live

sustained, and that the infant grandson softly
comes out of anesthesia to his father's
relieving tears, the primal water

that ancient consciousness construed
as "the deep" outside this universe
—the deep within, bulking, confused,

seeing every possibility and object—
mirrors, vices, seventy
kinds of oak tree or creeping vetch—

in a single cell.
So multiply made,
I still think I'm alone, waiting
for a phone call as if no one ever waited

before. No end to desire's stirrings.
This desire greens the tips of firs
and makes the pump-motor click in

that one may turn a faucet and drink.
At the end of phone lines intricately
linked wait well-drillers, botanists,

one who writes, since one word
prolongs the still-ephemeral.
The observed absolute death of a cell—

do you credit those scientists?
Yes. And their connecting stays on
after the end exists.

Metaphysics III: After Waiting

"So the baby is fine," says my youngest son,
          phoning after the surgery, untroubled
as the day moon afloat in sunset clouds tinged

fiery on the under edge. Rain gray dissolves
          above white billows, puffs. Dusk's
long shadow-streaks make the valley more lovely.

• •

To wait– why give time
such power? The not-yet
over now. Privacy

of dream, the stream's depth
where fish swim
under ice which hides and protects.

To imagine grim
disorder, death out of place—
that's knowledge addicted

to form, to making
myself continue, to belief in omens,
false significance

as if a morning's rain
"meant" sadness to come, or a man's
dirty shirt "means" he's unclean–

the poet's error. A blank
white envelope is simply unaddressed,
and light from a dead planet

not inferior or impure.
I take a fishhook off the line
and store it where it won't snag, or

not so badly, since I'm
still caught, and take the great
blue mountain-morning sky

personally, a good
infinite, intense, not my eye's
opening at all, not neutral

no more than the baby's
unexpected red hair and loyal
energy of his body's healing.

At the Aspen Stump Again

on hiking back up to Goodwin beaver ponds

More worn, settled
into the brown-bottomed pond
which mirrors its clenched roots,

the stump accommodates wet
grass-tufts, algae, the hot
clarifying sun. It falls back to the blue

sky-reflecting water, less raw
than years ago. It's the season
of early yellow-gold weeds like

dandelion, "false" lupine. Currents
hidden and swift ripple into loose
curves against the far bank. Flies

skim this quiet son's bronzed shoulder
as he drops a fish-line off a log.
Trout hover near a sand-shelf

undisturbed. Repose. Nothing to do—"no
attainment and no non-attainment."
No pressure to move the mind

which doesn't slow any more than
the exuberant diamond chilling
stream rests. It sends

its overflow into calm shallows.
Sky sleeps there. Tallest
firs point downward— further,

stiller—and slow pine-smell
sinks through the air. The stump
slopes jaggedly across the silted swamp

immoveable
as some lost thought.

Sunday Morning

(i)

No complacencies:
wren's nestlings hatched, flycatcher
poised on a dry pine tip

Nature's not enough, no
mother, and illusory.
Sunfire produces

green contradictions: sky-
blue the shade of emptiness,
but benefits

blind motor-bikers
as well as meditators,
death also growing

into the good, even if
TV commentators didn't
jiggle enameled eyes,

syllables, canned-pea
label in place of peas, hot
on a plate.
                    Desire
to be entertained—
what a mistake. But desire

that cuts out its own
heart and tosses the pieces,
sunflower seeds to

the Steller's jays, that's
the sun that gilds emerald
the wings of bank-swallows

and polishes gravestones.

(ii)

All powers are higher, being real:

Every night of full moon
    led a lonely poet-monk northward,
    pinning haiku on cherry branches.

Tu Fu meditated in autumn
    while mountain winds wailed
    in the *wu-t'ung* trees

and Li Po leapt into a pool of wine.

I sit with pen and ink
    on the splintered wooden deck
    with this silent son, it seems

    recovering

Who can rely on the forms on pages
        that collapse into formlessness
        as bird-twitter in scrub oak

mixes into sough of wind and creek-water
        tumbling among white-blooming cresses
        on the pump trail long untraveled?

Let's walk to the willow
        in which we saw a yellow-bellied sapsucker
        pluck beetles from a branch cleft

not "sucking sap" at all—

Think of form as emptiness:
        the cloudless sun at 10 a.m.

(iii)

Accept the challenge
which things present to words
—*Francis Ponge*

        Blueflax miscalled "chicory,"
or periwinkle, blooms by the cabin steps:
blue or purple as that myrtle—or flowering
myrrh?—in leafy banks

        under live oaks
and madrones at the old stone house in California,
where my father's study windows looked out
        over them.

That room he sat in,
struggling to write. That dead father, his face
and voice held beyond photograph or scratchy tape
on which he sang

I did it my way—

exact shading of the thing remembered,
for which no word:

Ephemeral petals fall by noon
beneath the stem whose furled buds englobe
the bloom to come.

Wind

sweeps through pine boughs.
Sough of water
over rocks: sound not

of wind but of wood,
stone resistance to
the unseen:

Word stirs dust off the leaf.
high clear dome
washed clean

not I, not I but the wind –

Necessary

My son must leave today.
Flight scheduled on time.

Subdued light: a haze
dulls green mountainsides.

Blue-flax petals, shades
bluer than sky, fallen in dry

grass. West wind may
soon brighten the snow-peaks

or it may not.
Lone flight of nighthawk.

Lone necessity to hang back
in rocky terrain.

Exhausted

standing in the whirl
of inexhaustible wind,

twitter of birds,
cloud-shift:

dumbed eyes, ears register
endlessly.   If

instead of clear, a mist
also wakes drifting

mind to heart's gist,
tenderness, a knowing, is

there a problem?
                                        Miffed
because the roof-fixer's

late – so what? It's
a finite world. Dirt

scuffs up between rifts
in floorboards, sifts

from ceilings. Pay attention to inter-
stices. Do wash and pin it

on frayed line winter-
worn. Give in.

Metaphysics of the Interior

Chilled gray sky lowers
          over the valley, and the mind
feels shutdown, mildly suffers.

Weather's not to be correlated
          with the personal: this diamond
intellect—anyone's—wakens

flash! like that, whatever
          light plays on it. Why
then this imagining of lessened

hearing, seeing? An inner scene
          crowds characters onstage,
who nag, rebut and disappear

a moment. Must write a letter,
          telephone, placate
them, hunch over the desk

indoors, keep after evasive
          freedom not obtained
by just this pursuit.
                              The view

from the front window
          is blocked by the same
near-black pine, green a day or two ago.

Clear Sky

High cool blue wind shakes
screen doors, wild roses, stones: clears
three words on a page.

Blanketflower, 'sugar-bowls'
bloom. Can a rug be called meadow,
cup an acorn, the whole

world a house swept out,
dishes on the sink-board given
to whoever's around?

No greed to hold, or
less greed, wanting after all
a longer day, more

hours before the stars rise
through clean blackness, unpossessed.

Moon and the Milky Way

(i)

Moon rising: a Chinese
bronze gong veiled in smoke

Cloud sinks: it brightens,
night's tiger's-eye

(ii)

After day's harsh wind
no sediment or blur between
mountains and sky

The river of stars flows over
pines in shadow whose tips
turn watery-black silver:

strongest light of far dark mind

Broken Meditation

Late afternoon stillness:
          shadow of fir-tree and cabin's roof peak
fall over meadow and scrub oak.

A corner of sun on the deck,
          on a deer skull and tin pot, relic
of abandoned mine or Cottonwood hermit's

lost camp, signs to preserve
          of this mountain's history. Serene
and glossy oak leaves glint, protecting

young firs among them. This quiet
          opposes my jitters over property
in California, my dead mother's legacy.

Money troubles me, unsettles
          my thinking, as if, like the Chinese
poets, I too might be suddenly

exiled, deprived.
                              The red
          bandana at my throat draws a sizzling
hummingbird to aim his beak

and I'm afraid he'll get me,
          cheat me like some west coast realtor
of something kin to that bureaucrat's security

which gave Tu Fu his brush.

Yet
he lost it, and seven mountains sealed
him away from the capital.

This free
I am also, with broken
meditation and a few mosquitos
in a paintless chair whose rush-woven seat

was torn out twenty
years ago by someone's kids. Cheap
yellow rope replaces it and interweaves

with plastic straps. Adequate
as the sun goes and the last clouds clear
from sky even more absently blue-green

than an old scribe's agate
inkstone whose repose freed him
for poetry and pointless dreaming.

****

Part Three

THE CHANGES

Untitled: [My Brother]

Again a cloudless morning:
          glazed-vase blue overhead
          a little too smooth,

dry stalks among green in the
          meadow, blanching dust on the old
          blocked driveway. Into

this drought, concealed, arrives
          remnant of an angry dream
          as I stand on the deck

looking east into the glare too bright
          and the dust-haze on dim peaks:
          uprush of ancient resentment,

a half-broken open feeling, but
          of what?
                    Disturbing, this lack
          of rain, this newscaster's "perfect

weather," as in the Napa valley
          in the seventies when my mother
          still lived there, distressed

by her lawn's dry patches marring
          the verdure, mottled like old skin—

Now my brother is driving in

to stay for a week. He's late,
upset—
his rental car's mud-streaked,
has
out-of-state plates
because in Trinidad, or—
or California or some
place—

someone made a mistake
disturbing the carefully made plans
which are his life's need.

But he's here, not fallen through
the gap of fear, his shadow cast
sharp against hillside weeds.

This mountain is a graveyard,
its stones the bones of the dead.
Our parents' dust flies

into the air under the hard
parching sun. We two are left,
disconnected. A gnarled pine

shades our greeting. A breeze,
cool illusion, passes
and I'm carrying my brother's bags,

helping him through the door. I see
dust unswept at the doorsill.
No excuse surely for wordless pain

when the day has this clarity
          and blue-green flowered curtains
          hang at the huge clean window.

Stars: For My Father's Memory

Vega, Deneb, Altair—
starry arch to brace the night wall.

Past midsummer's height
dark lasts a little longer.

The fixed stars never fall.
Faintly they shine on the gravestones

at Rosita cemetery among
overgrown thorns. My father died

on June 26, commanded
his ashes to be cast over the ocean.

No stone for him, for stars
to hover over, remembering.

Cold air, cold creek tumbling
beyond the dark trees,

a creek of stars overhead
to liven darkness.

Cactus Flowering

Purple-pink petals
on knobbled thorny antlers
of desert cacti

seen swiftly through
the windows of the air-conditioned car:

petalled silks of the rich playgirl
next to the dust-swept starving
Sudanese woman

on the TV screen.
One should stop, step out into

100-degree heat and get scratched
by those thorns.
I say to my brother,

"Look at the cactus blossoms
there—and there—"

He pushes his chin out
to look hard
but he can't see them.

At Rosita Cemetery

Pine needles settle over
the old stones, the nameless ones:

incomplete families
behind a picket fence, birthdate

incised in marble. No death
yet for a wife not visiting

a husband's grave on Sunday.
Here no chiseled death-date

for Floye Smith, who, speechless,
strapped down, died March 6, 1987,

in a nursing home, her ashes not
here beside her suicide son's

despite her carved name waiting—

So much for plans.

So do I want

a northerly corner here
between a cracked red sandstone

marker, weather-shattered,
and the Adams child?

It’s not important, just somewhere
someone might visit.
I place two
fallen pine branches and five pine cones
at Floye’s blank headstone,

having forgotten to bring flowers.

Useless Stars

after the evening news

The stars oppose history,
shine on all atrocities

—the machine-gunned dead,
a ten-year-old abused

by her father, to whom a judge
gives her for custody—

          Pity the poor
and the pain of the world

that the night, sweet-smelling
of eglantine, will not quell.

The stars offer no meaning.
Constellations have tricked

weak hopeful eyes. No hope:
the diamond light

cancelled out by daytime's
flat overwhelming white.

“Genuine Heart of Sadness”

Birds twitter, sun
          again hot and clear outside.
Mauve penstemon droops

in the vase. Husband naps.
          I sit cross-legged on the dusty
rug. My brother—how

to help? Impossible—
          The room is curtained,
semi-shadowed,

quiet and unquiet.
          Heartless now to raise
a lofty hymn to diamantine day:

The flaw in the jewel—
          let it cleave open there.

After Reading Tu Fu

Parched ground under day's-end sun,
long pine shadows over dry grass:
I pipe water to fir-tree roots,
write poems to bring blossoming
to purple lupine and scarlet gilia.
Mountain wind drifts to cities
where books rot in flooded basements.
It brushes this crescent moon rising westward.

"In the deepest water the fish's utmost joy."
In highest mountains empty purest blue.
A well a hundred feet beneath hard earth
draws from the source. A car passes,
kicks up neurotic dust. My son, why this
discontent, blaming others? Writing you,
I put aside the pen to watch the moon sink
behind Spring Mountain where the creek
                                        comes down.

Haiku at Midnight: At the Desk

Silence. Curtains hang
        between the lightless room and
Saturn's splendid rings.

. .

No sound. Icebox hums.
        Husband sighs, reading in bed.
Pen scratches page, pauses

. .

Speechless, my eyeglasses
        lie next to a small basket
woven of plain grass

. .

Much paper, milfoil-
        white, to be thrown away, much
to bloom in meadows

. .

To pacify the
        raucous red paste-jar, one must
turn off the late lamp

. .

Desire! You keep pens
in jars, and the gauzy veil flung
across the unseen overhead.

Once More at Rosita Cemetery

(i)

An old man stakes out the plot
for my grave. His frail arm lifts
a sledge hammer too heavy for it,

almost driving a pipe into the ground
with my name on it, not yet
memorial. In his soft gentleman's

voice he speaks of history,
his Civil War forebears, some for
the North, some for the South: "You know,

even afterwards the Southerners
were still convinced they were right—
couldn't persuade them to think otherwise."

Opinion hard as Barre granite.
History alleviates, can't cancel. "We
buried a baby here. And over by those trees

our plot—" And then he's pleased
to see the sunburnt blond-bearded
worker come to help him clear

fallen pinecones and prune back
wayward mountain mahogany. It's late
in the morning. They'll work all day

tidying graves, for those on both sides.

(ii)

Dawn thought:
meet the gentle old man
under the benign
Rosita pines

Noon thought:
grandson coming to stay in the cabin—
the sun
past meridian

Night thought:
Why afraid? Consciousness
doesn't make much
of itself, touches
lightly, breaks off,
resumes.

Evergreens spread
dry needles, a sign
that they live
for a while.

Rain

freshens grass-tips, not
deeper. Still a fire danger
in higher forests.

Dry holds underground
at the parched roots, more than
depression dust, fear.

Can poems help the mind
lying in wilderness, an
unbanked campfire?

Lightning opens low
steel-gray clouds. Thunder
rattles the doorframe.

More rain will soak in
to the meadow still half straw
and stunted blanketflower,

cut a runnel straight
downhill. Dry hearts, they're
passing you—the hungry

black man at McDonald's door,
the rag-heap sleeping on
the railroad station floor.

Heat Lightning

for the infant sleeping

Lightning plays in night clouds
to the east. Moon and stars in clear
        dark overhead. No choice

. .

        Still pine shadows crisscross
silver meadow, silver road. Child
        sleeps under silver roof

. .

        Wild silent light dances
protection over farm-lights, its
        timid imitators.

. .

        Night-obscured mountains,
books, ink on paper, patience –
        these let me sleep

        like the little boy growing
between thunderheads over
        far mining towns

        and the talus slope
always to be climbed.

By Moonlight

Moon on high: a stone
in the lake of the sky
invites a diver

as into an ocean
to go deep, deeper
to grasp a lighted world,

dive to rise
up through trees
of black coral,

a sea-creature
foreign to daylight,
its dry perverse pain,

drawn to the crystal eye
which changes,
truthful as dream.

Darkness

No stars but blackness past
          the porchlight's pale angle along
the wet grass. No sign:

eyes strained from typing,
          wrist arthritic. Night trees drip
invisible. That black cloud

blocks off what stage? It's
          after midnight and I'm not
finished. What made me think at dawn

of twenty years ago, my homemade
          olive green skirt and round-collared
print blouse, when the kids

slept in double cot-bunk beds
          behind olive green curtains
next to shelves of treasures

crayons, mica-stones—
                              that *deja-vu*?

Late

Scorpio low in the south,
Antares caught in a pine branch,
Vega's moved

only slightly past zenith.
Mind of quiet night expands
midsummer's gem

at heart. A painter friend,
her hair gone white,
opaque stone—lapis—

in her wedding band,
had her wallet stolen: "nothing
but driver's license

and 53 cents." Knows "changes
must come—maybe drawing
is what I do best."

Care for an old man
in an old house brings
her foot to the same threshold

daily. Fixed starlight's faint sheen
on an unnoticed
windowsill.

Part Four

FRENCH WINDOWS

From a Paris Sketchbook

Eiffel Tower over
plane trees, sidewalk tables,

smooth green lawn between paths
where nannies watch infants

roll balls, jump rope: *La Grande*
Jatte moderne, serene.

· ·

Place de la République
        at midnight. Amber *phares*
circle past cafés, pink
        fringed shades, geraniums
in boxes. A couple
        lean together, head to head.

· ·

On the boulevard a *flâneur*
        in shirtsleeves strolls
among tree-shadows, flicks
        a cigarette away, passes
into a dark sidestreet. Music from
        an unseen jukebox.

· ·

Darkness overhead. Who can see
          moon or stars when floodlights
burnish golden flanks
          of warriors' horses rearing
before the door of the *Cirque d'Hiver*
          posed in continual sun?

Notre Dame de Blanc-Manteaux

in the Marais

Our Lady in dulled aura
of uncleaned gold opens

accepting hands over the
holy book and microphone.

Clear plastic covers the
holy table's old lace—

no great light here
from the pallid clerestory.

Confession hour: the booths
empty, ecclesiastical chat

from some back room. Large
Renaissance Virgin's jarred

from her frame. By Vincent
de Paul's bust a display

of children's crayoned offerings:
Jésus ressuscité: Je crois, crois-tu?

Yes, I do—in the chipped paint
and one or two candles

in the brune disintegration,
slow sinking of too hard a floor.

Interior: Midnight

8, rue du Grand Prieuré

In the nursery, the hand-sewn quilt
that wrapped my daughter's infant son
and red knit pants outgrown sit stacked

on shelves. He's walking now,
wears bigger shoes. Tomorrow in the south
I'll see him, changed from the round

soft outdated photo-baby.
Stocking dolls my grandmother made
for me—and I played with them—

stand on a corner shelf. She
and her daughter have vanished.
My hair is graying. Where's my handwork?

At Musée Carnavalet, unknown painters
recorded the blood poured away
under stones I stepped across today

in the Place de la Bastille,
thinking them neutral, ordinary
like me, blank.
To record:

this stitch outlasts the hand that sewed.
His eye will read, or hers–whose?
Whoever wants to know the revolution

continuing, doing and undone.

In the Dark Garden – 10:30 p.m.

Rabastens-sur-Tarn, near Toulouse

We sit under acacias' feather leaves
after a passing storm. Crickets creak
in far fields a language both French
and English. Open shutters bring
cool into small bedrooms beneath
whose windowsills sleep hydrangeas
and begonias. One cry from the
child's crib; he turns over, sleeps again.

Another child next spring.
Overhead the quiet stars.

Siesta: Entr'acte

Big fly buzzes from
        back garden to front terrace
over this table.

I mended a hole
        in an unneeded sweater.
Sunflowers turn straw

on the hill. This sun's
        a heavyweight winner; I
demand another bout.

Rebellious mind wants
        up. Old body sweats. On the
terrace, purple, mauve,

pink-rose petunias,
        begonias wine-red-leaved
in russet pots, more

hot-headed than the sun.

I sketch
        rose de rosier de
                Rabastens, oeillet rouge –
                        ni mots ni l'encre inclus

At a Rainy Window, 2 P.M.

Gray-black clouds move north, shift south
over the cathedral and the cemetery.

The baby can't stop his temper tantrum.
Parents' feet pass up and down the hall.

French flag flies above the Occitanian
crusaders' cross, gold on red,

a heart-struggle still after eight centuries.
Une guerre d'annexion, king and pope

joined their powers against independence
of spirit. *Esprit* equals "mind" in French.

But in Tibetan, mind lives in the heart center.
It thinks before words. A nephew plays

with his uncle in the garden where trees
still drip heavy with rain. Sun arrives,

temporary, maybe. It's dawn in Minnesota
where a daughter-in-law starts chemotherapy.

Which power wins, hope or history?

Roses bloom for no reason. Appreciate!
Appreciate! Here comes another buzz of rain

which means take an umbrella while traveling.
And it's nearly time to go—the child

to his nap, cancer-ridden girl to her doctor,
and I to what, under what flag of lost causes

in a country thick with mosses, aged trees,
fields of weed where swallows nest in stones

from *châteaux* fallen in the fifteenth century?

Late Summer Meditation

Voices from the garden after rain:
two little girls exclaim over the hydrangeas.
My daughter sews during the infant's siesta.
I sit in the breezeless bedroom,
fertile damp soaking my fingers and eyebrows.
Grapes and tomatoes ripen in the farm-plot.
In this countryside, a horn of plenty:
Other lives complete. Loneliness of thought solo—
                    the best *donnée*.

After Ponge

(i)

The abyss between word and thing is total. Human desire makes it bridgeable. But it must be the right bridge, delicate and strong, a *pont neuf.* Is it always poetry? Is it worth disputing the label? The deepest desire is to speak the unspeakable. But these depths don't contain sin or evil. The unsaid is not the unsayable. The unconscious can open with simplicity; it's honorable, itself and not something imposed or external. The real word both touches upon and creates reality. Nor should it necessarily be called art.

Ponge's carnation: *oeillet*. Oyez oyez: hear, hear. For a child one points to an object. The carnation, *oeillet*, is a bridge between word and thing. But "carnation" and "oeillet" have nothing to do with each other, or the flower garden.

(ii)

The abyss between word and thing isn't total, or there would be no need to search for *le mot juste*, would there? Is this right word closer to 'the thing'? But what 'thing'? A word is also a thing.

(iii)

A word
is also a sound,
a violin
from the next room.

If Beethoven, deaf,
heard his music,
isn't a poem
evolved in the silence
between
the farthest stars?

In Provence, Near Venasque: Le Beaucet

After a dusk climb
to the ramparts
of a ruined castle,

sad Catalan music
on a guitar
half-badly played

before the altar
of the little church
under repair—

old paintings stacked
under a dusty sheet
lean crookedly,

bug-killer sprayed
for concertgoers' benefit
stings the eyes,

a missed note or four
on a dead string—

At intermission
on the unlit parapet
the guitarist smokes, shaky.

The battlement's rubble settles deeper.
Young volunteers, they say,
work on fixing the church.

Art is a skewed composure
of what isn't yet mastered,
a dismembered past,
disarrangement.

Tarnished gilt on a nameless statue—let it stay.

A Failed Watercolor of the House at Venasque

False eye evens out
the house too rectilinear
to start with. Crude color

and square brush in a child's
paintbox dab at contrast,
wall-shadow, but the vast

light won't be confined.
Would-be painter is the slave
of external sensation

mistaken for the "real."
But all materials are good,
workable, even this room,

tight and heating up
as the Midi afternoon
comes on—

straight black line out of the picture
on the right: electric wire, or the phone
—a mistake—no tie-line
from daughter to mother

I didn't clamp it
to the pale stone façade, but
it has to be there,

not the worst part of the composition.

Stone Water-Trough
at a Crossroads in Provence

Between Venasque and Saint-Didier
fresh water drips continually
into a basin that overflows
into a *lavoir* beyond the pillar.

Off of rough slopes, breezes
from vineyards with ripening grapes
ruffle the plane trees' fat leaves.
Cool of oncoming autumn.

Rocks are loosening in the slopes
ready to fall into crumbling gullies
among banks of drying golden stubble,
weeds and live oak.

It is 1950 in the Napa valley
at Stonehouse where my mother gardens
in overalls, her long hair
tied with a shoestring, and
my father

sits at the picnic table
reading *The San Francisco Chronicle*—
Bells of Saint-Didier sound from
Mont La Salle, the monastery's

blue-tiled tower above the trellised grapevines
of the Christian Brothers,
from whom we get—my father smiles—
our water and our wine.

In Paris Again

Cool autumnal blue
sky over narrow streets, more
cool in long shadow

• •

at the Musée d'Orsay

Sober Cézanne: brown
table, gray pitcher, fruit, white
napkin struck by strange light

His apples pour across
a blue-flowered cloth. In my daughter's kitchen
tomatoes in a cobalt bowl

on faded mauve African batik
beside curtainless windows

• •

at Café Procope

On the sidewalk by the
back door where revolutionaries
stepped, a red-faced
body sleeps stretched out
in grease-black suit, shoeless
smiling a little
as in America, inventor of revolutions

·   ·

Reading Segalen's *Voyage to the Country of the Real,*
imagined as he traveled in China in 1914,
so I go down steep stairs into the metro
                    at St-Michel

·   ·

Standing behind the great *horloge*
          of the museum, time appears
                    reversed over the Seine which flows
                              brightly in its unchanged
direction.

·   ·

the next day

Gray light behind
livingroom drapes, but open windows
show clear sky again.

Clarity comes back
if time does not: a tangled dream
no more real, nor less,

than light whose space seems
eternal. Time to take off
a faded nightdress, put on

a shirt bright as bougainvillea
and white summer sandals
to walk the city

whose sewers one may
visit, study how the water
of the Seine collects

its filth, is filtered
and re-cleaned,
continues its collecting.

In A Dream My Mother

appears in a chartreuse suit,
          tells me she couldn't find
the right shoes:

I shout, "She's alive—proof
          of physical resurrection!"
I walk with her, convinced truly.

Then by Canal Saint-Martin
          she sits down on a bench,
slumps, eyes closing. She's going back

to death's place, inaccessible.

Waking, not loss
          but opening of unseen connection
is the dream's sense—

          Haunted all day—*Chartreuse de Parme*,
                    the drink, a charterhouse,
                    her Girl Scout oxfords,
                    my foot pain –

Sitting late in a street café
          I try to tell my husband
how good it was, the dream,

and start to weep.

After the Museums, By a Window, Late Afternoon

Prajña, knowledge,
mothers the mind.
Empty sky provides

birthing space. Wind
rises, collects
bits of grit,

a crumpled paper
or two, passes
them on. In

the museum relics
of a bishop's cope,
signature

of a tormented poet.
Everyone dies. Daughter
will listen to

dream-mother's words
alive, remember as she
hears the street-sweepers

brushing up debris
first thing
in the morning.

Une Américaine à Paris

World of another language—
is it so unlike the American,
so word-made?

Narrower sidewalks, cleaning men
in green uniforms with green brooms,
odd electric switches,

water-heaters—these no longer multiply
differences. Street-noise the same.
A mother in the park

bawls out the bigger boys who push
the littler. Sunlight. The faces stare.
Paris doesn't make

all Parisians happy, either.
The well-coifed sun-bronzed woman
in sunflower gold linen,

patent pumps to match, looks off into air
as she passes. At home, backs to each other,
my daughter and I sit reading.

Larousse by me slowly aids
decoding of *Libération* but doesn't help
break down the wall between

thought and speech. But thought too
fails. Voices in the street—I can't hear
nor catch the tone—

fear, pleasure?—to which I want
to respond. *Plein air* alone,
what words make the transformation?

The Louvre: Egyptian Antiquities

Early morning. No one around the ground-floor tomb,
the *mastāba* of a man of means, a stonewalled room.
Thus I'm alone as he was at the house of death when troops
of women singlefile with slim white-draped hips brought fruits
of every kind—dates, figs—vegetables, grains to soothe
his life-hunger, and men lined up to bring him each a goose,
a hare, a fish, for death could not be very different.
They made known
the way into the unknown eternal by carving it in lasting stone.

The seated scribe, androgyne, sees into some far space.
He has high cheekbones, a straight spine. A scroll
lies across his lap. The words to come are essential. Wait.
Hieroglyphs dictated to the carver give testimonial
that the dead aren't so, entirely.
What then to leave in place
for those whose desert tombs are rubble, utterly effaced?

À Bientôt

September. Chill breeze.
          7 p.m. Clouds rosy under
gray at the end of

rue St. Antoine. We
          to New York tomorrow, our hosts
to Moscow Monday.

World scattering: last smile
          from the infant a voluble
break—
            not to take

possession means to
          keep on longing. How can sky,
that nothingness through

which we'll fly, connect?
          Emptiness also is form.
A daughter isn't

her mother; all genes
          are accidents passed on.
Stone arches of the

ancient Place des Vosges,
          then high modern cream façades,
shelter what kind of

midnight?

*****

Part Five

ON NEW YORK TIME

Re-Entry

New York, 8:50 p.m. 3 September

(i)

POW!   out of JFK Air France terminal a/c, oy vey
94-degree heat, dirt, crowd on steamy sidewalk
under
the Carey Bus sign. Zigzag taxis, vans,
bunged-up autos illegally zoom
into the bus lane, blue-shirted cop yowls
through bull-horn.
Ongoing oncoming zany headlights flash
on heaped luggage carts.   Late bus comes;
passengers crush in till jampacked.
Angry-faced redhead dame curses young black
woman bus driver:
"You
pushed me off this bus! I'll
report you! I must get on this bus! My luggage is on this
bus! I hurt my back pushing my luggage
into the baggage compartment . . ."

She's off. We're off.
Gross dark bleeds over the agitated
highway.
A migraine.

No pill for it.

(ii)

East 18th street:

ripped-open black plastic garbage bag
on the sidewalk covered by heaps

of greasy bags, pizza box, plastic wrappers,
used diapers leaking infant turds onto a pizza
half-eaten. Bums got
the 3 or 4 bottles returnable
for 5 cents each.

Kid off the stoop toddles
into the oil-slick gutter-water.

(iii)

Oh Paris! Azure sky over the still canal
and calm barges as an elevated train
swings away from the Place de la Bastille—

On Boulevard Richard Lenoir the foul marketplace
at sunset—staved-in boxes, stinking fruit and fish
scraps. Dark-faced Algerians slowly sweep up.

(iv)

Le trottoir, c'est moi, this sidewalk crowd.

Hobbling old gal in fuschia polo shirt
and slacks smiles too broadly
under her gray fringe and white sunhat.

Post-insomnia depression. Too late! Too
late! Hurry to catch up with the overwrought
          competitor—who? In whose
          oncoming eyes a threat?

My concrete heart and feet
          of tar, hard, hurt. Wrenched
          a wrist muscle tugging my luggage—

                    Mind kicks up
          this garbage and the frowning face
          of the plump blonde with germanic hair

braided across her head in peasant style,
          coming at me. Her ancient hunchbacked mother
          clings to her in pain

.

                    But no: the braid is a
          twisted scarf. I didn't see it right,

          not all of it.

(v)

Well, did you think you could always vacate?
The pseudo-organized employee goes out
          to understand New York:

          2-story brick façades
above shop signs LOCKSMITH
          FISH MARKET—
                    Deformed lettering

mirrored on bent car-tops
        receding down the avenue.
Accurate data mistaken,
          too much for the eye
          too large for an idea.

(vi)

It is late in the day.

Pressures. Sweaty

breath crushes the chest.
100% humidity.

Slick skin drips.

Mad eyes
of the Citibank beggar,

crocodile eyes
of the well-dressed dean

on the campus path
between untrimmed thorn-bushes

and a Civil War cannon
aimed at the bursar's office

welcome my return.

East Hampton, Long Island:
Nearly Midnight

Wind stirs leaves overhead
in darkness. Insects unseen whir
steadily. Peepers vibrate a half-tone.

Are there stars? Myopic
eyes see the same blackness closed
or open, conditioned by light

on desks, checkbooks.
Eyes cast their purplish fever against
the eyelids, trying to substitute for

or evade the quiet lack
of definitions.

                    Night: I'll never
give up loving poetry,
its steady uselessness.

The Next Midnight, Even Quieter

Afternoon in the mind's eye:

how silver-blue water
lapped the beach
under pale blue sky silvered

with cirrus, how white sails
reached slowly over
the silenced mirror

where gulls dozed as if
summer ease might stay.

        And now the tree-frogs
        also sleep
        and asters in the centerpiece
        suggest an autumn

dusk where now goldenrod
extra-tall at roadside
darkens its flashy pollens.

        A cycle of vanishing: at the beach.
        ebullient orange rosehips
        where the roses pinked the tangle

        and these darken too.

A Cornucopia on Columbus Day

in East Hampton, remembering my mother

Born 92 years ago October 12,
died on my birthday three years ago.

Her crystal birds, fat as tears,
sit on my shelves as they sat
on hers in the nursing home.

In the jewel-box's drawers lie heaps
of earrings she searched among to match
her outfits, red, green, gold—

plastic fruits, hoops,
tiny globes of
no intrinsic value

but to make the road still curve
past hilly California vineyards
where the grapes grow purple—

In this morning's chill
I cut the wild grape's tendrils'
fruitless grip

on the young *arborvitae*,
which must stand sturdy in winter,
and heaped the yellowing vines

around the front-porch pumpkins
not yet cut with a child's ghost face
for All Saints eve.

No need
to cut the bittersweet—
later it bears
red berries.

Note in a Sketchbook

Grapevine and bittersweet
intertwine. Bugs eat both. Veins
show intricate

against light, yellow
at edges. No end to tight
grasping tendrils, drying,

stray twigs caught.

Eleventh Day, Eleventh Month

Went out in keen sun
this afternoon to cut
bittersweet's orange-red berries
from bare twigs where
cool wind shuffles leaves across
a lost lawn, an ocean tossing
brown waves, shape of Hokusai's
spume curl or Van Gogh's sky.

Autumnal art of fading:
one cell melts into another laid
under the moment's microscope.
One face among thousands opened
into a camera as the Berlin Wall
came down.
                              So much falling
reaches the core. So many leaves
I watch at 2 a.m., sleepless,
as they gleam in the moon's spotlight,
knifed by iron tree-shadows
faintly rustling under
the suddenly brilliant stars.

Before Departure

To travel, to go beyond—
        only a quick flight
to snowy Minnesota

but to go, to leave,
        to separate:

        Only a few minutes before I stepped
                into the California hospital room,
                                my mother's breath
                        had stopped.
                her mouth the hard O
        I sat beside—
                                Only
                a moment of going,
                                invisible the breath,
                then no breath:

        Oldest son's sad voice
                phoning from Saint Paul:
        "Michelle's not getting better. . ."

I pack quickly, to fly

yet every day I leave
        some clothes behind,
notes on my desk

bring, do, write . . .
        string of words on the page
for them to find.

NYC Again: On Return

Gray light through
        the back window. Dull roar of
                trucks on First Avenue.

A scrawled list
        on the desk under the light's
                eye-beam: do [this]

or [that]. Phone
        rings, irritated boss: ". . . conflicts
                in my department over

your concert. . ." so
        I must dress, go, soothe—

                Nodes of anger
                        block the connecting lines,
                subways, flight courses, pattern
                        of the Australian natives'
                songs by which their ancestors
                        in the Dream-time sang
                the world into being—

Here's a "sort of song":
        impulse along a line across
                America, a neural web of mind,

these scenes conjured
        as if on a TV screen:
                one son sleeps on a sofa

near his sick wife's bed, another son
feeds his infant boy.
Around them sweep
winds that carry all away—
but not yet.
Phone lines sway

and the radio blips
the dead of the morning,
murders, weather, the traffic

jams, thousands of stopped
cars. In each, the driver
seethes: *I, I alone, must go on.*

Insomnia: the Darkness

cuts into day-life's logic,
        wakes up another mind,
                the one that won't belong

to schedules. To live now
        in the unlit hallway, kitchen
                where the streetlight-haunted window

rattles, to think how
        living is remembering—memory
                wakes you:

                        Don't forget
        how yesterday the little grandson
        ran his red truck along the brick wall—
        or fifty years ago the father
        strung the Christmas lights
        and one, a blue parrot with a yellow beak,
        shone in the fir branches

                    not long ago but now

in the timeless dark
        that floats you like amnion.

                Dark egg of the world,
how you open, how within you
        genes infinitely continue
                    to multiply—

Fiery Sunset

in coldest December
over the wilderness beach—
sky-curve of fire and gray purple cloud edge.

Night broods, stretches
above it. Fire lies on the water,
shrinks and pales. The off-sea wind blows

freezing. Lurid sensation and pain
I'd say—too much. No regret
to their going,
but I'd be lying.

Light vanishes. We stumble back
along a crooked path among tree trunks
heavily bent over, bodies of night.

A small moon muzzled by mist
hangs in a branch as black as this
lampless earth, and lights it.

Loss of my body
threatens me. If only
I can hold such fire a while—

Delusion. One goes, and others go.

But now remember how it happened,
that gift, much more than could have been desired.

Veil

Snow is falling again.
          The driveway light shows
a white membrane blurring

yew shrubs and leafless oaks,
          ghost flesh that vanishes.
I turn off the light, begin

to take on that ending.

• •

Deep snow by morning.
          A blizzard. I rush crazy
into the cold white

beating against my face.
          Got to catch a train,
got to get there—leave my house

of shelter to struggle,
          fight. A frantic windshield-wiper
doesn't clear my sight.

Wind piles drifts
          against the padlocked
railroad station door

and the train doesn't come.
        Mad Azerbaijani shot Armenians
to get their apartments

screaming Allah! Allah!
        Carry a gun, meet a gun.
This aggression carries into snowfall:

am I also insane, blind and buried
        by the inner avalanche?

Late Afternoon, East Hampton

Leaving soon. A pause,
nervous, before getting on
to the next thing

as if that not-yet-done
weighs more than
this flighty now—

Walked to the beach
to gaze across the moss-gray sound
to the north shore's minute ridges

Wanted to keep these
in my eye, not leave,
not leave finally

the frame whose screen
of skin falls cell by cell
into the shower drain

with loose hairs not
to be replaced on the
stubborn skull believing

in long life.

So a timer will click
the night light on for safety.
A machine will speak my voice

as if I'm here. Can't postpone going
to the train, whose iron step
will not give way

as I lift my baggage in.

Endgame

Purkhang: temporarily constructed
ceremonial oven for cremation of Tibetan lamas

Hiked that last retreat day
the rutted road under evergreens
whose black branches kept
massive snow-mounds frozen,
slick, blocking the log-roads,
feet slipping till I slowed
and held each step with care
not to break a leg crossing
till ice became mud and the way
widened out of deep gloom
into meadow where the *purkhang* stands,
isolated, white-plastered, square
on a lonely rise, bare bone against green,
its four oven mouths shut tight
facing the four directions,
its chimney-tower pointing
into directionless gray space
whose cold winds whirl
a torment of wet flakes
out of the bowed fir-tree tops
tangled and overgrown at the
shaggy meadow's edge that backs off
from the cremation place.

Here the remains of a body
that had once held a mind
and had decomposed to water
packed in salt had gone to fire

and then to air (but not this air
of now) and in that air set
an arc of gold, two arcs, green-tinged,
the hoped-for rainbows in the smoke
created by the logs of *arborvitae*,
juniper, sacred fuel of enlightenment.

The fire has long been out.
White paint peels from the ledge
where a few dry flowers lie
and coins, a velvet hairpin
disintegrating in the weather.
They offered what little they had
thought up on the spur of the moment
at this temporary furnace, reminder
of a transient life declaring transience
the rule, as everyone knew and knows
and won't admit, so to gaze fixed
on this crumbling structure is deluded
and generally useless—

A sudden furious flurry of snow
whips its wild white scarves
around the white pinnacle:
such a thunderstorm will not
come again soon.

You, my world, I got an eyeful. Your turbulence
isn't internal. You cry aloud: get up,
go, why are you waiting around
as if your heartbeat were not sufficient?

Heat

abnormal for March
        brings creamy and purplish crocus
                into the pigeon-lawn

at East 16th Street.
        From Paris my daughter telephones:
                the *petit-fils* born Sunday

sleeps at her side.
        Can one dismiss from mind
                so soon those blinding

winter snowstorms? Uniformed
        workers prune the excess
                branch-tangle over the grass,

startling the pigeons off
        their brightly blossoming carpet.

Night Again

insomnia: reprise

Night wind shakes the old window.
What thought lies beyond the wall?

I was scrubbing spots off the floor,
making a list of things to forget.

The frustration of mirrors: a door
is what's wanted, an opening.

The room widened and darkened
under the same mundane ceiling light.

Breath, ah—the wind lifts
the curtain, unseen, the transformer.

So late to be transformed and left
the same, shaky, rattling in the frame.

At 5:45 p.m. before Good Friday on East 18th Street

To close the book:
regret, accept the sun's decline
behind the hospital tower.

To open another book:
meet morning sun with denial
of afternoon. The gold lilies flower

long in a pale green vase,
longer than expected, a sturdy
buddha-bronze gold

that oxidizes slowly.
Ink also lasts long on closed pages.
To read invites decay

as exposure to light ruins fine art.
Still, one wants always to keep on
reading by a good night light

till the book must drop away—
Infuriating even to think
of tiring. It is still day.

The sun still shines on Horn Peak.
Wind riffles the watercolor paper.
Another painting to be made.

Underground, wild iris, *fleur de lys*,
deepen their blue. Soon
it will cover the mountain.

TRANSITORY

A POEM SEQUENCE

in memoriam
Phuong Vu, called Michelle
born Saigon, Vietnam, 4 April 1961
died Minneapolis, Minnesota, 22 February 1991
and
for Tom

. . . this transitory life

—*The Book of Common Prayer*

Death comes without warning;
this body will be a corpse

—from *Buddhist teachings of the Four Reminders*

Part One

AT FIRST

Prologue: Photo Album

Opening the book, here they are. Michelle and Tom at her graduation from art school in 1987.

He in a gray silk shirt, silk tie, sleek dark hair drawn back in a ponytail, she slim in a silvery dress, masses of black hair around her small face. Her large deep brown eyes gaze out smiling, pleased.

A Vietnam refugee, she came to study fashion design in Minneapolis and fell in love with my oldest son, handsome but unsure, with the wrong friends. He badly needed someone to love him, appreciate, shore him up. This time he was lucky. Her funny enthusiastic adoration of him, her energy and determination to succeed, these were overwhelming. How could there not a good outcome?

• •

A photo in mind, not in the album:

We sat on an old sofa in Tom's rental house. He was out somewhere. She's not his girlfriend, Michelle said—she was lying—just a friend, but she wanted to meet his mom. She waved papers in her hand, forms to enter a national contest to discover young designers.

She would enter and win the prize!

She had the best ideas!

With the prize she'd go to New York and start a business with her own designer label, Fashions by

Michelle maybe, she wasn't sure of the name yet.

She would make wild, happy, modern clothes, loud day-glo, metallic, and get rich and famous, and Tom would come too and help.

Tom's mom lived in New York—would mom help her fix up her English in the contest application?

Her black hair fell in her eyes as she bent over the paper, writing, hopeful. Who could refuse hope? Mom. It was an election. Two heads leaned together, reading the words, trying to find the winners.

News in Afternoon Rain

in the Sangre de Cristo mountains
Colorado, 29 July 1989

Rain getting heavier, but not an omen.
It wets dusted leaves and dry ground
beyond the wide cabin window.

My son Tom on the phone
from Minnesota "Michelle is very sick—
cancer of the colon—

they operated—cut some away
but it's—it's
completely incurable, they say—"

(break) "—in the liver ...
they say: she's got a year and a half
but she denies, says 'I'll get better.'"

Rain weighs down a black-green fir branch
on the roof edge:
his wish to have been kinder, steadier,

not so drug ridden to add to her pain.
He ran marathons for recovery, kept running
for strength, health in midwestern sun

too hot, bright, humid.
Now he walks
and waits daily by her ward-bed, works
nights and hasn't slept. It's worse

to lose one not loved enough, not married:
    no future and no right ending.

        Long enclosure in the silence

as gray rain plunges
    not letting up, not even with the shock
        of more frightening thunder.

The Question

looking again at the photo album

Was it too late for her, 14 years old in 1975,
on the last plane from Saigon? Did the fatal chemical
come with her in her blood?

Probably not. She grew to 19, 20, ebullient—
"I love Tommy"—with swift scissors,
without a pattern, designed and cut

with magical accuracy
the shimmering black-silver dress,
ruffled its skirt with silver-mauve netting

This precious human body,
free and well-favored, is difficult to gain,
easy to lose

Probably not the war.
More likely the careless doctor
who said she was "pre-tubercular"

—is there such a thing?—prescribed
but didn't warn her: if one pill
is good, two are not better—

No pattern for her. The graduation picture
conceals his addiction,
the stomach pains she didn't mention,

reveals her beside him, thin, thin,
a wand in silver,
his magician, holding him.

In the Laundromat

Westcliffe, Colorado: before
closing the cabin for winter

As a woman on the Ganges
rinses her saris, as the Chinese poet
heard the washerwomen's paddles
and the clip of the quilter's scissors shaping
winter jackets, cold cloud travels
along the peaks, cutting them off. August
brings mountain autumn. Winter asters
grow purple in graying oak shadows. My breath
too is cooler. Fingers with the pen crack,
Faint split of old branch in the wind inevitable.

A farm wife folds white sheets.
Pale bundles tumble
in the dryers' round eyes.
I wipe an ice-cream smear off
the formica bench, tidying up.

A nurse strips a bed
in St. Paul-Ramsey Medical Center while
Michelle sleeps.
A waste bag taped to her thigh slowly fills.
Cells awry eat within.
A clean canvas curtain—
very clean—
hangs between her and light.

Leave in the cabin fresh-laundered beds
for whoever comes next. Don't forget.
Snow will cover dust, together
melt into earth-clefts, join
wash-water in its compelled descent.

Shrunken Notebook

leaving the mountains

(i)

Floribunda: name of my good big
drawing notebook packed
and mailed.
Too good, too big
for my shrunken words.

(ii)

Hardy asters,
showy daisies
sprinkle the mountainside
where Felix the grandson marched
and Philip floated balloons
on his second birthday—

Abundant flowers
late in the season.

I'm very tired:
can't match the work
of those young parents,
my children who grew up
in these summer mountains,
here with their children.

"Alpine fir and blue spruce
taller every season,"

said Tom in June.
He hadn't come
for ten years, kept repeating
"It's so beautiful—."
I said: the grass is greener
this year from much rain.

Zip up the carry-on bag
to close down a season,
remembering he said,
"Michelle is getting better, but
didn't want to come.
I shouldn't have let her say no.
I shouldn't have—"

A choice, regrets

harsh beyond season.

(iii)

What is still here: clean cold water,
vast day-sphere hiding the stars.

A sage of old India believed
you see a million million

galaxies within
one pore of your skin—

so limitless the mind.

But can one think
the goldenrod into bloom?

One pollen grain
lifts itself
into air.

Night Airport, Back East

Below the descending wings
massed jeweled lights
rise up out of the darkness,

make you think you might
dissolve in their amber,
a pill in whiskey,

and after you land,
it's true—you've changed
as you cross the tarmac,

grown a rich strange
saffron skin not so different
from the decomposing

stink of the hot home city.

11:30 p.m., Late Fall

East Hampton, Long Island, New York

Crickets whirr faintly.
Low flying plane shakes
          door-frames.
Moon rises one night past full.

•   •

Do crickets sing the
"tale of their tribe?" It's late,
          late to be
repeating the same note.

•   •

Tardy moon mounts slow
fragmented by a black
    leaf jagged
on tangled branching.

Momentary Manifesto

To leave things as they are.
To write something every day.
To know no thing more
          than for its instant.

Whiff of earth in the air.
Phone number on a scratch pad.
Quick! Time for a walk
          to lean on the graveyard fence.

Notes for a Tombstone

No poem as long as death:
the minutes pass 12:03; 12:04
the train is leaving

        If fragmented life
death too then in jagged pieces?
broken glass in the frame
that held the whole

Shaky train
going to the country
for the weekend—

        Assurance that the 5:29
        on Sunday comes back.

• •

Music:
yawn of workers talking
        —"all of a sudden—. . .
        ... you shoulda—"
shudder   clank of wheels
        —"too seriously . . .
        no—"

Mind's siren:
        She wasn't feeling well
        today—vomiting—
phone voice-over in memory
        —not the chemo-therapy—
        it's the tumor on the liver

Man on the seat ahead
wears tight earplugs
wired to his own private amplification

Mom, if I go to Lourdes,
the Virgin will help me, mom—

• • •

Damn the French bureaucrat refusing to speed up her papers. She's ill, can't wait. Stiff brow, snide lips: "People lie to us for a quick visa—28 working days. Nothing will hurry it."

• •

Through the dirt-stained window
thought I saw a child
in a garden, half-hidden
by a tree branch.
Train
jolts—no,
clothes only: a scarecrow.

• •

Quickly change trains.

Will it be like that?
What makes you think
it'll be a journey?

We plan
her journey to Lourdes,
to the healing water
pouring from the earth we're used to.

To heal:
Earth must do its own
healing. It must be
a healer.
That severance.
Always severing. To
go to the country,
lose the city. To
stay. But who stays?

. .

Old trees rot slowly
in grass at trackside
under the withering red
sumac-leaves.

Monuments to solidity,
brick walls also
drip water that erodes
their mortar.

Deep-dug foundations
open concrete coffins
for new walls to be
built above them.

. .

What evidence, however, proves
that continuity prevails,
that dying and being born
are in one package?

Is the body
a package for what lives
within?

Blood, nerves, walls, tracks
intertangle,
not a convenience for
transportation.

The body scientifically analyzed
consists of many millions
of constantly changing
densely-packed cells
that have no substance
yet thought of as particles
divisible into smaller
until the smallest
is nothing but
an energy charge—
thus a constellation
of energies
not
a body.
It's a fantasy to think
one has a body. Or no body.

. .

"Being" is social,
a name put on a birth certificate,
    graduation list, police blotter
    —label: female
    or Vietnamese.

A doctor signed "cause of death"
    for my 89-year-old mother: "pneumonia."

    For Michelle, shall they say
    "Agent Orange" or—
        but the right word is "birth."

Bureaucrats won't stand for it:
any confusing of the certificates
that verify the body's arrival or departure.

. .

Trying to think of my death:
open a door into darkness,
find another unseen door,
try to back out into light
    but think: no,
    this time no going back

. .

On the Manhattan-bound train
doze off, wake up.

As the sun goes off
amber lights come on along the track.

        Does thinking ahead prepare?
        Michelle will see Paris
                and drink the water of Lourdes.

        She will go down stone steps to sewers
        beneath a great city
                where the vaulted tunnels
        receive visitors
                Persephone to Hades
                lost bride to her groom

Tom goes with her, learning the way
that can't be learned

I'm thinking the way
that can't be thought

        .   .

Never the same people going back to the city
Though I take the same train weekly

The morning subways at the same hour
at the same stop contain no one I've ever seen

Many trains, many million cells
beyond mind and memory.

"A life has to be more than lived;
it has to be imagined."

Write it random,
the pieces, bits of paper
larger than the whole.

They Leave For Lourdes

(i)

Slowly they moved
out of sight—Tom's dark
jacket, dark hair,
Michelle in black
became shapes among others
darkening as they passed
up the curved tunnel of TWA's terminal A

My eyes hold them in sight
as I held them
in the narrow basement
on Van Buren Avenue
and in the shabby
double room on 27th street
where Tom sat sick with heroin, denying

And hold myself
in my mind's eye in East Hampton
as I stared into the carpet,
its even tan sheen
not telling me to phone, nor
not to—
        Can much
be changed in the raw pit
that I think is what I am?

An open window,
a net, a grid,
a permeable membrane—
this mind full of holes.
The wind rushes through
these meshes,
ruffles these scribbled pages.

(ii)

I sit in Terminal A
because security says
"Passengers Only"
to the gate—
and I
should have broken the law
and gone to be with them
till they boarded,
not let
the break happen sooner.

O Lourdes, your water
isn't so powerful,
is it? May she live.
May I live. Isn't it
the continuing wish
that also knows
it's denying?

(iii)

The break—was it
umbilical? I won't
sever: I hold her in mind.

She wears my mother's black
cashmere coat for softness
and warmth and my black
beret and a red
plaid scarf I bought her
on the sun-down street
across from Bloomingdale's
as we walked while
Tom talked of coming
to the Central Park duck pond
when he was a kid

And I hold in mind
before the divorce
the 9th floor apartment
on Avenue C with eight-year-old Pat
in his baseball suit
on the terrace where we ate
hamburgers on high stools
at a narrow table and watched
pigeons on tenement roofs
and the East River as it curved
around Alphabet City
before we moved to Avenue B where Tom
came home crazy stoned for the first time,
the first time we knew of–

this family that can't be destroyed
although it's broken.

So memory in fragments recurs
to build a gaze that holds
something,
a moment
as we three sat waiting in the café
of Terminal A, a rehearsal.

(ii)

This stiff hand oddly writes
in the cold wind
on the subway platform at
Howard Beach

unexceptional words, no style, functional
as a plastic café table, scene
of the action, plain fact symbolic of itself.

He lives to help her live.
No junk, booze or fantasy
because death is stronger,
everybody's fix.

• •

Night flight
into night's heart

this subway car worms
its passage back
into the congested organism

as if coming and going
were mere mechanisms.

Part Two

WAR

December Sixteenth in East Hampton

(i)

The snow lay on the ground
The stars shone bright
When Jesus Christ was born
On Christmas night

An old hymn
sings itself on the snowy driveway
among dark pines that grow
a foot a year to cast a longer shadow.

What children's Christmas tree
of memory stands multi-lit
and hung with paper chains?

Grown children elsewhere—
no more church in which to sing
lauds to illusion

Unto us a boy is born
the king of all creation
Came he to a world forlorn
the lord of every nation

What patina now on the dark pews
Of Trinity Church, St.Louis?

What if—again—the young mother
walks through the rectory door

into the festive living room?
There two tall strange dolls,

gift of an unknown giver, stand
on the mantel in medieval dress

of blood-red velvet, surcoat, wimple.
Lord and lady of a castle, they

don't look at each other.
                                        We
watched the kids tear open their gifts.

They're happy. We meant well.
Our gifts to each other I can't recall.

(ii)

Not to make too much of memory.

The exact detail blurs.

It isn't the one day itself
of shiny wrappings and ceiling-tall tree
but all the days stored in attic boxes,
handmade ornaments to hang again
among the boughs—
          a child's red-crayoned Santa says again
          "I whit you a Merry Christmas"—
but that the day was or was not,
is or is not gone.
Vain to repeat in ritual the past.
Vain to think one doesn't try.

"Pleasure and pain are ornaments
it is pleasing to wear"

I twine lights around the pine
nearest the driveway.
Wind shakes these earth-stars
in the blue dusk,
but they fling their ellipses wider,
hold tight.

Remembering the House of My Childhood

Though our California house outside was ordinary stucco, not even tile-roofed, inside our living room contained heavy dark teakwood chairs, sofa, high round table intricately carved with writhing dragons, trees and branching flowers of inlaid mother-of-pearl. These greatly strange somnolent creatures turned the room into a lair. Its gold wallpaper and deep black-brown woodwork increased its interesting uncomfortable strangeness. Not like other people's houses. We weren't like other people, but was that a good thing or not?

Beside the fireplace stood the peacock screen, embroidered birds in stitches tiny and subtly pearly blue and blue-gray tinged on the pale gray silk. Glass protected the delicate fabric held in a dark teak frame on pearl-studded feet. Once, perhaps in China, where Chinese women had stitched those pale and graceful birds delicately perched, this screen had protected an open brazier, but now it couldn't be used as a real fire screen before our western fire. It was art, rich, inaccessible, valued, out of its place.

We were to live always, my brother and I, with "the Chinese furniture." It came from our artist grandmother. It was our legacy.

Once the Chinese sofa and the two slenderer chairs were sent to me in St. Louis to the house of my first marriage. Later I sent them back.

The peacock screen is posed near that sofa, those chairs, in my unmarried brother's apartment where there is no fireplace and nothing moves. But my remembered and present life emerges out of obscured and denied labors as richly embroidered as the peacock screen, a jewel-encrusted accident.

In Transit, At War

opposing Iraq, 1991

(i)

To New Haven, January 16: On the Brink
7:45 a.m.

Engine roar fills the stone tunnel
in which the waiting train sits:
gunfire constant in the ears
filling all space. It piles up
overhead, stone on stone crushing one.
Cave closes in. It is dark.
It roars. It's hard to breathe.
It's not my death but what I must witness.
It hurts. It won't stop.

(ii)

To East Hampton: January 18
1:15 p.m.

My train seat faces backwards but
not to look at the old private
war that other son Jeff wants
to start up again.
Think back, my son,
to the mountains
and Goodwin trail—
how you ran far ahead
to find your own spring or bend
for stopping-place.
But we all met

high up and looked out
over the Wet Mountain valley
trying to spot our house
in the dense green.
                Couldn't see it, ever
                but always got back there.

(iii)

War By Television: January 19
5:00 p.m.

Radar TV sees a bomb hit
a thousand miles away
but it is not far-sighted.

In the desert brash colors
of aviators' uniforms
and blue sky are transmitted
onto our flashy silvered TV screen:
        the Israeli ambassador in pinstripe suit
        at ease and dignified,
        Lesley Stahl's blonde pageboy,
        her serious questions—

How many screens screen off
the bully Achilles dragging Hector's body
through the dirt,
        that old fury and degradation?

Blind eye registers blue clarity,
sleek steel of bomber's wing.
What does the sharp detail show?

Can his mother see past
the pilot's white explosion
over Baghdad?

CNN live audio hears no news
that bleeds or stinks. No news
at all, as if there were no killing.

On Martin Luther King Day

in East Hampton

Many cars fill the snow-packed driveway
up to Calvary Baptist Church.

The hero's demeanor is enough.
No need for weapons beside truth.

If black goes on screaming "black"
and white "white," what peace?

A son rages at his mother-vision,
believing in that white ghost,

the mother a viper, a fiction,
much as a dictator believes

in his own power.
                    No missile
settles any dispute, but the sky

is full of them. Why are you sitting,
my angry son, behind your newspaper?

This mother walks patiently as a white
woman's black maid on the streets

of Montgomery in the 1960s,
won't ride the bus that says "bad mom."

Segregation isn't workable when a bomb
takes out the communication center.

The need to reconnect the lines
comes first. You send back gifts

and you won't phone. Aren't those tracers
in the blacked-out sky? What if Israel

won't attack?

Three-Day Weekend

the Gulf War continues

(i)

Warming the Car in the East Hampton
Village Parking Lot; January 24

Warriors say "The war is going as we expected."

A gingerly war. The missiles send telegrams:
"let's talk—stop—let's talk."

A mother writes a son—let's talk.
        Sea sky here is streaked pale blue.
        Black smoke clouds the Gulf sky.
        Does the oil underground catch fire too
and burn always, not sending signals, as coal mines
burn continually under northeast Pennsylvania?

Car motor quietly hums, like breath,
        neither for you nor against you,
        a language unknown but learnable.

(ii)

Nearly Full Moon: January 26

Through bare branches
the moon moves as if
the luminous blue clouds do not.

Cold wind.
Tick of a dry leaf
like a loosened safety catch.

(iii)

Day Sky: January 27

Dulled hazy noon chills
this East End sand-spit.

Troops in camouflage suits
look at sky slipping
into darkness over desert.
Is this the same sky?
My mind or another's?

"We'll watch The Super Bowl too,"
says a girl to TV's desert cameras.
"It's better than just
putting on our chem suits
and chem masks—"

Late, Alone

(after W.C.W.)

The train
whose car is empty
except for
one carries
through a rainy night
its gloomy
lights and mud-grimed
windows where
reflected
a gray head and
gray bunched collar
hunch into colder
wet and darkness

Dream

The house is cold,
old, its passages blocked.
Black is the fitted suit
I wear but black and white
wide-striped the blouse.

I came without
suitcase or a toothbrush.
Can't find a bathroom
or anything to eat.

Two old ladies—
servants—pass ignoring me.
I hunt for people,
find some, none
I know, but one has a baby,

blond like Jeff.
His mouth is bulging strangely.
He's strangling.
Deep into his open mouth

I reach and remove
a huge weed burr,
and with full hand-sweep
pull out a whole crushed
hardboiled egg

still in its shattered shell.
"A whole egg!" I announce.
No wonder he was choking!"
And the baby starts to cry.

Manifesto Under a Subway Ad

The train has gone into the tunnel.
Fake planes fly on blue poster-board.
We imagine the war we see on TV.
Lights flash by outside the windows.
There is pressure on my ears, hurting.
Let my words be like that pain,
not a corporate jet.

PART THREE

MINNESOTA

Minnesota, Night and Day and Night

(i)

Flying To Minneapolis By Night

Too sleepy to write.
Engines roar, as black as what's out there.
They keep the lights on.

(ii)

Being in Saint Paul By Day

Sleepy again beside
the dying girl's bed set up
in their living room.
Wanting not to watch her eyes
only partly open
only the whites showing.

Half awake at dawn to roam the apartment,
see my son's tangled hair
nearly as black as the pillow
he's buried his face in
dead asleep in the black-curtained bedroom.

Meditation on the Sacred Heart

Flying in the night
the great engines pumped
as if I dozed
inside a giant heart endlessly
pumping, as if
an ocean of empty space
could not fail to pass
through auricle and ventricle,
'sacred heart' of the universe.

Then the plane set down.
The engines shut off.
The 'sacred heart' was beating
faintly in the recessed lighting
of the long terminal hallway.

Over the kitchen sink, framed Jesus points
to his heart.

In the bed, Michelle's body
holds its swelling tumor.

Sacred heart, sacred swim-bladder
to float you under the weight
of dark water.

Sacred tumor if it leads
to eternal life—

no one thinks this.
No consolation for this going,

ordinary and inevitable
as finishing the orange juice
in its bent jug on the sink-edge.

Sitting in the Half-Dark Beside the Sickbed

Channel Four displays
scenes of this new war.

Outside the loose windows
cars whoosh north, south

on Snelling Avenue.
Michelle's morphine machine

whirs and clicks its programmed dosage
into her neck-vein.

She groans. Bird-thin hands
twitch on her chest.

A slight frown over
her drug-closed eyes seems

to mean a bad dream
is bringing her breath into gasps,

precious desperate witness
to the body which must

soon give up its civil war.

The sounds of warplanes fill
the room. Snelling traffic

roars as if on an overhead bridge.
The screen dims and brightens.

A rocket follows military music.
She speaks a name or—

I can't hear. Her eyes,
puzzled, briefly meet mine

and close again.
Loud jukebox from below

in the restaurant,
drowns out—not quite—

the whir and voices
of Iraqi prisoners of war.

If I went downstairs and said:

"There's someone dying; would
you please turn down the music"

wouldn't they say:

"All the more reason for us
to push the decibels higher,

to blow away death,
prevent the little whir

and ominous click
as the needle lifts from the disk

to leave its dreadful silence."

Portrait of Grief By Morning Light

Feast day of Our Lady of Lourdes, February 11

He stands in the empty dining room.

Light from north windows touches
his left cheekbone and jacket sleeve.

He faces her hospital bed in the living room
but is browsing the latest *Newsweek*
that just came in the mail.

It's later than he meant to leave.
The two birds chatter in the metal cage
on its stand by the window.
She has had her morning pills.

He has flushed the vein-pump and
gotten her to eat three bits of melon.
His car-key is in his pocket.
He kissed her, said "goodbye,
honey," and then paused

on his way out of the living room.
In the front hall he picked up the magazine,
whose cover reads "The science
of high-tech WAR"—
and his head is bent over it,
absorbed. The light edges

his chino trouser-leg. One foot
points slightly toward the door.
He's taking in news of the war.
He can't quite make himself move
to leave. It must not
be time to leave.

An Ordinary Day in Saint Paul

(i)

The windows are sealed with clear plastic.
Snow beyond the glass runs in dirt-brown
        furrows along Snelling Avenue.

The home-visiting nurse discusses morphine
        dosage with Michelle: "down to
        2.5 an hour?"—"yes"—"or 2?"—"yes"

Tom is impatient, weary: "the bolus
        should be more—"

The little machine is set. Yesterday
        she had too much, so today
        she thinks she doesn't need painkiller.

(ii)

The thermostat is set at 80°.
        Its dial reads 68°.
        The bathtub drain backs up
as I wash a shirt in the sink basin.
Michelle groans. I rub her back.
I throw out two dead carnations from
        the old bouquet whose baby's-breath
        is drying and put two fresh
        red blood-clots in among the pink.

Asian New Year: year of the Ram.

I draw an auspicious red dragon
with marker on pieced-together
typing sheets and tape it over
the doorway HAPPY NEW YEAR
MICHELLE. Red for good luck.

Cartoons come on the TV.
It's 4:00 p.m. and getting dark.

(iii)

Dark at 6:00 p.m.

Tom comes in without her *photai* soup:
Vietnamese restaurants are closed
for the holiday.

Michelle spits into the pink
plastic basin under her chin.
She lies on her side.
Pain keeps her from closing her eyes.

Tom bends over her.
He empties the vomit-basin.

The landlady knocks at 11:00 p.m.
"They're complaining below that
water's coming down—"
I let her in to look at the tub.
Tom, angry: "No, no —
don't let them in—"

She takes my hand, says "I'm so sorry"
    and her two boys watch
    with terrified dark eyes.

Tom empties the vomit-basin.
Afternoon spit was faintly white.
Now the spit is red-flecked brown.

She lies in the dark.
The TV flashes a re-run of *The Love*
        Connection.

The red carnations on the table
        look black.
The red dragon flying over the door
        looks black.

Two Dreams of the Week of February 17

(i)

It's 1:15 p.m. and I'm a student who should be in English class. I know this but something holds me back—not exactly that I can't find the classroom but that I—somehow—just—can't—really tell myself I must go. Something is more pressing but there are no words for it.

(ii)

I go to the three-story Victorian house of which I've dreamed before—the one with the secret fourth story, the door to which I discovered in back of a closet. Up a dark narrow stairway a huge attic packed with luxuries—trunks of antique brocade gowns and jewelry, rooms under the eaves piled with antique tables, chairs, paintings, valuables which I sensed more than saw—but above all, space is there, rooms that can be cleared and the treasures taken down and examined, space I always woke before it could be penetrated . . . and this time I go to the door of the house and declare firmly, "I know this house has a secret fourth story and I want to go up into it." They say, "But look, it's boarded up and the stairs have been removed. You can't get there." As I gaze up at the white-painted bevel-siding, the outlines of two windows rounded at the top appear clear, where the siding has been fitted in and painted over to match the exterior of the house. What tool to pry loose the veneer and take possession? I cannot find it.

A Tomb for Michelle

(i)

Friday night: she vomited till dawn.
Michelle's eyes are dark
in the bedroom darkened by the black
          curtain covered by huge pink peonies.
Red-brown fluid dribbles from the
          corner of her mouth into the kidney-shaped basin.
I empty it repeatedly
    into the mauve plastic bowl
    beside me on the floor

until I can't stand to look
down into that little lake
          of darkness deep as the world.

(ii)

Saturday she sleeps, vomiting,
lulled by Compazine.
Sunday she eats two bites
of pineapple sherbet.
Jazz plays in the background
until the five CDs go round
and shut themselves off.
One day into the year of the Ram—
Aries her birth sign too.
The stars too weak to change
the mad cells' course
cannot be seen in the gray daylight.

(iii)

Monday comes: "I want to go
to the hospice—they give me
shots and demerol—it's better—"
But the hospice can't take her
till Tuesday, the 19th.
She sleeps. Tom adjusts the morphine,
goes out to work awhile,
comes back to her,
all nights of the black universe
in her black hair,
all earth in the pale yellow-brown flesh
shrinking across her cheekbones,
all-healing Lourdes-water futile in the glass
with the straw on the table beside the bed.

She refuses to drink.
She hasn't eaten on Monday.
Tuesday is coming—the day he knows
he must lift her from bed
into a wheelchair
and with the medi-van driver
take the chair down the twenty-two
green steps to the street door
and wheel it into the van—
He shuts off the thought.
No morphine for it.

(iv)

Monday [Interlude]

Tom is away.
It's noon.   Suddenly she
must use the bathroom.
I pull the wheelchair close
and pull her upright as
her long claw fingers tightly
clasp mine.

She steps onto the floor, reaches
for the wheelchair arm,
misses, collapses onto her knees
on the cold brown hardwood.

I can't lift her,
slide a blue comforter under her
partway and cover her slumped
body with the comforter
of white roses,
but comfort isn't possible
against my horrified helplessness.
"Mom, mom!—" Tom cries out
over the phone: a plaint.
"How could you let this happen?"
Wouldn't I protect if I could?
I too am a ghost,
a phantasm, empty space
held together by a white shirt
and blue pants, crumpled cloth.
I sit on the floor beside her, mourning.

Tom comes
and with her stick-thin arms
wrapped around his neck
and with his tall body
and long arms around her
raises her up again
for a little while.

(v)
Late Monday Night

He sleeps on the sofa.
Light flickers from soundless TV.
Four tall pale rectangles of the
east windows beyond the raised
hospital bed corner fail to
illuminate heaped furniture along
the walls, unintelligible shapes.

Her voice—"to the bathroom"
Tom also a shape in the dark
murmurs: "can you get up?"
The comforters turned back,
she lies on her side. Too late.
By feel more than sight
I cover the bloody stool
with tissues and take it away
and with other tissues wipe anus
and soiled sheet trying without light
to make it clean.

(vi)

Our Lady of Good Counsel Hospice

Tuesday afternoon sun
through the south window whitens the floweret-sprinkled
whiteness of the sheet that covers Michelle
as she smiles from the bed
at Sister Denise in her white coif
and white Dominican habit
whose long front panel covers
a nurse's uniform and a pocket
containing silver shears—
          Atropos, the inexorable one.
A rosary hangs from her belt
as if to say: healing comes from more
than medical instruments in
uniform pockets.

Michelle is happy.
Light and cleanliness surround her.
"Now give me demerol—"

Patiently Sister Denise stands by as Sister Luke explains how it is not possible to give injections and demerol, how the morphine must continue to drip in through the vein-pump, how those things cannot be done that were done in the hospital before, that had given her hope.

Tom sits beside her, holding her hand.
She wears a white gown edged with lace
and dotted with tiny blue cornflowers.

The sun is going down
and puts a deep gold edge on snowy roofs
beyond the window.

(vii)

Evening: her father from Houston and cousins fill the room with their dark shapes, heads surrounding the bed. They crowd flowers—daisies, yellow chrysanthemums —onto the corner chest, the table, the small shrine with its candles and crucifix. They talk with her, turn away weepy-eyed. She wakes up. Her voice is strong, speaking in Vietnamese, now telling them—their eyes tell them—she is sick. She hadn't told them before. We don't know what she tells them now; this is Our Lady of Good Counsel Free Cancer home. Now they know— something. She is chatting as if—as if —

A dish of sherbet melts untouched under the chrysanthemum leaves. She is past eating. Her father in his gray suit comes out into the hall and holds his handkerchief to his eyes.

(viii)
20 February

Wednesday morning: she's weaker. Tom says "Where's Father Bob? We were talking about getting married, but we didn't get around to it—"

Tom goes down the hall to the pay phone. It's Father Bob's day off. Tom leaves a message.

Michelle's father comes, her brother-in-law. They say that her mother and sisters are coming tomorrow.

She sleeps. Tom paces. Her father weeps beside her.

The sun is bright through the curtains.
A fan plays through the red roses and baby's-breath that her father put near her head.

She talks to her father. She sleeps.
When I sit by her, I stroke her arm a little, say foolishly, "Love is everywhere around you"

I'm fading away too, more slowly, intensely deluded, into whatever is that reality.

Light and breath
there and absent:
cells of the body
galaxies in collision;
each molecule a "red giant"
or "white dwarf" or madman
in the desert arming warheads
with chemicals, multiplying

Tom says, "Michelle, let's watch TV."
The little set swings on an iron arm over her bed.
The noon news says the Soviets propose peace for the Persian Gulf. Iraq has not yet answered.

. . .

In the afternoon the priest comes. Tom in his clean white striped shirt and dark tie stands by the bed where Michelle lies propped in a new white nightgown. Father Bob holds the prayer book so they both can read. Her father watches, and his mother.

"I, Tom, take thee, Michelle, to be my lawful wedded wife for richer for poorer, in sickness and in health, so long as we both shall live, and thereto I plight thee my troth."

"I, Michelle—husband—for richer poor in sick and—" The priest prompts her, pointing to the words on the page, "and there I ply tro..." Morphine thickens her speech. It's okay, says the priest.

"Where's my ring?" she calls loudly, pointing to her fourth finger. His mother takes off her wedding band and gives it to Tom, who places it—too big—on the fourth finger. She tries it on different fingers and settles it on the third right.

"I therefore pronounce you husband and wife."

Every cell a cosmos
opening ever outward,
luminosity that pressure,
timeless Alpha and Omega

"You're my husband." She is smiling completely.

Tom holds her hand with its weight of gold. Keeps holding it.

Mad cells duplicating
in the dark, you are nothing
that will go beyond death.
Who can say you have not
spawned diamonds,
the jasper and carnelian
of the new city
that shall open out of heaven
where the blest
meet and kiss and pass into
each other's pure spirit.

(ix)

Michelle's parents, cousins, sisters swarm at her bedside all morning. They've bought her a gold ring for her to give to Tom and a smaller ring for her—"so you can give back your mom's ring"—but the mother cannot take back the gift given and Michelle wears two rings.

Tom looks at his ring—crown of thorns that circles the world, heart of the god one wants, pure gold that nothing can tarnish or soil, pain no morphine can expunge.

(x)
February 22

Friday afternoon: lips dryer, mouth more open,
        chest heaving, oxygen brought.
                A look at a distance, a terror
in the great brown eyes that—but who knows.
        She looks without seeing. Oxygen

no help. Tom—ah!—lays his hand
against her body a moment. She finds it harder
to breathe. She is seeing—or hearing
the sisters in angel garb in the dusk:
Hail Mary full of grace
the Lord is with thee.
Blessed art Thou—

Sister Luke takes Michelle's hand
places it in Tom's hand.
Don't go, don't go.
I thought we'd have
at least another day—
so fast—no

(xi)

Mouth an O:
that utter motionlessness.
The hand that feels like skin
will not move.
Where the body is, the woman was.

Is death physical?
The physical body is here:

but where are you?
You are here—
aren't—

O Michelle—
a name to wake you

(xii)

Circuit of the sun,
          winding of the moon
between fixed stars
and stripped branches:
          such trivial changes
by comparison.

*   *

Part Four

AFTER

The Poltergeists

photo by Sean Chen, Pratt Institute

An artificially aqua-blue dragon by nightlight, greenish subaqueous, parades beside a man whose black sunglasses show a white glint like the white glint—bigger—in the huge black pupils of the balloon bug-eyes of the dragon. Four yellow antennae emerge from the black pupils and moss-green irises, like needles that stick in eyeballs but produce no pain. Great fin-like fans of aquamarine ears flare out behind and above the balloon eyes. The jagged upper lip hangs monstrously over orange tusks, just as the stogie hangs from the bronze lips of the little man in sunglasses, hunched at the bottom right under the dragon's shoulder. The dragon's huge blue chin droops over a ruche, the parody of a woman's fluted blouse-collar.

Next to the man's head, almost out of the picture, a skeleton's white bony hand clutches at something too black to be seen.

The dragon appears to spring from the stogie-smoker's ear, a huger version of his monster self, his death-hand raised over his black hat, flexing its grip.

A Wedding at the Vernal Equinox

Friends Meetinghouse,
110 Schermerhorn Street, Brooklyn

Light from high rectangular windows
on three sides
outlines the foursquare benches
replication
of other meetinghouses whose plain style
also back then
reminded those keeping silence
how powerful silence is:
how it makes you face yourself
as you face
strangers in the Friends Meetinghouse

who are not strangers. They inhabit
bodies temporarily
and have come to the bride and groom saying
in silence: you're brave.
You take on difficulty, are willing to
know that bodies
go soon into earth and light and
that forsythia blooms
only a short sun-lit time, changing
to uniform summer leafage,
and to stripped branch sooner than anyone
will admit—

• •

No words in the meetinghouse.
“Drop, drop slow tears”
at the *hieros gamos*:
          Tom took Michelle’s hand
          “I, Tom, take thee, Michelle—’

          •   •

and light came simple
through windows, simple as time passing
and the frail yellow spring blossoms gone

          •   •

Tears for unknown friends,
for goodness that passes.
The light of a foursquare window
lights a foursquare city
entered by the gateless gate

          Tom lays his head
          on Michelle’s breathless body.
          The light is breath

as Lee and Susan sign their names
on the marriage-paper
and others sign as witnesses
befriending loss and death
under the temporary windows.

City Birthday Haiku: April

Early white peach tree
blossoms by the gray building's
tall shadows

. .

In the long shadows
of sooty brick buildings
pale petals open

. .

White hair too symbolic—
I dye mine. White-petalled
spring passes

. .

as expected. Much
isn't done. A tree's new green
blends into gray

patches on a concrete wall.

For Tom

East Hampton

(i)

Daffodils bloom under the yew-bushes
next to the house.
A good watering brought back pansies
parched in the window-box.
New green leaves tip the azalea shrub
though its blossoms withered.

Think on this: next year
there'll be blooming again

90° heat last week, abnormal
and dulling.
Rain came lightly last night
so the grass has something,
a reassurance. But the big oaks still
hold up bare branches.

Think: next month or later
the big azaleas, the red ones
will be opening

(ii)

Another midnight.

Forsythia in bloom
but above its starry yellow,
three long dead stalks.

I snipped these. The yew
stretched out dark feathered arms.

Alone in the cold house
I think of books—how long
they last, how late it is.

Spring in Return of No Return

Waiting at the station
for the 2:22 from the city:

Mozart plays on the radio
while the wind buffets the flag

over the lumberyard.
But now it's Wagner's *Liebestod*

and gray clouds pile up
to the west. Train's late.

Tree-buds not yet opening.
My love comes toward me

somewhere down the track.
Tom's love is underground

where Hades' black hand
won't let go of her black hair.

He would like to be waiting,
listening to music in his car

at midnight, waiting to go back
to her.

                    But what returns
is no return. The trees

refuse to green in the park
where he runs again for health

and hope, where it grows colder
instead of warmer. He goes

home where the clothes-filled closets
are emptier than ever.

Empty heart, empty checkbook,
neither winter nor spring.

No train yet. Some accident—
the essence of existing non-existence—

keeps the one I love as separate
from me as if it were all over

under the sullen shaken branches.

Haiku for Fr. Perry's Ordination Anniversary

Art student crowd in the courtyard,
Pratt Institute, Brooklyn

Bashō's frog—plop!—in pond
of blue paint, frayed jeans, tempers
—how come no-smell turps?

. .

No one spoke–the book,
the cut grass under mowers,
the white collar.

. .

Benches backed to walls
beside unwashed windows. Someone
hangs over the sill.

. .

By the pagan fountain
under the six-story fire escape
a whole-world chapel.

Tom Says Goodbye to the Apartment at 761 North Snelling, Saint Paul

He stands in the doorway
of the empty dining-room,
looks toward the empty living-

room where the hospital bed
had held her belly-swollen body.
No curtains now. Outside

the sign "Henrich's Cafe"
in crude red paint. The spine
of the college chapel beyond.

He'd swept the space clean.
No furnishings. Car keys
in hand.
The casket closed

again when he took her blouses,
dresses, shoes, jackets, put
them into boxes and bags

to give away. Each box shut
away again the face, her large eyes,
the slim fingers playing

over her sewing machine. She's
there. She speaks, living
in the light and air. He can't

leave her, but she left
and he has to leave.
Her life fills the place, but

it's time to go.

Do you ever leave anything behind?

I was little and fell off the step
of the old house in Saint Louis
and bent my tooth—

In New York, Gerry and I smoked
by the fountain in Stuyvesant Park
near Friends Seminary—

Gerry with a wife and three big kids
in Bayonne—and I go to Houston
to work, following her corpse.

It's hot. Is it the same apartment
whose windows filled with snow
the morning after she died?

The same. The same.
I the same but not walking
in New York, not hearing my mother

call me by some silly name
Tom Tune, Tom Terrific—
                              Never
the same, but holding Michelle

inside, as if—it must be true—
her body's cells, the healthy ones,
cling to mine. Strong muscles,

something steadily pouring into my heart.

The car waits.
The door closes. He turns the key
in the lock. He walks down
the twenty-two steep wooden stairs
as he'd carried her wheelchair
and her bath-robed misshapen
dying self watching him.
Silent eyes.
                    The last journey
to the hospice, and this place
makes him repeat it.

He gives the key to the landlady
in the hardware store
as he'd lifted the casket
into the hearse. Gets into
his dark red car, packed
with his life's remnants,
shuts the door,
                    starts—
because there is no choice—
another journey.

Distant, in the Colorado Mountains

Desk, book, list of chores
in writing: what to compose.
I read "correct" poems, revised
so the *words* are right.

> *Think of the poet who fixed and re-fixed*
> *poems to her surrogate son, fixed them*
> *seventy times seven*

Does tinkering make poetry?
Does suffering make poetry?
Does it matter to make poetry?

> *This planet and the stars themselves*
> *may vanish, and they will—*

> so "cultivate vast mind."
> Vaster than death? Still
> that too vanishes.

This evanescent now provides
enough water and air
to let the mind endure its thought

of knowing that it will know
when death is coming
and won't want to let go.

And know that these furiously
correct words tightly cling
to imagined reality.

Something breaks through.

I'm standing in the doorway in Saint Paul
while I stand by my desk in the mountains,
saying goodbye.

I will my writing to the air.
Let it be a tall fir-tree
and a deep well by the back door.

Dusk, With Music

Walked out to do work,
        cut wood, fix, mend.
Got stopped.
        In the east one peach-pink cloud
against a wash of gunmetal haze,
the receding storm.
        Westerly orange fire
        of the lost sun.

As grass darkens,
        invisible birds raise voices
increasingly loud,
        lively signals. Listen
as looking fails.
Music in place of light
        rises in the blue dark
        where the lost creek runs.

Out of sight, past working,
I want bird-song in my last night.

Epilogue: The Ghosts of Memory

(i)

The ghosts of memory tap on the windowsill.
It's raining again.
                    On Tom's wall

a photo's edges crumble without a frame
but it doesn't fade
                    It is Michelle

who clings to a pole as if blown horizontal,
a wind-whipped banner.
                    She is flying.

Red chiffon streamers furl and spread
wings along her body
                    and beyond. Magic,

a photographer's trick pose.
She is laughing
                    and the wind still blows.

(ii)

One morning, visiting Washington D.C., I happened
to find myself at the Vietnam War Memorial.

What was it, this monument thrust up out of earth,
its incisions bared as if the writings of a lost planet?

Who were they, this crowd of witnesses—tourists,
mourners, seekers, not identifiably any of these?

They moved slowly by, their shadows black on black
across the list of the dead inscribed in this day's diary.

They concealed what they felt, mostly. One woman
reached out and let her fingers rest on a name.

I looked down at the ground where foot-scuffed dust met
verge of grass. No Michelle Vu among the 55,000 ghost-
names written on the wall.

What of their dead?

*Have they a shrine in Saigon draped in orange for
the death agent?*

*It's still in the soil, grows tainted vegetables and
mutilates the fetus in the womb—*

If there were release, an antidote, however momentary,
to stand against suffering and death, could it be the poem,

some blunt-edged saying of the unsayable,
these long-lined transient streamers in the wind.

NIGHT LIGHTS

I am what is around me.

—*Wallace Stevens, "Theory"*

At some point you realize that it is not you looking
at the moon but the moon looking at you.

—*Chögyam Trungpa Rinpoche (1939-87)*

PROLOGUE

In Silence

Walking by flashlight
because the path is dark

the moon rising past rocks
spills white

over marshy gravel, showing
where to step away

from mud.   No mud there.
No cloud here—

the willows quieted that
twittered with a pair

of yellow warblers earlier,
unseen water

running somewhere—
this tent farther

from a few voices,
nearer the moon's stripe

across the hilly meadow.

Part One

SHORELINES

Night

off Madeira, ocean and sky
indistinguishable

No night comes the same
as any other, though similar. Change
is its signal, as in the sough
of waves that slap against rocks
broken below cliffs. Night seems
timeless with stars in place
at first look, yet slowly passing
to another station, if late,
later, sleepless, one looks again,
and the sound, ceaseless, then
is also not the same
but subtly shifts its music
within a range and sometimes
bursts more loudly, strident
almost, if wind upsurges.
Night
is steady, constant, at
a standstill in thought. Ocean
and sky hold seamless,
untampered with until slowly
at some point
the immutable blue-black lessens
and time starts up. It moves noisily.
Night shrinks,
disintegrates
and those thing have to happen, whether
one sleeps or seeks freedom, or denies,
or wishes—after all—
not to look at shadows.

Transformations

(i)

early morning, Madeira
from the seaside hotel balcony

The long cirrus-shelf spreads across the world-width,
grows inflamed from the fire-point of the sun surfacing
just above the dark water-girdle rolling straight from
farthest left to farthest right, the eye-line now all crimson
blazing *red skies at morning*, enrouges the pink façades
of hotel towers sunk in pines where mossy verdure vests
umber-brown cliff-sides in rubeate amberesque light
intensifying green leafage and the hotel pools aquamarine
through gold filters—and slowly the sun edges its copper disc
up under low scumble of grayish opaque cloud white-streaked
and soft steely as a luminous ray, a girder, goes aslant
the blurred bundle of a barren island and its smaller ghostly twin
while the flame dissolves into a wash of pale yellowish
vacancy between ocean and emptiness invisibly lit as the fire
sinks back as if sucked down into the earth's volcanic core
and daylight normalizes into its generous equality of fire and light.

(ii)

the evening elements in all directions

mist
surrounds
full
moon
white
foam
laps
rocks

pale
clouds
streaming
outward
into
night
silence
sky

(iii)

Wind is rising
        and so is the moon
                out of sight
        in a cloud whirl
                in blue-black
                        overhead and
straight out two
        amber dots, a tanker
                at rest now not
        a ship but a
                penetration of
                        darkness where wind
whips the unseen
        sky and waves into
                constant sound

Now, and Memory: Quai d'Orsay

walking in Paris after a concert

Romance of the guitar. No escape
even in sharpest winter cold on
the Quai d'Orsay.

A surrender to now beyond body,
material, hour as it goes on
within—and on out

not stopping but stopped as
over the Seine in the blue
metal dusk shone

the great gold sonorous moon.

*

Steely clouds to the west still hold
a little light while the moon
full in the east

repeats itself in small gold moons
on the rain-wet drive beside the river.
Bitterer wind

on the old, old stone bridge harries
the footsteps of the long dead,
the soon dying,

the composer gone to music,
the player gone with it into
the ripple of lights

on the mutable *bleu-marine* Seine.

By the Rockwall on the Boat Channel

East Hampton: thinking of
Michelle Vu dying young

Orange gold wash
of sky above the lost sun:

blue darkness
rises from jagged black
of bushes, rocks:

tall weed's skeleton
rattles in the sea wind

dark masts pass
quietly into the dark harbor

*

Never again this sunset.
What confidence

that one can leap up at dawn tomorrow
raise a white sail,

clip safely outwards
on the sparkling solid blue.

At the Mouth of Three Mile Harbor

past sunset, no wind—
a fisherman on the black rock jetty—
Water and sky gray-blue.

A ruddy flush on the horizon
darkens the channel
where the beach slopes

sideways back into reeds
by the old fishing station and
six picnickers have lit

a small fire. They look across
into the inlet's wine-dark
cedar trees and shadows

on the other shore
which thicken, move and rise,
evolve into a ship

with three tall masts
and blood-rose lateen sails,
purple as the dusk.

It glides out of hiding.
The deep blue hull parts
the waveless waters

under quiet power.
It heels into the channel.
The picnickers wave, call.

A horn toots. A flag
ripples from the stern
as it passes the jetty.

The masts point upward.
The sails grow taut
where harbor, bay and sky

meet night.

Water

> We can repay our debt to our parents
> but we can never repay our debt to water.
> –*Japanese proverb*

The canal at Islington
runs straight gray
between low concrete bulkheads.
Straight bike path
runs beside it until the lock,
not much used
It's a mess there—
cottonwood fluff, algae,
tiny green specks afloat, caught.
Rebel backwater.
They should open the barrier sometimes.

*

Verticals of modern apartment buildings
with chrome-edged curtained glass
border the concrete channel.
Two swans cruise the water-road.
Their necks curve white against gray,
black masks over their knowing eyes.

*

at the Tate Modern with a friend

From behind the nearly-invisible glass
walls of the museum, the level Thames
that created London draws its fundamental
line, defines the squares, rectangles
of brick, halftimbers, basalt, girdered

steel, St.Paul's dome ornate and
light-attracting, establishes the business
of living firmly upheld by the gray-green
movement in stasis of water—and
across it the silver arc of the Millenium
Bridge and over on the right, a crane
constructing a high-rise, lifts two bright
red poles up out of the half-built
mass into the air, and from it a cable hangs
ready to hoists effortlessly many tons.

"Water is healing, isn't it?" she said,
pensive, beside me.

*

Melancholy. Is it bodily?
The body is mostly water
but its form is not water.

Is melancholy
thought or water?

*

The canal widens in an arc
overgrown with weedy shrubs
and trailing grasses where
the water is roughed up as
a red-hulled motorskiff,
tour boat, turns back at
the lock and goes under
the curved bridge, sort of noisy,
and the bike path bumps

toward exit stairs which
present a choice of whether
to go on beside the water,
which would be succumbing
of desire to follow the canals—
a map shows how—
all the way across London,
the whole city—
          and out into the countryside
of 19th-century English landscapes,
under soft windblown azure sky, just as
here this afternoon.

*

a concert March 13, 2004

Heartbreaking to listen
to Shostakovich's Chamber Symphony
          "against war and fascism"
                    —Stalin censored Shostakovich—
    to think of the Madrid dead for whom they played
and "in memory of the victims" this music, the long
          trickle of water on a single violin.
A trickle but ascending drop by drop
          against gravity, against the weight
              of destruction
          —buildings, bodies, millions
      many millions of Coventry, Dresden
Stalingrad, Hiroshima, an escalating
scale of destruction.
          Against it a few violins,
a relaxed unhurried wrist
and a bow necessary
              for sustenance—

but violas crowd in, and cellos
agitated, furious
                    this inner shriek
                    of—you can't say
what neural thread grates under
the gut-strung bows pushed to extremes

Music is like water,
flows, swarms over obstacles,
formless, makes the form that holds it.

*

on the train to Durham

Rainburst after sunny clouds.
More sudden sun dries
train windows, rainbow
vanishes. Low thunderous clouds
eastward vanish. White thunderheads
bulge south over "England's
green and pleasant land"—
the uncertainty of water.
Water overhead and wind
stronger. Less light. Gales
and rain. Will an umbrella
be needed, or will it change again
before the train reaches the station?

*

Tyneside, Newcastle, coming and going

The train slows over the Tyne.
Noon light stipples the river,
opens its fan wide, wider

until the vestibule fills,
with light, light, light.
Light-blindedness:
no water nor bridge nor glass,
no eyes. Inundation detonates.

By night slow tide of the Tyne
slides for one moment
a blue crescent across the window,
not blue then but lighter black, lost
ribbons of black, here and here and here,
a larger darkening:
no land nor water nor roads. A few amber holes
in unlit space, fewer, then none.

*

Proverbs of water:

1) Water enlightens. Water and earth enlighten.
2) Water is not sunlight; earth is not darkness.
3) The sun of knowing resists the moon of unknowing.
4) Day for night to film, water to spread nightlights.
5) Rainy by day; misty at evening; invisible sleeping.
6) The lion drinks water, therefore water is stronger than he.
7) Beware the oxymoron of "holy water".

*

Commentary on rainwater: an echo

Not a thing
depends
upon a thick

black
stick glazed with
clear
nail-polish beside
the bleached
pulpit

Much depends
on seeing
rainwater

*

Too conceptual this notion
of water as the feminine,
the unconscious, shapeless.
She is the vessel, not what
is poured into it

*

Psychoanalysis of water: keep looking.
Don't read too much into it.

*

Literarily, water is limpid,
crystalline, a mirror, long fingers
touched to a damp forehead.
Forget it. Literally, it is—
            well, how can you say
             what anything is?
            "Is" is not

*

ah
ah
ah
falling water—
how water must fall
hidden waterfall
as it pours through the body.
The mountain stream flows
over and around rock and crags—
how it must fall away

*

The Danube flows lazy
wide and gray-green between
the castle on Buda hill
and parliament on the shore
at Pest, joining
and separating.

Water is wise.

*

Music—Bach, Brandenburg
in the gold and green concert hall,

thus a mind only of music
and then the full moon over the towers

of Budapest. Gold floodlights embellish
the classic columns of the museum

and against the night sky light up
a winter tree's twined branches

in gilded curves of Secession art
hung with seedpods concealing

some fruit to come, consonant
with the moon and the gold,

an opening up to which the mind,
like the river, constantly moves.

*

Hard water.
Mineral rich and a problem,
as, for instance, the need
to clean it out of the plastic cup
in my daughter's bathroom
in Paris, the one the boys use.
Hard-water scale has built up
inside the cup's bottom
and grease on the top and
outside where fingers grab it.
Not noticeable. An absurd
obsession to scrub and dig
to scratch the scale away
and peel back the scum with
the round end of a nail-file,
the only tool at hand. Not

worth the effort, of course,
but I think it makes the water
taste a little better.

*

Looking at "Montagnes célestes,"
Chinese paintings at the Grand Palais

The mountains and waterfalls,
peaks among mists, are spiritual

though also fine-ground black ink—earth—
and shaded grays out of a wetter brush.

Bone-stroke makes a branch broken,
nail-stroke the sharp pine needle

against the white brume rising
from the abyss, the unseen depths

where the white isn't water but paper
left blank, an emptiness, radical freedom.

The mountain is still there, a thousand
jagged edges, half-peaks, cliff-sides

hiding the path on which the tiny figure
at the bottom sets a hermit's foot.

PART TWO

MOUNTAINS

Five Moons

over the Wet Mountain valley, Colorado,
in the driest summer to date

(i)

Crescent growing   also falls in slow arc
into darkness   rising behind pines:
dish of pearl dips
into marine blue black

(ii)

Half a lemon ripens   at tree height,
its juicy gold geometry above
a rouged sunset:
wishful grace of drink

(iii)

Gibbous   hefts itself   swings icy high,
effaces stars on the stilled
black curtain: straw dry meadow
looks midnight snowy

(iv)

Bronze discus, huge, round   dwarfs the far hills.
Soft gong throbs silent light.   Cloud
lowers iron shutters,
jagged edge of knife and omen

(v)

Now just this: the earth not in the sun's way.
A perfect ivory mirror reflects the eye
opening. Simply full moon,
pine trees, dusk on the road-curve down

Jazz Festival

in the town park, Westcliffe, Colorado.
in the Sangre de Cristo mountains

without much beginning—a few bass
notes, a tryout, slips into the main
theme, come sax, comes drums, now
a latin riff, maracas knock, shift,
brass ocean-surf surge on cymbals, while
the sax runs and seeks—something—going
on in fun, a hurry, trips over its own
notes, snare snapsnapsnapBANG irregular

gold aqua tentroof stripes over
walmart chairs, yellow white grid,
white green back, red t-shirt shoulders
—festival t-shirt—Monk tune, Miles,
Sangres blue in the distance, clouds
gathering for maybe rain   woman reads
supine on an army blanket amid the chair army,
young midriffed suntans on the grass

GNU BLOOZE loud through the sax jounces
pinkhaired hand on a near knee   sky graying
brings far mountain into keener focus,
olive green slides Horn Peak into Comanche
Basin, high dark bluegray pines spread
up to treeline, not surely defined at any
particular altitude but then ending
in stony scree   and bass whomps like water

pours when we hear the persistent creek
among the alpine fir-straggle on Goodwin
lake edge but nothing like saxophone,
that blatant man-metallic voice wobbles
into its non-ending, a human handful, so
many hands clapping is one footclomp or
what sound? Break   Clifford Jordan:
Blue Monk's stronger brass and gut job

lets go as the southmoving cloudbank
blurs the high not so far peaks into a flat
steelblue gray line against lighter gray so
mountains appear and disappear inseparable
from form and color.   And art, isn't it
the quintessence of interpretation too,
the melody line like an unstateable divagation
from nothing previously known, hence

no divagation nor anything divagated from,
and a final mellowing out and sun
from somewhere. *In Walked Bud* more
Monk Theloniously to raise the question
of again piano inseparable from its note
and elusive as mountains covered by
vapor, fog, something evolving out of
nothing   or am I always making a mistake

thinking of what to do next while
piano notes unfold precise as aspen leaves
when random sun hits?   no one body
in this audience is like any other nor
blade of grass under any picnic cooler
nor has any horn ever blown out quite
that exact reverberation   a deaf boy
signs to someone near the end

of a chair row. What comes through
his hearing-aid is mostly all we hear.
Three young guys out on the lawn who
played before and maybe-teen girl in black
shirt, buttocked in denim cutoffs—no
way to record each one solo who
will disappear yet leave a past
behind   Piano endless in takeover

like mountain, like water, a
reclamation. Lightning leaps over
Spread Eagle Peak. Thunder *'Round
About Midnight* as the broody afternoon
gives warning to my arms with its
lengthening chill. Not even music
guarantees continuance. Blues seventh hovers—
pauses—improv, stops. That's it. Face it.

At the Summer Solstice

Last night my father's death-night
twenty years ago
who was born

the eve of the solstice,
the longest day.
Tonight overhead

the sun gone, the stars
in their far niches
bright as if

for us, for me. What to say
of their truth,
his truth?

On the cabin's unlit deck
the protective railing
about to give way,

star-molecules bind with
swimming cells in
this body, named

and futile in decline, also
perhaps with stray
cancer cells there—

like his—or here.
The darkening light
reveals sky

as it is, mostly empty,
yet seeming full
of tiny fires,

burning worlds so distant
they relieve a mind
unthinking it will go,

will go.

Night Lights

from the cabin deck, looking toward town.

Ranch yard lights in the valley—
scattered, not many.

Isolate. One drop of water,
one musical note, one thought
where the black lake overruns.

*

Deep blue early night
held the crescent moon.

Clean light, a high curved
window opened a slot
until a dark peak closed it.

*

It's more quiet
than I've ever heard it.

The color of ink.
Not a cross hatch, not blank.
The basis.

*

Nightfall under steely clouds.
Amber arc-lights ten miles away
at the ballpark in town.

Are they playing?
Always.
It is the play of the mind.

Behind, through a window,
a crescent moon, misty.
Is the glass unwashed?
It can't stay unspattered.

*

Six starry floodlights
have come on over the ballpark.
"Without thought"
the crowd watches.
The creek whispers ease
downstream in that direction.

*

You know those lamps
with motion sensors
that protect doorways?

Pain comes on suddenly
that way, a hot blossom
too white on the sidewalk.

You don't know where
the invisible line is
that set it off.

Someone else must have placed it.

*

I drove south of town alone
in the entire blue-black night
without end. The half-moon darkened it.

Gone valley, gone road
past the headlights' shallow pool
into desert.

Roadless road into the deep Huerfano.
Homeless.

Twenty years ago the radio played
Bye Bye Miss American Pie.

*

The guitar plays
recuerdos, memories.
Midnight condenses

chilled mountain air
on the old deck-rail
that leans outward.

Unsafe. It is breaking.
Feel it—the splinters.
Silver notes. Needles

in the eyes.
The million-eyed
River of Heaven.

*

Holding the little boy
the night before they left,
meteors streaked the sky.

The thought returns as the Perseids,
their little light-bursts. A gap
—*I have driven a road*

by starlight alone. And will again
It's hopeless,
this lack of fear, this fear.

Someone leans heavily on the rail.
It creaks. The very distant
lights of town squat unblinking

but the massed black pines
intervene.
"Oh look, it
lasted long—"

More quiet.

The far high night is breathing.

Permeable Membrane

(i)

Note on the telephone pad
beside the seven digits: *n.a.*
no answer

but music from radio to ear
permeates, answering
no word.

The bell rings at the Great Gate
of Kiev, a picture
exhibited.

Where is here? The skin,
that fascinating organ
of the body,

manufactures its useful raincoat
to keep one thinking
of an other.

(ii)

Another—it is all "other.".
Outside, the blue sky over-swept
by clouds registers
          as if eyes
                    saw something. A mind
          reads the alpine firs among
          scrub oak and thinks "time"—

To know they are there
growing. The words don't do it.
You don't have
          the right idea.

                    The blue-jay caws
what word? No idea
          fits the knowing. Natural
and unnatural align
in *no answer.*

·

The radio's off but not
the ear. Beethoven deaf

          —how did he do it?

(iii)

So this imagined self within manufactures
as protection its imagined skin

while the imagined other—but not
so imagined, or one couldn't open an eye.

—it's a crazy business, those who see
UFOs, hear voices, hear the stories

they want to hear, as if manufacturing
their own dollar bills.
                    But a bird's

sharp note sounds outside and
it is not distorted mind that rides it

into the pines whose needles fall continually
and whose brown-black branches crawl

with a golden parasitic flower that kills
the tree, eventually, in which now sits

the warbler, *empidonax*. Scientists
have named it in a book, and so its breast

streaked pale yellow and its wild fly-catching
are truthful, though hardly a guide, not music.

Divided Creek

meditating on nations in a wet season
when the creeks run high

Creek divided
by willows and boulders,
the white water plunges

under the hikers' bridge.

*

Rebel whinny
of a horse
somewhere in the campground
where they stake them
before the rodeo.

Has one escaped?
Where can he go?

*

Division "of opinion"
over Iraq, Israel, Palestine.
Past midnight
a long resounding shot.

*

The quiet night is one night,
moon in the sky all morning.

*

When I walked
under city streetlights
through leaf-shadows,
my feet grew shadows.

Enlightened, endarkened
I was walking
on hard trails.

*

No more whinny.

Did they catch him?
Where did they take him?

Would you think the absence
of headlines a trustworthy sign?

*

Long division
of breakage and dissolution
one may not speak the word for—

say "prison" or "patriot"

say "Rosita cemetery"

*

So, my friend, the cop ticketed you
for a moving violation.

Were you just pissed off
at the slow-moving asshole
on the freeway?

Do you think you're justified—
it's the other guy's fault?

You don't think
this has anything to do with
Israel vs. Palestine, do you?

Or Serb vs. Croat
or Taliban, the way it's
starting up again—

*

Under the bridge
the creek comes together.

Its clear pools
hold a sky-fragment.

Then it splits again six ways
under the thickening willows.

*

The mountains are high
hideouts.
They keep clear water
falling.
You can peel and eat
the inner bark of willow
if you are starving.

That shot—
who fired it?

Did it miss?
Where is the gunman?

The Hikers

internal monologues, below thought

Father

Middle age pulls mother
after, pushes son ahead.
Not to push. Try to do it
the way we did, I
age 9, going somewhere

Older son

BOR-ing! So slow. No
thing goes so slooooow

Feet heat knap-
sack just going. Bugs.

Bugged BORed. What
is this nothing
happening for?

Younger son

Bounce. Run, run
back to my brother.
I get to carry
the canteen. (bounce)
I keep up with my

brother and my father.
Go, go, with my brother
who carries the fishing pole.
Trail up. Slow. Trees.
My brother goes around
the big tree curve.
Hurry up so I can still
see him

Oma

Fireweed, bed-straw, hare-
bell, Indian paintbrush,
kinnikinnick—also called Indian tobacco,
bearberry—showy daisies
orange and black butterfly: fritillary
white butterfly: cabbage

yellow? another kind of cabbage?
It chooses to land on yellow flowers.

So much unnamed

Mother

We and the woods are one.
The boys, big and little,
green growth. It is slow,
cool, sunny—a relief.
They are far along the trail
and I walk at leisure
left alone, finally,
in the silence of
sweet-smelling pines

Philosopher, trailing behind

Who writes the poem
when the waterfalls
plunge over boulders?

The reflected aspens
twitch on the pond's surface.
A green thicket of willows

over swamp muck.
Nature is too unformed.
I want a hand in it,

my pen on the mottled page.

Rocks and Water

(i)

Water falls over
rocks. Rocks hold water. Fallen
trees hold moss above

and in water. A bridge
crosses rocks under falling
water. Little boys climb

between beams holding
the bridge. They sit on rocks
beneath the wooden

planks. They look around.
One fishes in a deep pool.
One carries a peeled

aspen stick. One says he wants
to do things "tout seul,"
climbs away

from constant water-flow.
The others' voices not
audible among

water-sounds and tumult
of falling, staying,
growing. Not solid,

neither rock nor water.

(ii)

The trees are tall, their trunks
bare until the top. The tallest
trees lie fallen.

The stream cuts a deep gorge
out of which the trees rise,
their new green tips

lashed by wind that brings down
alpine fir and aspen both.
The wind and sky

invisibly hold each branch
or strip it. Each leaf
or needle separately

falls into the painting
in the mind's eye. The boys crouch
happily under

the bridge which shades them.
The shade passes. The sun heats
the rock. Flies alight

because they like sweat and skin,
ephemera that die in a day
on the great slab of stone

embedded beside the bridge.

Part Three

LAKE PARADOX

Fireside

at Lake Paradox in the Adirondacks

The cricket's flutes, tonight
are broken. . . . .
Oh I am alone!
Who knows my tonight's feeling!

— Yone Noguchi,
The Summer Cloud, 1906

What can be said to a woman
whose daughter has set fire to herself?

The night is cold.
The mother lit a fire in the parlor
after she phoned the hospital
in Tennessee.

Packed in ice, unconscious,
will live, probably.

Silence before the unstable flames.

*

Alone, the fire burns.
Give it another long-burning log.

*

Here is an old book with misprints
mistranslated in skin-grafted language.

Awareness is said to be
"the fire that consumes the fuel
of conceptual mind."

Is awareness madness?
Oak wood there
fanned by updraft
glows neon.

*

Questionable, the death wish.
The incandescent log hums, a holdout.

*

She gazes into the fireplace
    I am alone . . .

Rust-orange leaves,
an armful, curl and dry
in a smoky vase on
the parlor side-table.

A red taillight's comet
zips past the window.
        Who knows my . . .

*

Science of flame, of burns,
how to promote healing—

this is written in a magazine.
She reads it, I read it.

A log breaks, drops
behind the fire-screen.

*

“Let die what must die”
means “don’t let die
what must not.”

Third-degree thoughts eat
past the outer layers.

The burned one’s temperature
falls. Nurses heat the hospital room.

*

It’s not enough—“non-thought.”
Living is thinking, hardwood.

*

. . . *tonight’s feeling?*

Tonight doesn’t exhibit
personal emotion. It is

simply tonight.

A trace.
A line of ink.

*

The solar fireball isn't
always there, luckily,
to cause its mayhem.

Science of doing good for others.
Find that book and read it
          by its own light.

Moongazer

in an Adirondack camp

The ivory moon moves silently beyond the
drooping black lace of the cedars.
The night air holds the cedars' slightly acrid
odor in silence.
How lovely is the moonlight—how soundlessly
the old song sings
*I walk a-down the meadow with no one
near me—*
Invisible the deep damp grasses beyond dense
shrubbery's soundlessness.
A slant of light falls through the screen porch,
a faintly pale orange blur.
The darkness darkens as it rises through the cedars,
a palpable presence
amid the forest shadows—feel it, the pressure
of the changing night and the moon
not quite full, a potential, but in brightness
already enough, *how lovely*—

No Moon

Overcast sky, moon hidden. It seems
that lights indoors must be sufficient.
The sun-aged brown of the high living-room's
unfinished walls makes the lamplight gold
on the upright piano, the desk, end-tables.
The lamps on bases of bronze or amber glass
stand as if flambeaux in a medieval hall or
sconces in gimbels in a ship's hold, enough
to see the thick timbers and crossbeams
and support-posts that rise into dim heights
above the windows' many opaque panes,
where, last night, the moon took precedence
in chill simplicity. Tonight is less sublime:
rugs underfoot, books on the sofa, heaters
turned up, and ordinary conversation.
A magazine rustles, a page turns: inner life
as if the piano's ivory keys played themselves.

Rainy Night Thoughts

Green, green, I want you green
–*Lorca*

It rained all day.
Rain is green,
Greeny masses—trees,
leafy bushes—grew greener
as rain drenched them
and the grass swam
in greening pools beyond
the porch screens.
Rain is sky outside
glass and cloud
over gray glass lake just past
dark-gray pines dripping
silver, and an inside
sursurrus on the tin roof,
the whir of the green
engine and constancy
of water. It is raining
all night. Sleepless
rain thrums its thoughts
hard on the roof: irregular
overabundant green,
green light within.

Meaning the Random

Sometimes it's too much effort
to search for meaning.

Why search? It'll still be there.
We talked at the dinner table.

The pool of light over the pansies,
yellow in the small vase, means as much

as the silent girl to whom we
never thought to put questions

to draw her into the conversation
on Bulgaria and a bank card

stuck in a Barclay's ATM—or
the night before, at another

dinner table, lace-covered,
fine Wedgewood almost oriental

in design, held the flan, and the nice
white-haired Olsons, midwest born,

chatted with pleasure at being
here visiting their cousin Sara —

they were doing a puzzle in
the living-room, a 500-piece

jigsaw, and we each after much
searching found one piece to fit in.

Today, a Victorian Painting

at Lake Paradox

Through sliding glass doors, clarity:
Frost still glitters on the deck outside.
Slice of hot sun on the scarred table top.

Gold knotty pine walls and low-beamed
pine ceiling grow a tamed wilderness
around the old high oak chairs.

Corner tea-cart carries green cacti. Its
overflowing red blossoms fall to a faded
blue mud-rug where sprawls a brindle cat,

white belly upturned in warm white light.
A woman sits reading in a red shirt
and dark fleece vest, a red knot

at the end of her braid. The wall clock
stopped at 2:45 early in the last century.
Its intricate brass-flowered pendulum

catches the modern moment's all-
pervading shine and heat of each
lustrous object: out there utterly far

huge sky beyond the apple tree's
clinging leaves and snow-trace among
weeds down the riverbank.

Brilliance shapes the table edge,
the reader, ivory pages of the book, a knife
silver on a glass plate and biscuit

half eaten. The salt cellar's chrome
turret blinks a tiny beacon under the deep
fern-green fronds out of which rises

a flower-mountain of mauve heather
and lilac phlox among wine red
freesias opening their gold star centers

in a swath around six perfect roses whose
just unfolded petals, apricot-peach-orange,
hold onto the morning light and make it last.

Part Four

ARTS

A Suite For and From Paula Rego

I. The Painter Depicts Her Mother's Death

– a diptych

(i)

The plump white baby holds
her doll mother straddled on her knee.

The pompadoured mother pouts
lipsticky lips at the baby's inert mouth.

Not a baby but a ponytailed child.
Now one sees the mother less small

in blue business suit and high heels.
The baby-child clutches her doll to her,

strong left hand pulling up the blue
skirt. The mother kisses goodnight

the tearful girl-child in the chair marked
with crosses of blood on the slipcover.

The blood comes from their spread legs,
the monthly ending, a streak of red

where the mother presses against
the daughter's baby-fat belly.

The eyes of both are shut.
The time for seeing passed unseen.

(ii)

The strong black-browed woman lifts
the mother's porcine body, a meat package

in loose paper, as a teenager might
carry her pet German shepherd.

Her arms are lost in the burden's
black folds. Terrified mother's face

looks away, mouth wide in outcry.
Daughter's eyes, ink smudges, sink back

into the need.   Ink-stroke mouth
neither droops nor smiles. It sets

the raised foot's direction. The woman
wears sensible shoes, black loafers,

and a free-moving plaid skirt with red
crosses in its folds. Water dropped

on the paper and made a cloud
over the mother's distraught white hair.

Green underfoot—is it grass or
floor, as under the baby's armchair?

The daughter carries the mother forward.
The daughter's sleeve is blue, not quite

the blue of the mother-doll's dress.
The woman's cheek has the faintest pink

of warm blood circulating under the cold
white paper that sharply holds the pen's edges.

II. Looking at a Woman's Paintings in Time of War

Yale Center for British Art

(i)

The gallery's high, cooled white rooms
with discreetly placed track lighting
opened space before the framed terror

of women alone but exposed, seen
where no one should be looking, as
a policeman's flash bulb has to record

brutalities, the mangled corpse, fatal
accidents—so the woman looks up
into her own camera as she squats

over a tin bucket, self-aborting.
She wears a crude cotton print dress
and clunky high heels while she's bent

doubled over in pain for the terrible
impossible choice of holding on
to her own life at the cost, she knows,

of another's—impossible not to have
that knowledge placed permanently
in the accurate black strokes of the

brush. Don't underestimate
her necessities, says the painting.
Know she will bear the unbearable.

*

That day the television did its concealing act
on a bombing. Many dead, but it ran
the same loop of "reality"—one wounded man
on a stretcher wheeled again and again
into an ambulance. No way to see
blown-up bodies, the maimed, the walls
fallen, or what is crushed under them,
or to look into the eyes of the grief
of the mother who wants—wants—but
what can be known of her wants
once the cameraman leaves?

(ii)

Another woman cowers
in a wingchair, knees to chest,
feet pulled up off

the terrifying floor
away from the stout, unconscious
—dead?—old female body

flopped out supine
beside the chair, too close,
front and center

in a shiny cheap slip
lace-trimmed, those legs
spread, thick and white.

In the mirror, the chair's
back corner and the woman's
crooked elbow, yellow sleeve,

and a child—a girl who holds
a large mask, crude with eye-holes,
in her arms like a doll.

The viewer, beyond the frame,
becomes the child who looks
with minor fascination

on the nearby lust and horror.
On the far left, a thin black
supervisory matron in profile

benignly gazes downward,
walled off in another room. She is
that other viewer who does not see.

The body on the floor
does not appear in the mirror.
When will the girl put on the mask?

So far she hasn't.

III. The Painter Does Little Red Riding Hood

–a six-panel installation

(i)

In the old tale the mother is missing almost altogether. Anyway, she's no help. She has only useless advice to offer the daughter who's going into the deep woods of sexuality. "Ta-ta," she said, "now don't go off the path," meaning stick to the virgin path of bourgeois marriage leading to the sexless safety of old age—"grandmother's house."

Now, in the new tale, the mother is very much present, protective. She knows the dangers as she embraces the daughter, both in their deep blood-red sexually luxuriant dresses. The mother's lady-like high-heeled left foot is placed between the girl's feet, blocking the way to what lies between her legs but also balancing and supporting her. The distant grandmother, half man half woman in his/her running shoes and red boxing shorts, head draped with a peasant's babushka, looks on, a bit out of it, androgynous, not clear in the child's mind.

(ii)

But the daughter is on the edge of adulthood, edgy, trying to escape from childhood. See those sharp blood-red lacquered nails. She's ready. She's gotten her period. She knows there's something highly interesting outside the window she's poised to climb out of. Sneaky and not quite innocent, though appealing with her plain little girl's mug, looking back to see if anyone's watching.

(iii)

The wolf—well, yes, like Coyote the trickster, the shape-shifter, he looks just like a man, except you know he's not a man because he doesn't wear shoes. He's a meat eater, found on every street-corner and in Mike Leigh movies. He's scruffy, unwashed, arrogantly showing off the tattoo and the hairy chest, a little too old, but the young girl's eyes can't see that. Naturally he chats her up.

(iv)

When she takes off her red riding-hood, you see she's wearing a green dress. She's very green, inexperienced, but doubtful wondering why her grandmother has a beard and moustache. Children find old women most odd, smelly, misshapen, speaking foreign words, Another species of being, possibly from another planet. The peculiar eyes, big ears, big teeth. But she doesn't have time to know she's made a mistake in playing the game of this guy purporting to be trustworthy. He just eats her.

(v)

The child disappears from the paintings, and the mother re-appears in her red dress. Is this the good mother, who's usually dead in fairy tales, come back to life? Not quite. The child is gone. She has become her own mother reincarnate out of the blood of her broken hymen to take revenge. With her satanic pitchfork, she's going to rip open the dead beast bloated with misused power that killed him. She's freeing herself from everything that swallows up women. No doubt she'll pitch the damned deceiver into a Dantean *bolgia*.

(vi)

She takes what's useful that is left of him, his pelt of self-assurance. She adorns herself with silver-tipped furs, the wolf's inert black head conspicuously caught under her arm. She's quite smart in her scarlet ensemble and her red-winged hat, looking off to her left just as the girl did earlier but with more knowing skepticism. Is it a job interview? Anyway, she's qualified. Experience has not gotten the better of her; she's mastered it. No external rescuing woodsman needed here. No one can rescue you but yourself. One more phony myth of women's niceness and weakness bites the dust.

Two Plans for Soho Street Performances

Real Life: The Movie
– *headline NY Times*

(i)

Put on a huge black mourning veil,
waist-length all around, over
an opaque skin-colored stocking
facemask with 3 equal-sized 1"
holes for 2 eyes and 1 mouth
& 2 tiny 1/2" nostril openings

But the black veil will be thick so
the inner face will hardly
be visible

Wear a shabby loose print dress
ripped black stockings & scuffed
thrift-shop Reeboks

Walk along the streets of Soho,
invisible eyes downcast
head bent forward

Carry a placard 8-1/2"x11"
lettered large black on white
& pinned to the back of the dress

under the veil but readable

SHADOW

Sit on selected doorsteps. Plan
point of entry, secluded & place
of departure. Time it.
In a cracked black plastic handbag
carry & play a tape of female dialog:

Q. What is your name?
A. *My name is Lee Jun*
Q. Are you a nun?
A. *I am none, no nun*
Q. Are you doing art?
A. *No art*
Q. Are you crazy?
A. *No insane*
Q. Are you in mourning?
A. *No morning, no evening*
Q: No?
A: *None even*

Sit down on the sidewalk
next to a mailbox
or fire hydrant.

• • •

Think of a way to end this performance.

(ii)

Female figure in very high heels, very tight
'50s suit with huge rhinestone dog collar
(real dog collar from pet store) leans

on a cane. 8-1/2"x11" sign on her back

CLOUD OF UNKNOWING

Head covered by white sheer stocking with
holes for 2 eyes & mouth under a white
cloud of bubble netting, made by

stripping paper off a big Japanese lampshade
(round) so the thin metal arcs support
the netting–
but better:

a male figure (evidently) in very shiny shoes,
tight-waisted Italian silk suit, necktie leans
on what feminine object: broom?

Same head but
in an invisible cloud
with an un-seeable sign.

What is the drama to be performed?

The Protectors

Musée de Guimet, Paris

(i)

Light and glass expose and protect
the ancient terracotta figures
twenty-five hundred years old.
Seated women, hair piled high, play
musical instruments. A horse
arches its splendid neck and turns
its sad eyes toward a stone groom.
It mourns its master, for whose tomb
it was shaped. The fingers gone
to dust still live in the curved clay,
more than mortal, less than
eternal, a reminder paused
under fixed spotlights.

Shakyamuni walked
from village to village in India,
reminding women and men that everything
changes and makes us suffer.
No lasting self then or now
in those sculptors, but there are the objects.
A few notes of music
pass the viewer's ear and vanish.

(ii)

The savage dark-blue Mahakala,
"protector of the teachings,"
reaches out from the thankha's canvas.
His eyes roll and flames surround
the flailing arms that knock away
one's ego, arrogance and fakery.

Could I have felt his power if
I hadn't dreamed her, a woman
in an aureole of fire blocking my path
up marble monumental steps
in New York City? Blue-black, intelligent,
ferocious mother-self, she turned me back—

to what? But she was with me.
And these are with me too, these
painted lotus-seated ones among
their red-orange jade-green thoughts
row on row, luminous, who reach out
of an enormous floor-to-ceiling scroll
to chain the sun and take on death.

Draughtsmanship, or What is Not in the Portrait

an exhibit in the British Library

Albrecht Dürer with one hand drew the other finely,
at age thirteen himself in silverpoint, which can't be corrected

The fine eye, the real tool, is only in the mirror.
The replica ruthlessly insists on being taken for reality.

The real hand is gone; the stroke it laid in copper stays.
Fine line next to finest builds to likeness recognized.

This my hand, veins bulging, makes its clumsy mark.
Proportion is truth: the eye is smaller than one supposes.

The ground blue-green or ivory set off inks now brown.
In charcoal shading a lighter gray defines the jaw's curve.

It is line next to line that assembles the semblance of faces.
Those eyes watch. What else but go on to another drawing?

For the Sculptor of Heads

for Marcelle Quinton, of whom it is said truthfully,
she has "lived a blameless life"

A blameless life
given to the sculpture of heads.
Here they are on shelves, evidence:
White oval marble on a plinth, black-glazed
on side tables and ranged
on the ascending cornice in the library.

The head holds everything, after all,
within its globe.
The sculptor in her studio
strong-armed the earth into its proper shape,
the one skull that protects
the brain's entangled re-chargings.

She saw the head in its full truth
from all directions, witness
to the right seeing that leads to
making it right. No wonder
sculptors and conductors
of music live longest. The arm

swings wide and grows strong without
taint of aggression. Single-minded,
enjoying it, she hurls the clay
or chisels resistant marble until
the head takes form, and change
becomes permanent grace.

On library shelves below the heads
the books arrayed contain the thoughts
that swarmed in those friable skulls
now bronze or stone, words in profusion,
other worlds. Thought without a thinker.
The heads are reminders, presences.

Live Painting

as in "live music",
a word-paint experiment with Lynn Umlauf

(i)

Live painting, or live paint:
you wouldn't say
        it is any thing.

        thing   think
        Ding an sich

the thick paper
(not made any more
cut from a human-body-size
        sheet   had already a
        mark—*remark ?*
on it for a start

        so no
violation of a pure
smoothness
        So we went on
        the painter first
fearless of course
bold black, porcelain turquoise,
        that Chinese stroke
                and the poet
                in terror
to make a mark.
        It isn't my thing

dared some chalk.
Cyclamen red came out
of two hands.

(ii)

Space makes
whatever is in it, though
that hasn't anything to do with it
either.
Safe in danger,
two figures at a table
on which lie the dirty chalks,
inks, brushes

A circle of cadmium yellow
but not a complete circle
the open end free,
a lack of completion.

A worse danger.
A whole hand palm
spreads a brighter gold
outcry
down left—
and the phone rang
so the one hand waited, held up
covered with pollen
because sometimes in respect
for the other's loneliness, one
can't go on.

(iii)

One is afraid and goes on.
One's not afraid and goes on.

Lacquer nail-polish-red paint
swooped —couldn't bring myself
to that, so the long
circular black strokes
at the side wobbled

Amateur, you see it
but it also didn't seem a black
mark,
or three marks—
"Don't put on more green,
you're going too much to
the center, you're spoiling it."
Yes or no.
when to stop. Just then,

I thought walking home by Friends Seminary
under the leafy trees.

(iv)

He turned on the music. Suddenly
Beethoven's piano concerto #3.

It is about the two hands
and the ephemera of the permanent.

Not heard before just like this
but you recognize it,

not light or space but not
separate, either, from them,

but not an intrusion on the ear
which accepts the notes' wordings

that fingers have left behind.

(v)

Those artisans who placed the gilt
mosaics into San Clemente's vaulted
heights over the crypt of Mithra
and peeling frescos of Constantine,
they were just working, like
the ones who first put the temple
there to light and darkness.
It was work in a high place
even then, over a subterranean river
that runs a long way,
is still running.
                    Treble works in
with the bass, neither new nor old,
painting alive, live music, not
          anything more than
                    ongoing.

Part Five

CITIES

A Folk Singer in Penn Station

in memoriam, again,
for Michelle Vu

High pure notes of the girl's tremolo,
sad-eyed voice in last slow endings,
she sings where the escalator's slant chrome
bears upright bodies down onto marble
hard floors under TV schedule screens.
Cloud-moving winds of the faint guitar

and the birdsong sadness in a few faces
changes a little, mourning concealed in tall
black men—two in work jackets, not trees
swaying but they stand in breeze echoes;
in the swirling crowds a few also pause
in gray raincoats, numb purses clutched,

brushed by an invisible falling dew
or half-tears for whoever's lost, Irish
lad, or—oh my son, to have had to lose her
to the slow earth far under the stone
floor, too slow and dark to come back
to green leaf music.
Here under mechanized

ad signs' ill glow, travelers oblivious to
journeys longer than a day flow high, higher
or sink, ignoring effortless clarity of air
and mountain stream spray flung out to vanish
past bird-call and evanescent lake silver
—my son, you listen to her lost voice

speaking on a tape, the lasting notes
replayed in lasting midnight darkness
in the long concourse this side of
the river of forgetfulness.
                                        The screen shifts.
The train announced, the herd swarms down
other gray stairs where the great metallic worm
swallows and abolishes the water-notes descending.

Perspective

The jury room exudes utilitarianism. No one's utilizing it
so, under the general fluorescence, it becomes a painting.
Teal-blue leatherette chairs with faux walnut arms set up
a greenish wave—several waves—across beige linoleum,
the next wave-series more blue, then darker blue. White
light lines a foamy edge to each plastic curve. Peach shirt
lumps on the right. Cobalt shirt against the walnut wall
punctuated by a tiny brass lock and hinges. Up front,
focal point, a shiny gold half-globe top of a waste-can
raises its robot helmet head among the black curled
or coiffed spheres afloat over the ivory shirt, white shirt,
spread newspapers and half-open book in a high hand
poised above the waves. A nose in profile, mostly hidden,
contemplates the page held up to partially obscure
the rose-brown paneling, pale tan rack of magazines,
blue sign white-lettered NO SMOKING by the bright
brass-finialed red and white slant-slashed American flag.

Progression

Never a day without a line of poetry
–*Horace*

a meditation in shih form

(i)
Inbound on the Long Island Rail Road

Never a day without writing a line of poetry,
never a journey that ends with wheels' silence.
The body, ill, sits in the iron tunnel unmoving
as the fire-wheel vanishes and the ice-wheel rises
on the computer screen of space, specks of dust
emptying out. Overground the city's cryptic icons.
Underground the purring power muffles ego-sleep
of selves, shadows, lights passing the lethal track's repairs.

(ii)
East Side, 10 a.m.

November day without a line of poetry but
doctors, defiant walk for health in mind beside
the silver river and concrete hospital bunkers.
Warning lifts its smoke threads out of Con Ed's
ominous chimneys. Resistance of footsteps
on the walkway over blind traffic-roar. Little
pump under the breastbone, counter-music
relentless, recycles its inner Leonids' star-storm.

(iii)

Midday: street sounds

Wrench, pluck, extract a line of poetry
from where?—to override loud dread of silence
in the radio-laden air. Pipe a new line to earphones
walking deaf under the medical center canopy.
They die in there, other selves, wired to glucose
and monitors. ". . .be late," a cellphone maunders.
Brakes shriek near thing, engines snarl forward,
away, away. A friend is dying, and it is soundless.

(iv)

Sundown: hospital view

The fire-wheel falls again behind high-rise towers.
Window-eyes ignite in million-watt surveillance,
mimic protection. Night softens the ice-wheel's edge
bent over the black river. What line of poetry for one
who, saved by surgery, weeps for his friend who wasn't,
for failed chemo, ticking I.V., whatever hides beyond
a door signed "oxygen in use," for himself a shadow
trailing the street-siren's long cry: pain, disaster.

(v)

On the outbound train

Stitched belly barely healed, the body sleeps
underground, now lit, now lost as the power breaks.
Track repairers pass in orange vests, armored signage.
Overground, the city empties behind. Instant
windows frame the Queens necropolis and lose it fast.
For the funeral attended, for the dying eye's swift blink,
for hopeless postponement, never a day without
a line, never a journey that ends in wheels' silence.

Toronto in Winter

(i)

At sunset

the sub-zero world outside
the 35th-floor hotel window
requires a pearl gray palette

for the lake's distances.
Peach gray sky rises to
palest overhead blue.

Glass walls' green gray
embossed by gold loopholes
darkens as steam heat plumes

upward past the highest spire.
The rust brick blocks
thicken below. A snow rim

edges a roof garden sinking
back into blue blur. The sun falls
away off on the right

beyond the string of harbor lights.
Tiny taxis, beady-eyed,
travel tiny black gray avenues

at the bottom of the perpendicular.
            It is deep gray inside the
                        the pearly sheer drapes

that frame the multi-cubic vista
            as the spume unfurls higher into
                        mauve efflorescence

and lights in other towers come on and on.

(ii)

With moonrise
from the 35th floor hotel window
the darkness of skyscrapers
comes alive.

Cargo laden glass-sided
bulkheads almost move out
to sea.

The moon, a tossed ball,
faintly silvers the spire,
the mast

of the monumental city ship
anchored in the freezing
blue black.

Boxes of light wrap bands
around the towers
between

bands of hollow box-caves
of unlit windows.
The great

buildings take their stone
out of mountains, glass out
of sand,

their size out of oceans
and physics. Under the moon
they enlarge

the sky. The towers
are bioluminescent. Light
always astounds.

Inside the 35th floor window
the heated dark deludes and comforts.
The moon paints

a pale rhombus on the carpet,
as if one might forget the heights
or the intense cold.

For the Psychoanalyst on Her 70th

If you look across First Avenue
at the windows in brick high-rises
—at least 70 windows in sight—

you could think of the 70th
as 70 windows you looked into
or 365 times 70 mornings of seeing

into minds and foibles, and they too
through their curtains looking back.
What a mix—the blue-eyed sky,

sunlight, the straight heights,
too stark and boxy for the lives
contained, a base out of which

they spill into what they're doing
to fix up the grounds—what a mess
of constant up-digging,

gray excavations, slime,
earth-movers, but surrounding
new green, like that—also daffodils,

tulips red leftover, a few, and
sudden Japanese-y pink puff-clouds
on wet black boughs, and dogwood

white expansive blooming where two guys
winch some impossible weight up
a shrouded wall. The ropes

sway. Patiently they loft it there,
up over the top, whatever it is—
70 years, like that—

Reunion

at a Quaker women's college

Classmates, we are a Society of Friends,
the true internet, non-electronic, kept together

by reunions, e-mailings, phoning and photos.
The past links to the present in a worldwide web.

These words are part of it. One thought-thread lightly
flung out catches another's and lightly connects.

A door opens. You look into a garden, seeing
butterfly-bush that bloomed in your own backyard,

although, as in Vermeer, the doorway with its slant
of sun is the point of most interest. This internet

of women's lives began for us many years ago
through mere proximity, by accident.

Making friends is not agenda-driven, like
marriage or love that insists something should happen.

Your friends at a distance watch the work going on
in you, mute. Unknowing they sense it. The thread holds.

Rilke said poets living together should pledge
to "respect each other's solitude," for the form

of a poem—or of the ultimate artwork,
a life—will only come out of formlessness when

given space. A canvas, for instance, depicting
windowed half-light that shines on a pregnant woman

holding a balance scale in her right hand. Not much
overtly is known about what's growing within,

but death and life hang in a balance unspoken—
not unsayable but too much—and thus the net's

gaps mean as much as its knots. The seventeenth-
century Quakers sat in meeting, silent,

enjoined from speaking till the great urge not to speak
had risen, not to break silence frivolously.

But when the light within came to a woman,
she spoke, and no one forbade her. A world-change.

We are her heirs, heiresses, wealthy in speaking,
distributing the wealth. The network expands that raised

stone archways and let light through library windows,
that made our minds libraries, studios, gardens.

It is Indra's net of stars, always moving outward.
It's ourselves dead or alive who keep coming back

to re-compose the college's green grounds. A new
shape takes form, a new union when we meet

our friends' new faces, sit and enjoy their kind society.

Islington in Spring

(i)
a new wing to the house

The bright white-lit glass pyramid
surmounts the ivory-walled room,
its pine table, chairs (four), green

ficus—new leaves—beside an orange
abstract oil painting towards which leans
a brass rod to raise sky windows,

and a brass flamingo-tail will open
glass doors to a tiny walled front garden
with pots that send up shooting greens.

Ivory, rust, and green twine curlicues
in the Spanish floor tiles. And all this
rests hot and cool in the high sun's silver.

(ii)
looking into the back garden

A black cat sits
          on the brick-topped wall
above trellised vines,

evergreen, whose knife-leaves
          point downward.

Behind the wall, a tree-trunk
            gray and winter-bare
does not conceal a mass

of new white blossoms
            on another tree.

The cat turns slowly to
            regard the wild white cloud,
pointilliste, on slender branches

Emergent spring proliferates
            beneath still shuttered windows
                        opposite.

The Rain-wet Garden, Islington

after seeing an exhibit of Aztec sculpture

Lime-green tips overtop the side fence.
Pale stars shine, two or three, new
in deep green fernery. The white
cloud-tree thins. Its petals drop
on the brick and moss catwalk.
Low lemon-lime umbrella leaves

open over rain-washed stones laid in ochre
gravel in subtle patterns, invoking
Tlaloc, god of rain and Aztec
fears. Do we need him, his ferocity,
unpredictability, to hold off
unseen dangers? Now he's stone

dug from under a city artificially watered
and placed in a museum's perspex
cabinet. The walled garden
teems over its boundaries. For this
the "goddess of filth," Tlazolteotl
carved in aplite, teeth bared

in hideous pain as the baby's head
comes out of her cervix, perpetual
birth shaped in pale green stone
faintly speckled as if with dirty
wash-water. She eats pollution,
frees dirt from mistreatment,

"purifies transgressions"—

The rain-wet

garden is pure. Under its lushness
the peopled trains of London gently rumble
where water seeps down, and the diggers
keep thinking the digging is over.

Waking After a New York Poetry Reading

from lines of Denise Levertov

In the night, the poet's words
soaked in. It was like that,

I thought, waking up, although
unlike her, I didn't see my parents

standing in the doorway
but rather a line of clean light

under my window-blind,
the same as thirty years ago

when the boys banged out of bed
on Avenue C and headed off

to school, or not, if that day
one of them cut, couldn't take it—

Later in the bathroom
I was spraying stain remover

on a worn blue-green shirt
I'd dribbled down the front of,

to wash and hang it up—and saw
the furious seven-year-old

run to the rag bag, yank out
his ugly rust-brown tee-shirt

with kelly green stripes and twenty
holes in it, and pull it on. His.

Mending an Umbrella

for the anniversary of my mother's death

A strut has broken.
        It cut a hole in the black cloth.
Impossible to mend, but
        the two bent ends can be wrapped together

with duct tape, so it flexes—
        but it's a waste of time. The old thing
should be tossed.
        Instead, it's a multi-winged bat, caught

under my arm, tucked tight
        so it won't flop as I try to reach in
and secure the little bar
        with a black thread-loop so it won't wobble.

My painter friend painted
        her mother as a white scrunched-up
bundle carried awkwardly.
        She hated to lay that bundle down

and feel relieved.
        It wasn't relief, exactly, to have to give
her up. The end wasn't just
        failure of a mechanism—although what else?

Because the one place
        got mended doesn't mean it offers much,
this black umbrella. Rain
        usually brings high winds, and you see them

everywhere, busted
        upside down in curbside trash baskets.
This one stands neatly
        by the hall door, an inverted exclamation-point.

Memoranda: 15 September 2001

Lower Manhattan, New York City

Four days after, near the hollow between
standing buildings—but not near enough, or
too near—the pale ash lies on cars, awnings,
architraves, hubcaps, on the high lamps' long
aluminum arms, in sidewalk crevices,
on curbstones, gutters, grills, ledges under
the plateglass windows of investment banks,
on manholes, drains, fire hydrants, in cracks on
macadam beside marble steps that lead up to
the modern sculpture whose bronze geometry
blurs in dust; in every wire twist of fence
round wild weeds in a vacant lot, each grass
spike coated with fake gray snow, and bits of
flying paper, larger flakes, blow around—
Millenium Hotel, the rates for luxury
suites impaled on auto antennae, flattened
on walls, stuck in street mud, while everywhere
the nearly invisible mist of ash keeps falling
onto eyelids, eyebrows, hair, skull, and enters
stinging eyes and nostrils, ears and mouths.
The utterly pulverized, pure, fine atoms of bodies
of the dead sit on the opened tongues of the living.

Takeoff, Taking In

a flight from Madeira to Paris,
soon before the birth of Ellen Ann Morley

(i)

Seated on blue-gray plastic
with pale gray plastic tray
snapped in place as the plane

shakes awake, moving along
the runway, passengers hear
three languages of safety, see

Exit, saïda, red arrows and
video of yellow oxygen masks
and wonder when the yellow life-vest

will come into use, for safety
can't come from voices reasoning
but from the omnipotent engines,

the push, roar, the drag back against
seatbelts as the black windows pass
studded with amber lights. Liftoff

speeds power as no effort for
the tidy immoveable enclosure:
votre sécurite in cocoon. Goes

without seeming to go to those who
believe in help from hidden cameras'
slit eyes, *défense de fumer,* red Xs.

(ii)

Conscious of enclosure
under the warm light,
consciousness itself breeds
the way the blood-rush circles
through the amnion, nourishes
the baby to come—the *souffle*
of waves, of airconditioning—
audible through the stethoscope
held to the pregnant mother's belly.
And here as takeoff presses
the body, the mind gestates
and develops new being, differing
fully though out of the same matrix.
The heart beats, the small fists
press, the umbilicus feeds. The time
approaches and the hoped-for safe
passage through the tight channel
and the mother's pain into the dangers
of landing—bump—in dangerous
light and air over hard fecund soil,
the exercise ground.

History

remembering the friend killed July 10, 2002.
in the Sangre de Cristo mountains
– not only for his wife in mourning

A span of time. The literal
and the rupture

(i)

fragmented mind "heart broken"
but
it beats, or, that is, a muscle
contracts
relaxes—

But that mountain man slipped,
fell, struck his head, died instantly

nor does anyone know
when "it tolls for thee"—

The mountains stand, called "Blood of Christ"
(shed, it is said, for—)

But they are far, misty and blurred
witness as one looks up
from the cemetery gate,
Rosita, Colorado
with its sign: 1870.

Dust of pioneers mingles in mind

at the
great cemetery where in Manahatta, 9/11/01
the towers stood flaming
tipped slowly, fell, thousands dead

—dead dead—

Repeatedly the man falls
a hundred stories

on his black-jacket wings
Video/audio tape records
sound of the body hitting the
ground—THUD—another, then
another

Dead, dead—

and now the tapes in storage.

What use to sit by
the mountain man's body,
That *no-longer-he* who should not
—she has to say it over—should not,
like all the other young should not

have died.

(ii)

MISSING
a xerox photo pasted on the supermarket window:

under it this:

Rosalie Paisano,
30 weeks pregnant

[a digital banner in mind
above Times Square, its
moving white lights, dot
a f t e r   d o t   a b o v e   d o t   3 0
3 0   3 0   weeks

The dark smoke closed in—
(*You cannot save your child*)
"I cannot save—
I   will   try ... "

No "I" now, but that
name, body, heart forever
in the ash of the gray body
no body
the weeping ghost of ash
that walks out of the smoke.

A movie reel unrolls, replays
and walks

(iii)

". . . nothing to do," a woman finally, months
later, told her girl-friend, "but walk
back to Harlem
(*refugee, as from
Tibet, or across Poland)*

But at 57th Street I began
to cramp and bleed,
and so I lost it—"

(iv)

The great gap,
the great invisible mountain of blood,
fire, flesh that
towers in the empty sky over the river

The vast sky
over the Sangre de Cristos
into which the wind
carries the mountain man's ashes

not to rise again

(v)

Stand in line. Walk out on the temporary
plywood deck. Take out a camera.
Click.
A child starts to write his name

DANIEL G

in the history
of the living who filed past
the plywood wall but
hasn't time to finish. The crowd has to
move on.

Develop the film.
Not a good shot. You couldn't see
to the bottom of what will never
be
buried again.

KRAZY: VISUAL POEMS & PERFORMANCE SCRIPTS

Crazy, *a.*, of unsound mind, insane, mad, demented, often used by way of exaggeration of sense: distracted, or 'mad' with excitement, vehement desire, perplexity, etc.

— *OED*, p. 1148 (Compact Edition, 1971)

Women Are Crazy, Men Are Stupid:
The Simple Truth to a Complicated Relationship…

— title of self-help book by Howard J. Morris (Amazon, 2010)

The constellation, the word group, replaces the verse, becomes the center of a field of force, a "thought-object."

— from Eugen Gomringer (1957), pioneer in Concrete poetry

Preface

KRAZY is a collection of visual poems in the international avant-garde tradition of "concrete poetry," also known as visual poetry. In the visual poem the form evokes meaning and sound as spoken. It radically re-arranges the printed poem's convention of letters in lines on a page and presents a new object for the viewer's perception and contemplation. I began to work in this format in the 1970s, strict black and white, using commonplace schoolroom materials, construction paper cutouts, stencils, pressed-on letters, and the typewriter as the principal art instrument.

As these visual images were being created, the sounds of speech emerged along with them. The sound of a word, even a letter, carries emotional weight — O, for instance. The letters U and I, arranged on the page, rapidly manifest as the primal dichotomy of self and other, female and male, talking to each other. The challenge for me then was how to do a public poetry reading that would integrate these aspects. I put the visual poems into a slide show, the voices into sound poems and wrote a script to be read as the images remain on the screen.

This book mirrors the experience of the performance. First comes the visual poem on the facing page and after it, on the reverse, the words of the thoughts it generates. The texts also contain stage directions for the poet-performer, who stands semi-invisible in the audience in the darkened room, operating the equipment, historically a slide projector and an audiotape player, now DVD or Powerpoint. Occasionally a second voice comes in, identified in the script only as "tape." It is sometimes male, the voice of patriarchy, sometimes female as internalized subconscious conflicted thought. Sometimes a helper runs the projector, live actors perform the texts, and the poet is present only in the poems, as in this book.

— Jane Augustine, 2015

PART ONE

FORM/inFORM

Form

Form in Form   Form as Force

— a manifesto

FORm FORwards FORmations FORthwith
FORm FORtifies FOR FORtune's FORge
FORm FORgoes FORgery and FORces FORtitude
FORm FORstalls the FORtuitous and FORwarns FORagers
in FORmlessness
FORm inFORms conFORms deFORms reFORms

Observe the FORmS

2R DE 4CE
(i) 2mult

2l
2r
2t
2th
2mb
2be
2lips
2cans
2ners
2rniquets
2steppers
2rquoises

Two times two times two
or
two times one is two, times two is four,
times four is eight:

tool tour toot
tooth tomb tube
tulips toucans tuners
tourniquets two-steppers turquoises

2R DE 4CE
(ii) 4mations

4
4t
4ce
4mat
4skin
4stall
4malize
4warning
4nication
4tuitously
4tuneteller

Instruction for construction
of formation:

add one
to build *la tour*
from the top down:

fort
force
format
foreskin
forestall
formalize
forewarning
fornication
fortuitously
fortuneteller

Core

core

to the core   heart
heart of the matter my core
mon coeur   heart of me
courtesy
core to seed
cordoned in the core of me
laid bare   like this
a slice

Deep

deep

deepens   depends   deep ends
at the deep end   two halves
mirror
each
not
quite
white sinks   into black
black rises   around white
night
reflects moon
moon
night

Hollow

hollow

[tape replies as from a distance: "hollow — hallow —
hallo— oh oh oh . . ."]

hollow hallo hallow hollows wholes
complete holes open
holds open:
hold out hold on hold
in hollowed holders
hollo — O O o o o o o o

[tape echo: oh oh oooooo oh]

Inside

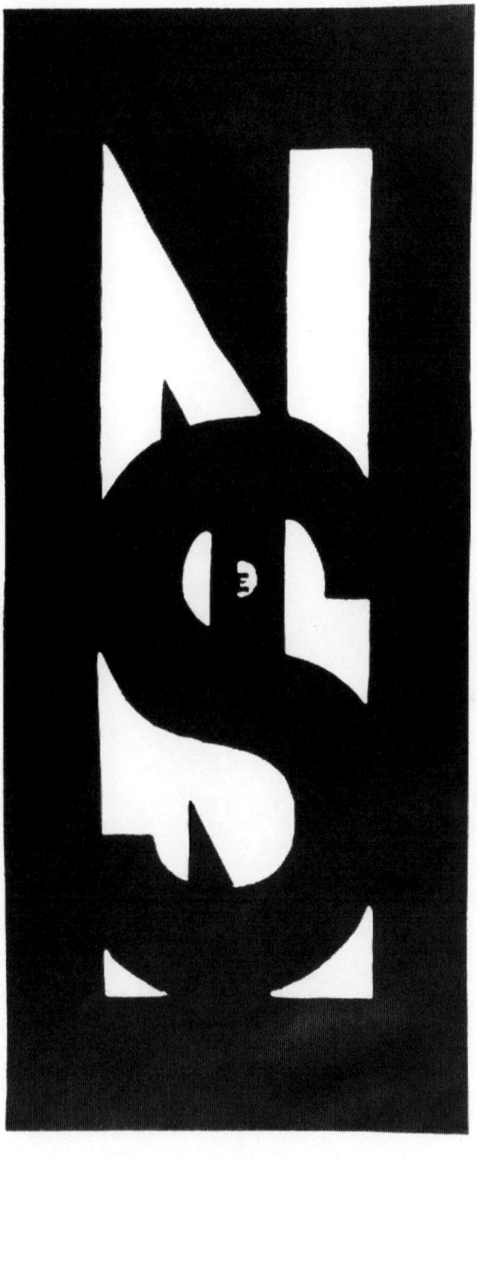

inside

I
N inside of I
S inside of N
I inside of S
D inside of I
E inside of D

INSIDE inside itself
self inside of self

Part Two

YOU + I SERIES

I: Relational Triptych / Form One: U + I

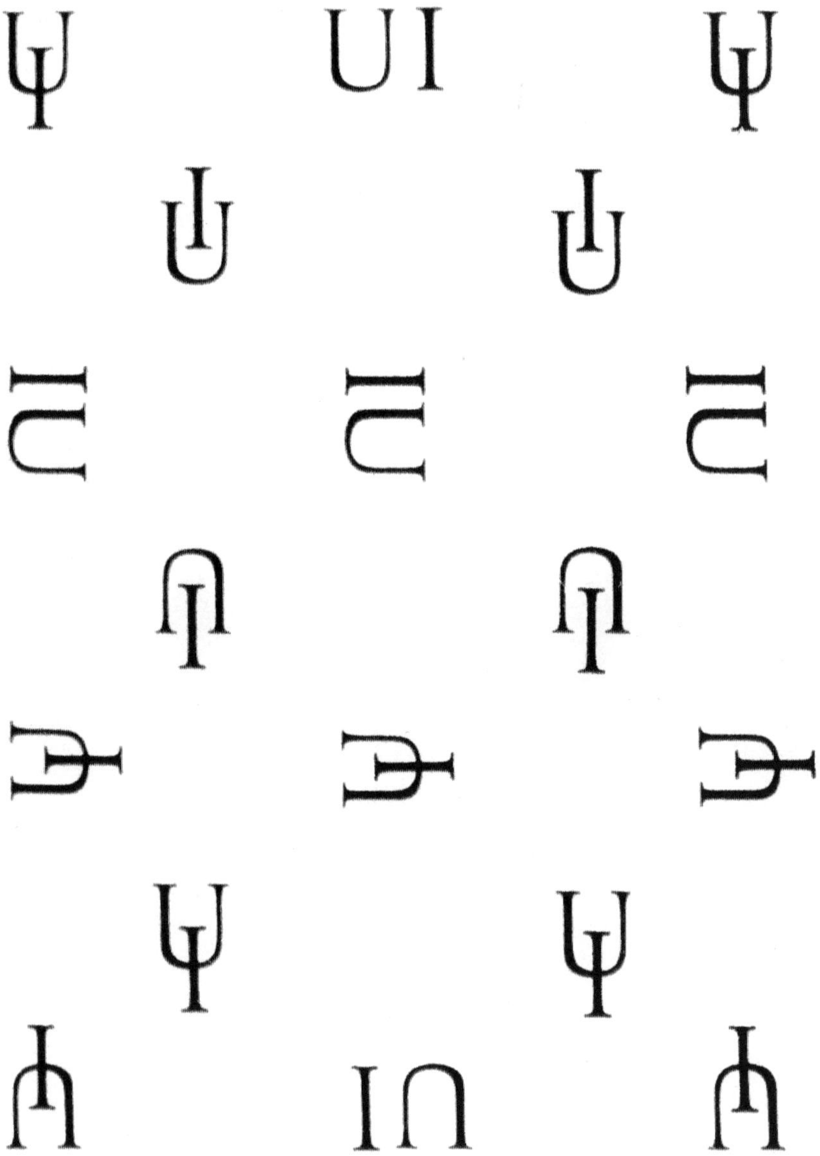

U on top of I U next to I U on top of I

U under I U under I

I beside U I beside U I beside U

U over I U over I

I in U I in U I in U

I under U I under U

I on top of U I next to U I on top of U

EROS ROSE SORE
ROSE SORE EROS
SORE EROS ROSE

EROS SORE ROSE
ROSE EROS SORE
SORE ROSE EROS

[antiphonal: tape speaks words in italic caps in parens, poet lower case; underlined spoken by both.]

EROS the little god, born of Venus (*ROSE*) the penis
the drawn bow, the standing arrow
ROSE, arose, is rising, has risen to the rosy (*SORE*)
bowed infolded flower, the rosebud
SORE with rising *(ROSE)*, with standing, with holding,
(SORE) with drawing; erratic arrows in erotic errors *(EROS)*

ROSE thorns prick the prick, *(SORE)* the prick thorns the rose
in auras of anger
SORE at the source, *(ROSE)* the little prick's fallen arrows,
too quick pricks, dozing roses; sore is
EROS backwards, eros is sore backwards; not ecstatic but erratic

SORE in erroneous zones *(ROSE)*, for rosy auras around orifices,
for arrows in arrears, errors in affronts oral & floral
ROSE has risen again on exotic errands *(SORE)* in erogenous
areas, and the rose encloses the arrow of
EROS (*SORE*) in amends for affronts, for arrears, for stalling,
for swearing, for getting, for going *(ROSE)*,
for was for were, for on for off, for am for are,
for is <u>**EROS**</u>

amamamamamamamam amamamamamamamam
arearearearearea arearearearearea
AMAMAMAMAMAMAMAM AMAMAMAMAMAMAMAM
AREAREAREAREAREA AREAREAREAREAREA
amamamamamamamam amamamamamamamam
arearearearearea arearearearearea
AMAMAMAMAMAMAMAM AMAMAMAMAMAMAMAM
AREAREAREAREAREA AREAREAREAREAREA
waswerewaswerewa waswerewaswerewa
waswaswaswaswasw waswaswaswaswasw
werewerewerewere ewerewerewerewer
waswaswaswaswasw waswaswaswaswasw
WASWASWASWASWASW WASWASWASWASWASW
WEREWEREWEREWERE WEREWEREWEREWERE
waswaswaswaswasw waswaswaswaswasw
werewerewerewere werewerewerewere
waswerewaswerewa waswerewaswerewa
AMAMAMAMAMAMAMAM AMAMAMAMAMAMAMAM
AREAREAREAREAREA AREAREAREAREAREA
amamamamamamamam amamamamamamamam
arearearearearea arearearearearea
AMAMAMAMAMAMAMAM AMAMAMAMAMAMAMAM
AREAREAREAREAREA AREAREAREAREAREA
amamamamamamamam amamamamamamamam
arearearearearea arearearearearea
waswaswaswaswasw waswaswaswaswasw
werewerewerewere werewerewerewere
WASWASWASWASWASW WASWASWASWASWASW
WEREWEREWEREWERE WEREWEREWEREWERE
waswaswaswaswasw waswaswaswaswasw
werewerewerewere werewerewerewere
amamamamamamamam amamamamamamamam
AMAMAMAMAMAMAMAM AMAMAMAMAMAMAMAM
waswaswaswaswasw waswaswaswaswasw
WASWASWASWASWASW WASWASWASWASWASW
werewerewerewere werewerewerewere
arearearearearea arearearearearea
AREAREAREAREAREAREAREAREAREAREAREAREAREAR
AMAREAMAREAMAREAMAREAMAREAMAREAMAREA
waswerewaswerewaswerewaswerewaswer
WASWEREWASWEREWASWEREWASWEREWASW
werewerewerewerewerewerewerewe

IS
IS
IT IS IT
IS
IS

LIKELOVELONELIFE
LOSELINELOVELOSE
LIFELINELONELIKE
LONELOVELINELIKE
LOSELIFELONELOSE
LOVELIKELINELOSE
LIFELIKELONELINE
LOVELINELONELOVE
LOSELIKELIFELIKE
LIFELOSELONELOVE
LINELONELOSELOVE
LIFELINELIKELONE
offoffoffoffoffo
onononononononon
offoffoffoffoffo
onononononononon
outoutoutoutouto
inininininininin
outoutoutoutouto
inininininininin
isisisisisisisis
itititititititit
isisisisisisisis
itititititititit
OFFOFFOFFOFFOFFO
ONONONONONONONON
OFFOFFOFFOFFOFFO
ONONONONONONONON
outoutoutoutouto
inininininininin
OUTOUTOUTOUTOUTO
ININININININININ
isisisisisisisis
itititititititit
ISISISISISISISIS
ITITITITITITITIT
isitisitisitisit
isitisitisitisit
offonoffonoffono
offonoffonoffono
inoutinoutinouti
ISISISISISISISIS

[tape speaks lines in caps, fast, poet lower-case also very fast; underlined words create iambic pentameter or trochaic. Tape is spondaic, loud. The poet's repetitions are muttered, hammered, or intoned, chant-like, as desired.]

am am am am am am am am am am
are are are are are are are are are are

AM AM AM AM AM AM AM AM AM AM
ARE ARE ARE ARE ARE ARE ARE ARE ARE ARE

was was was was was was was was was was
were were were were were were were were were were

WAS WAS WAS WAS WAS WAS WAS WAS WAS WAS
WERE WERE WERE WERE WERE WERE WERE WERE WERE WERE

Were we

OFF on OFF on OFF on OFF on OFF on
in OUT in OUT in OUT in OUT in OUT
IS it IS it IS it IS it IS it

is it

[tape begins faintly, builds up crescendo as subliminal mind becomes liminal, shouts more more more, then once in a while yells MORE in the middle of the following poem which is read at top speed]

want more   want want want   more more more want more
always want more   more want
more time   more time for   more time for wanting
more time for wanting more food
more time for wanting more food drink
more time for wanting more food drink sex want more sex
more time more drink more sun more fun
more fine more pen more pine more heart more burn more lust
more love more love more more more more more more loose more
loss more space more spin more shriek more tear more come
more go more come more more more come come come moremore
MOREMOREMOREMOREMOREMOREMOREMOREMORE

MOOOOOOOOOOOOOOOOOOOOORE

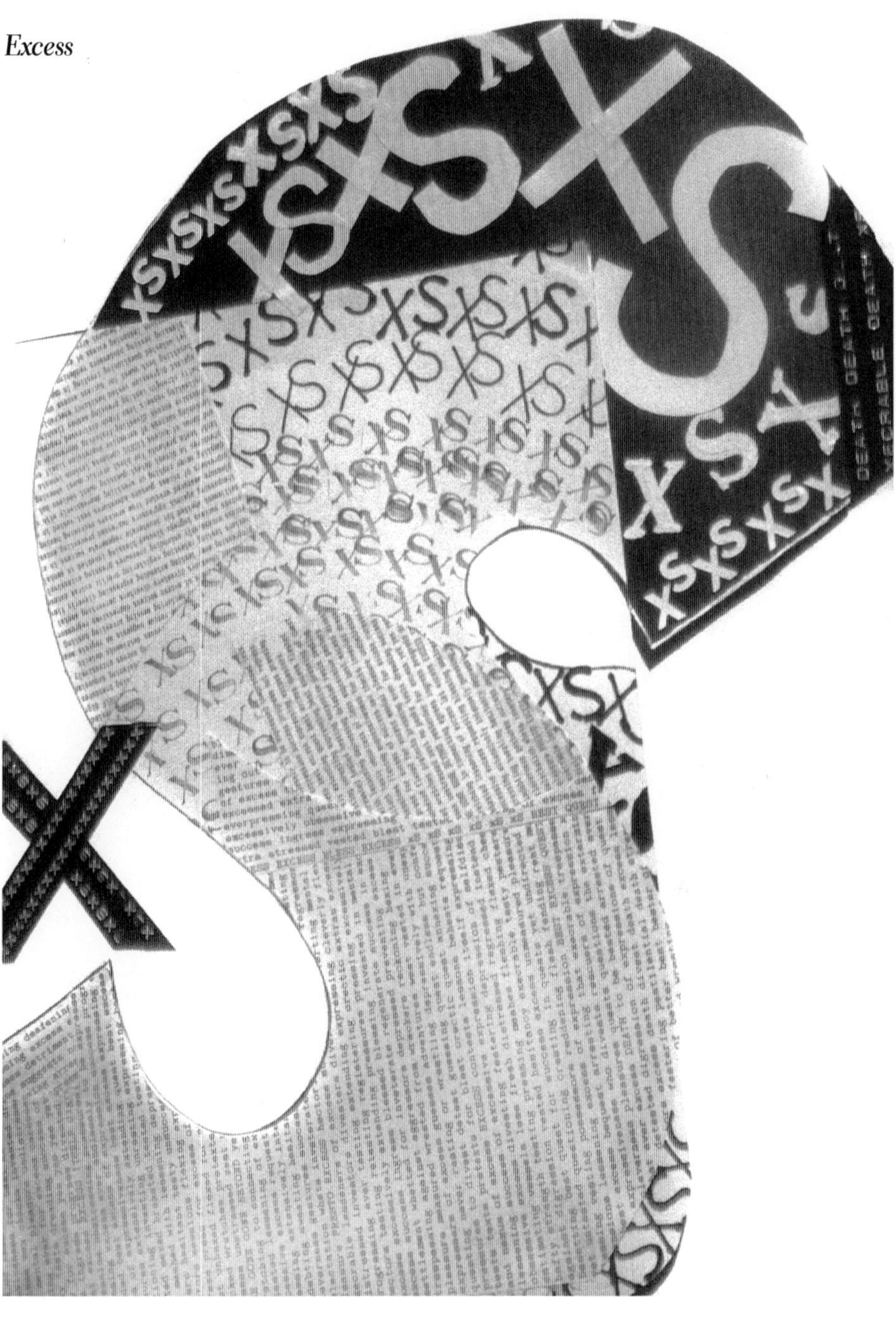

exCESS

of x'es   of s'es
xxxxxxxxxx
SSSSSSSSSSS

Enough — or too much, said Blake:

I say too much
excess of death

stress excess of breath

Slash

S
L
A
S
H

l
a
s
h
a
s
h
SH
sh shhhh

who—?
none
done it

Waves

waves

wash out   wash up   wash over   wash away

One word makes waves:
page arbitrarily ends
what need not end:
the line in black.

Clumsy felt-tip
imitates Hokusai's fine point
upsurge

about to overwhelm

Dripping

dripping

It’s ink,
isn’t it

virile black
from a loaded brush

commanded by
gravity   a natural
force

and runs in blood
down palace walls

Washout

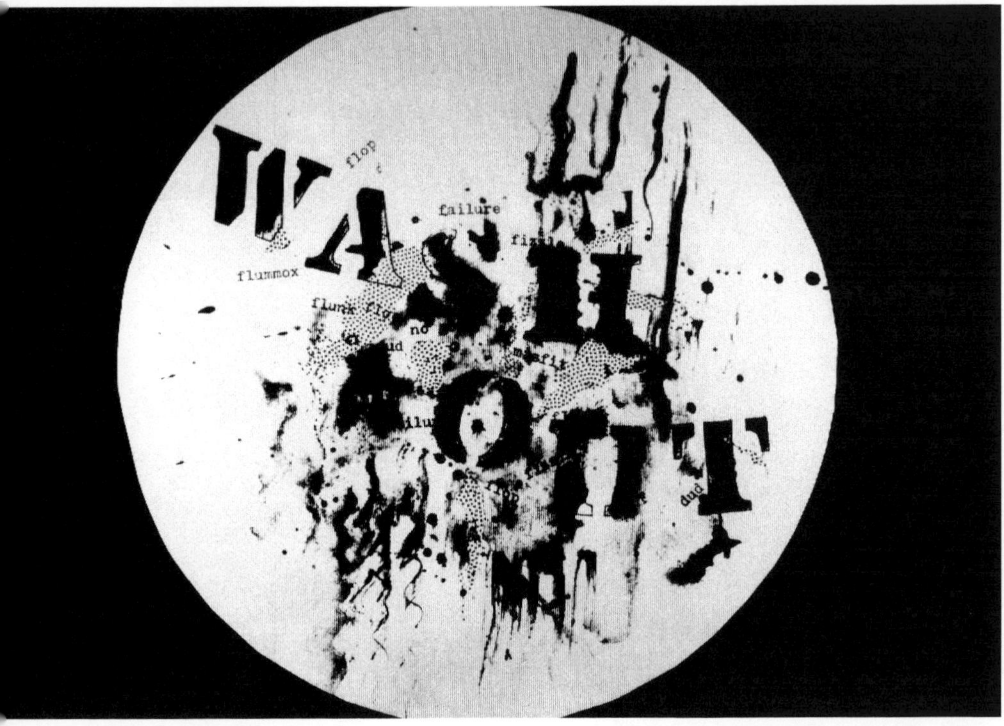

washout

[poet ad lib to tape]

FLOP DUD FAILURE BOTCH MESS NO GOOD
FLUNK FLUMMOX FIZZLE MISFIT LOSER FIASCO
BUNGLE MANGLE BOGGLE FLUMMOX FLUNK
FLOP
DUD
FAILURE
WA
SH
OUT

WA
SHOUT

Split

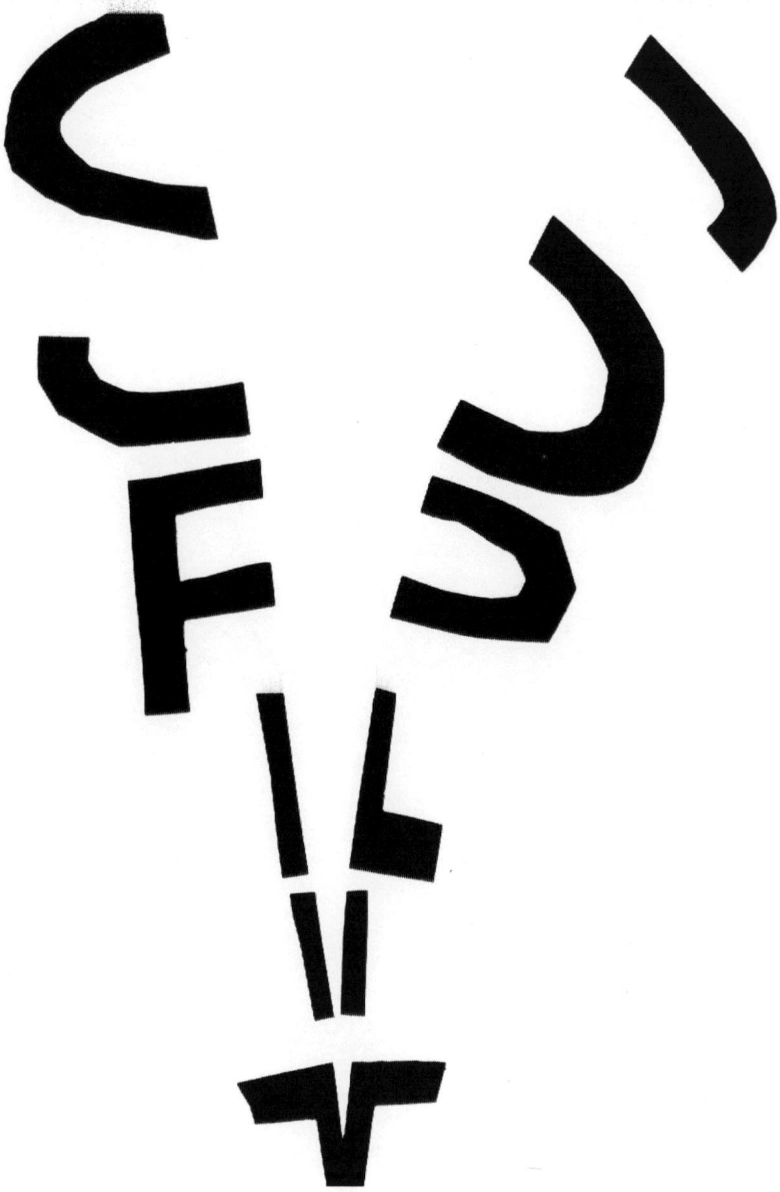

To split
you need a
hatchet which you
raise over your head
with your right or left arm
depending — put boots on first —
and bring down hard in the center of
the stump balanced on a larger level
stump and you get two pieces —then you maybe
think it would have been better to have left it one

Part Three

EXIT SERIES

IT

X-IT

*Nine meditations on Bartlett's, Roget
and the Oxford International*

Exits and Ends

XXXexexexexexexexexXXXXXXXXXitXitXitXitXitXitXXXXxxxxthe/end/the/exit/EXITEXIT

EXIT

called to make our
pursued by a bear
ten thousand doors for men
to take their

EXITS
and their entrances

ENDS

are out of sight, both
at my fingers'
delays have dangerous
divinity that shapes our
end me no
every man for his own
human, ultimately answered
neglecting worldly
of the earth, come from the
of verse, cheered with
of which were twisted
old odd, of holy writ
out to the undiscovered
private
seldom gain their
sought his
this strange eventful history
thou aimest at
violent delights have violent

--indeX, Bartlett's

exitEXItout/the/event/ex-doutXXXXXXXxxxxxxxXitXitXitXitexexexexexexexexXXXXXXX *[irrational sub-voice on tape shouts EXIT, EXITS and ENDS as title and intermittently mutters "ex it out/ the event ex-d out" as the rational voice reads the quotations. Both voices say the last word:*

ENDS]

Ex-d-out: Nine Traces

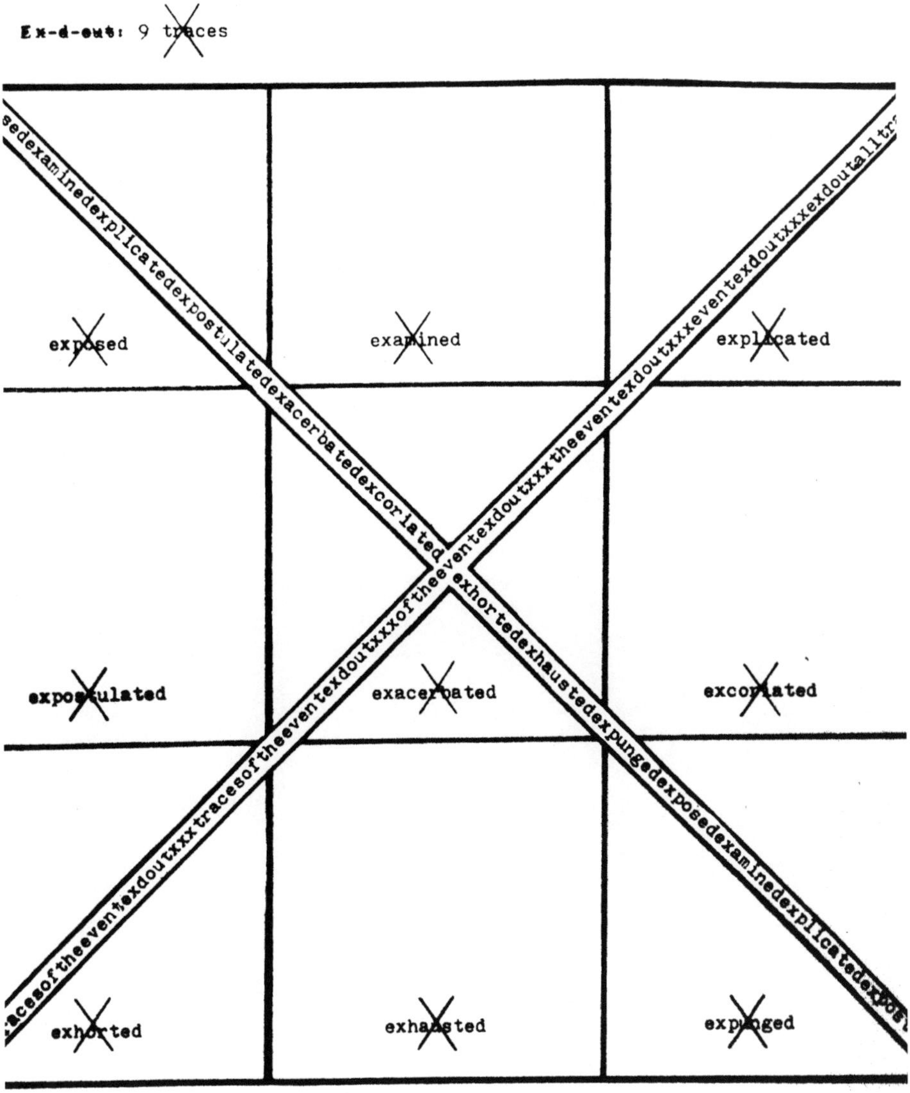

[tape says "ex" every now and then]

All traces of the event exd out

traces of the event exd out

of the event exd out

the event exd out

exd out

exposed examined explicated   exd out

expostulated exacerbated excoriated   exd out

exhorted exhausted expunged exd out exd out exd out

Ex-d-out XXXXXs

-Ex-d-out: XXXXXs

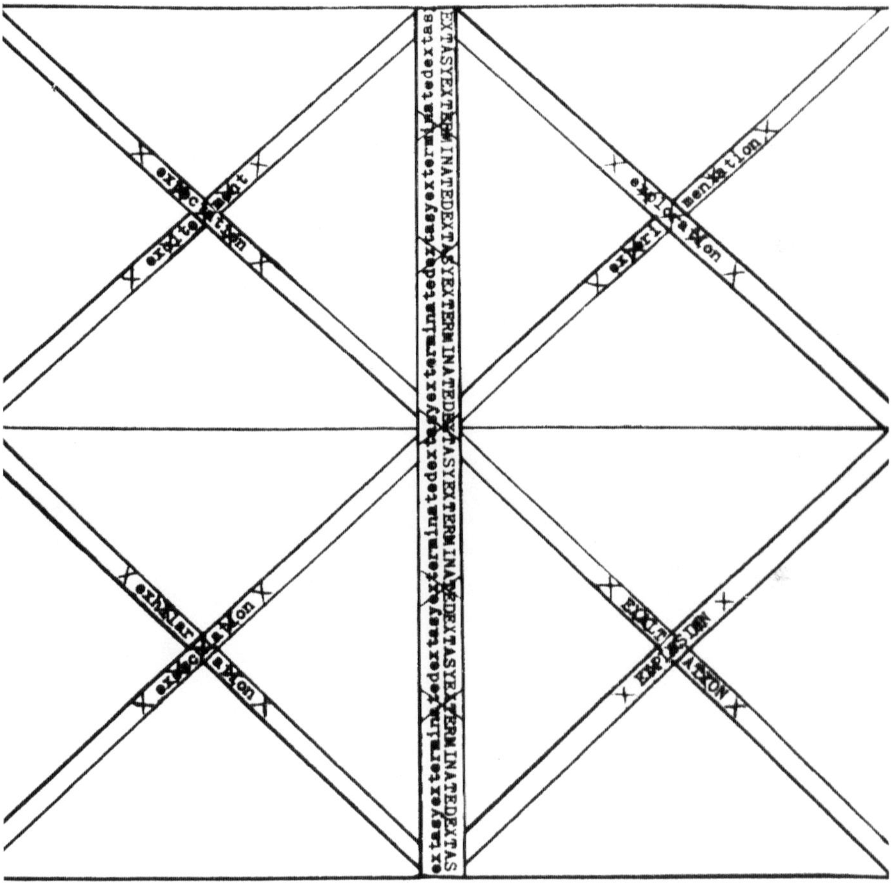

“Th’ extasie” exterminated:

exd out expectation   exd out excitement

exd out exploration   exd out experimentation

exd out exhilaration   exd out exfoliation

exd out explosion   exd out exaltation

extermination exd out:

EX EX EX

termination

X definitions

X definitions

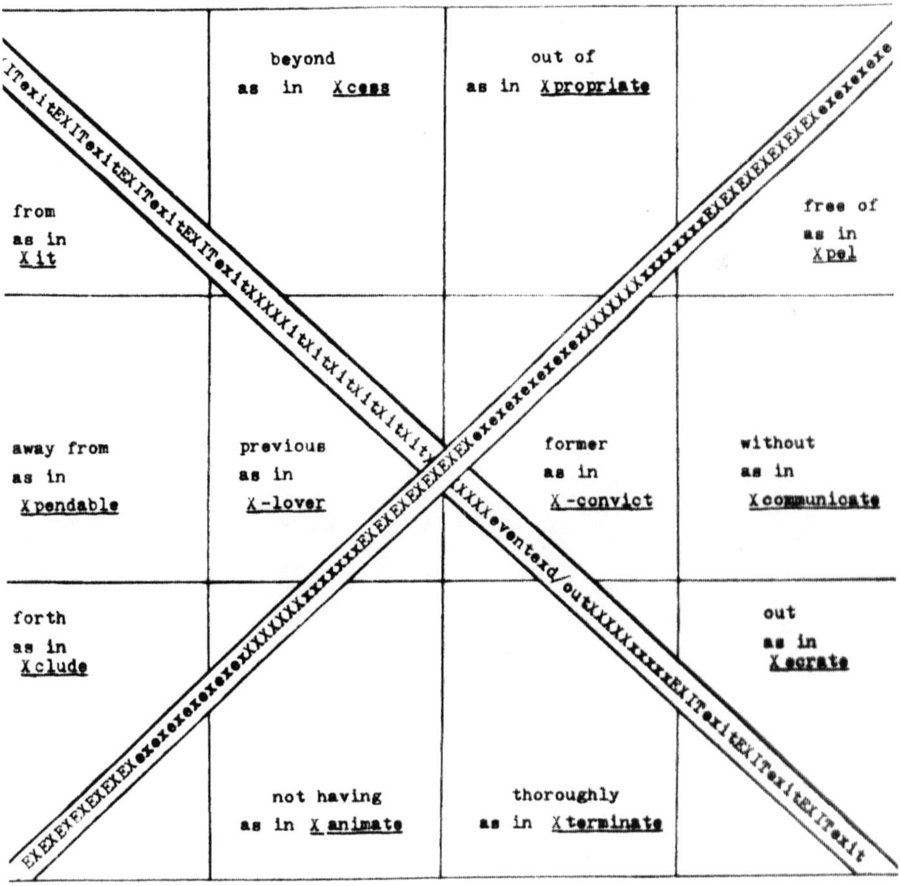

beyond
as in Xcess
out of
as in Xpropriate
from
as in Xit
free of
as in Xpel
away from
as in Xpendable
previous
as in X-lover
former
as in X-convict
without
as in Xcommunicate
forth
as in Xclude
out
as in Xecrate
not having
as in X animate
thoroughly
as in Xterminate

[tape goes on shouting EX occasionally as the poet transmits the linguistic information on the screen]

X	from, as in "exit"
X	beyond, as in "excess"
X	out of, as in "expropriate"
X	free of, as in "expel"
X	away from, as in "expendable"
X	previous, as in "ex-lover"
X	former, as in "ex-convict"
X	without, as in "excommunicate"
X	forth, as in "exclude"
X	not having, as in "exanimate"
X	thoroughly, as in "exterminate"
X	out, as in "execrate"

X-tensions

X-tensions

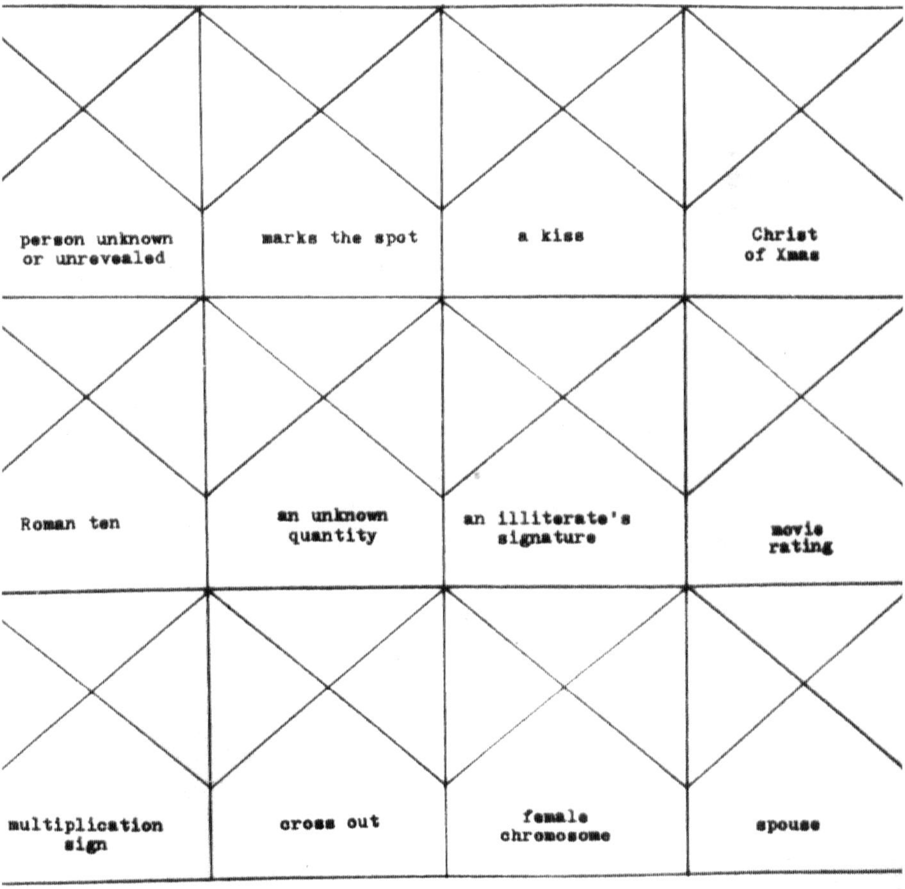

[poet says X; tape completes sentence, or the reverse]

X signifies a person unknown, or unrevealed
X marks the spot
X grants a kiss
X substitutes for Christ in Christmas
X gives ten to a Roman
X —algebra's unknown quantity
X signs an illiterate's name
X rates a movie
X multiplies numbers
X means "cross out," delete
X indicates the female chromosome
X is for spouse

Xit U + I

Xit

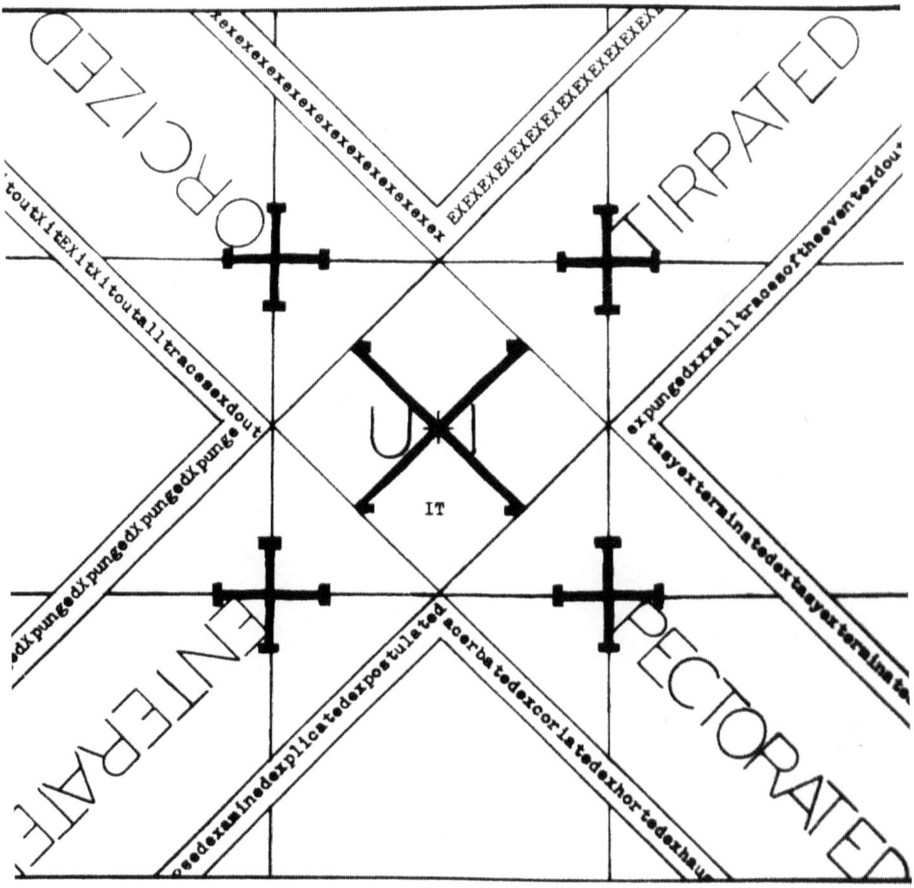

END

[antiphonal: tape says word in caps, poet lower case, repeats refrain, both voices on EXIT]

Exorcized	expunge the event; all traces of the
Expectorated	event exd out; traces of the
Exenterated	event exd out; of the event exd
Extirpated	out; exd out

X it out   X it out   X it

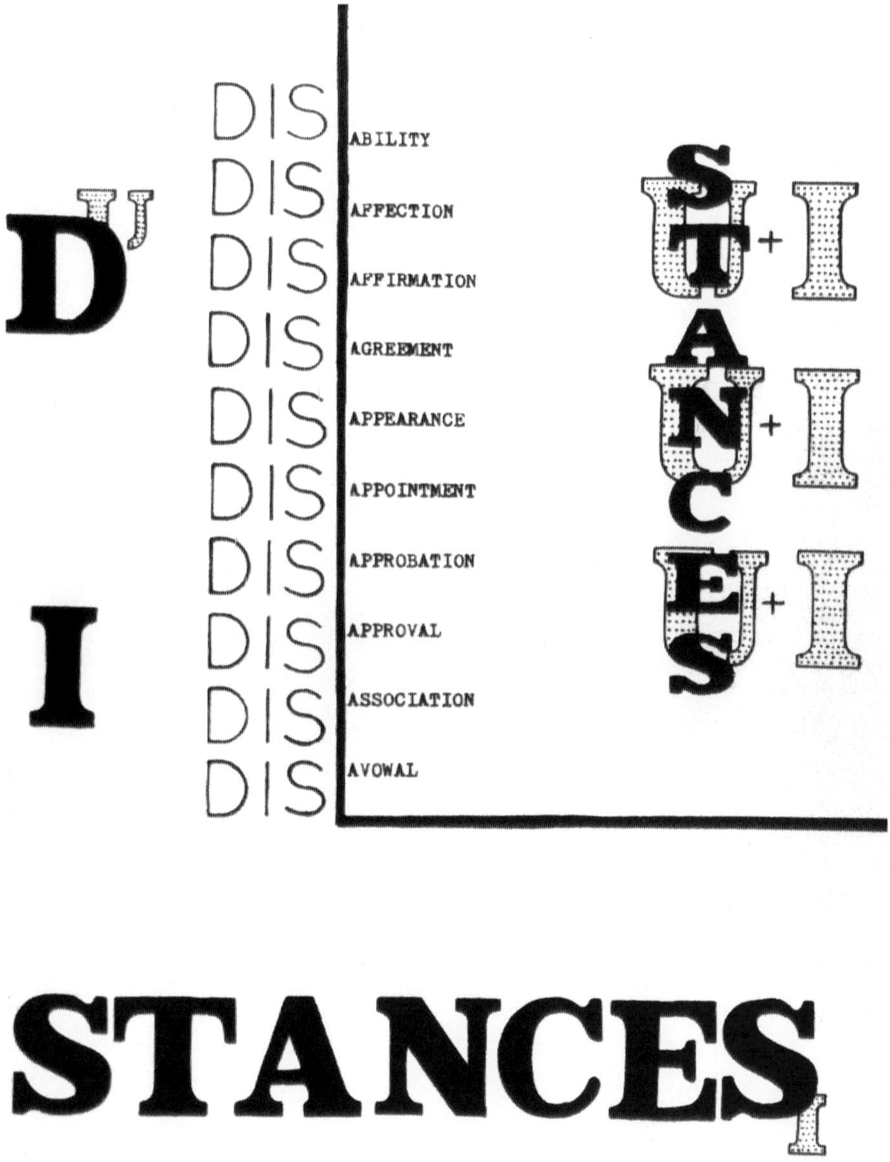
DISABILITY
DISAFFECTION
DISAFFIRMATION
DISAGREEMENT
DISAPPEARANCE
DISAPPOINTMENT
DISAPPROBATION
DISAPPROVAL
DISASSOCIATION
DISAVOWAL
D
U
J
I
S
T
A
N
C
E
S
U+I
U+I
U+I
STANCES
I

in alphabetical form

DIS-stances: U + I

— and these are only the a’s

Dis-sing (ii): Disjoin

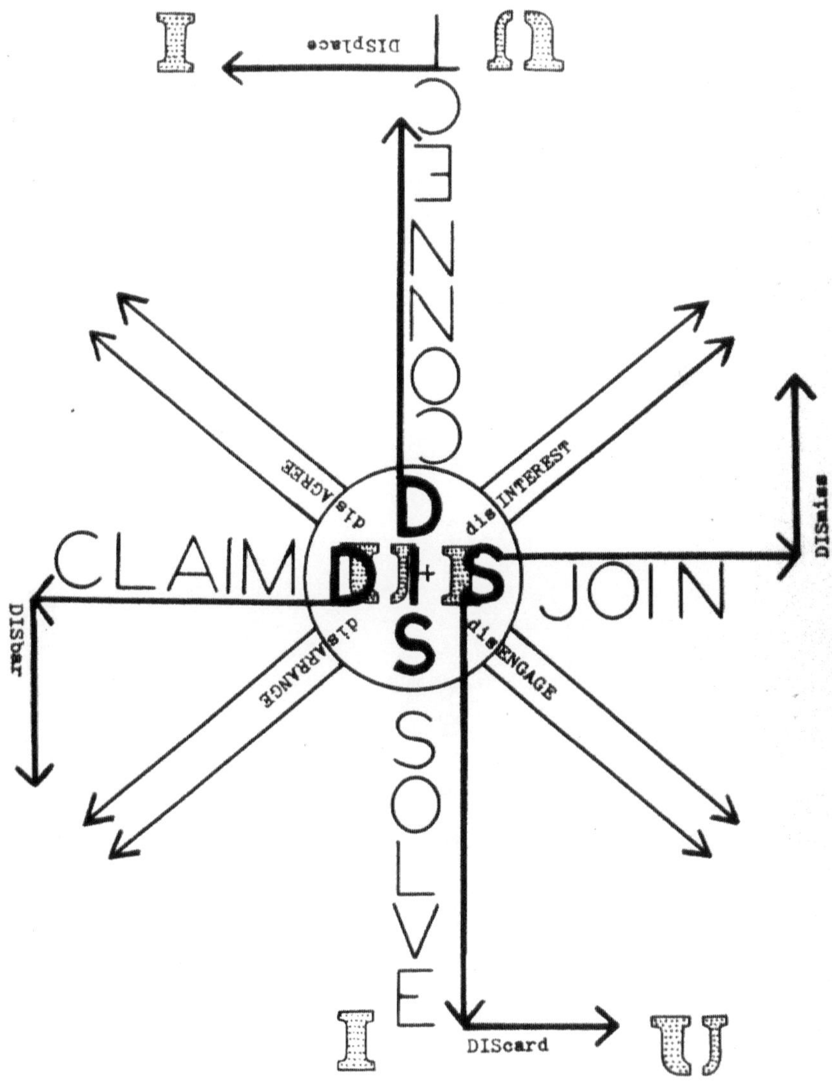

in philosophical linguistic form

DISjoin   DISconnect   DISclaim   DISsolve:

Dissolution requires solution

Solution:
(I) action or process of solving
(II) action of dissolving
or changing from a solid or gaseous state
to a liquid
(III) action of breaking up or separating;
dissolution,

bringing to an end.

Dissolution:
(I) separation into parts or constituent elements
(II) reduction from the solid
to the liquid
form
(III) action of bringing or condition of
being brought

to an end.

Solution = dissolution   no solution = no dissolution

—Form is emptiness; emptiness also is form

therefore no poem no non-poem

no dissin' no non-dissin' no stance no dis-stance

Part Four

KRAZY

KRAZY

ion neurosis,
hock, hysteri
chondriasm, h
k madness", s
of personalit
delіracy, del
ure of the br
wandering, di
rium tremens,m
il, siriasis,
sion, fantasti
tmare, incubus
iocrasy, idioc
on, twist, men
t, freak, magg
infatuation, o
ealotry, monom
ddiness, whim,
um for the ins
psychopathic
loose, have b
ve rats in the
topside, ramble
drivel, drool,
lose one's h
rack, run amuc
r,derange, unh
ead, befool, i
crazy, craz
sound mind, n
loco, touch
ss, insensate
nsick, crackb
not right i
n one's head,
t, stark-mad,
loony, batty,
hopathic, psychopatholo
cile, idiotic, rabid, r
frantic, beside onese
delirious, phrenati

insanity, unsanity, craziness, dementia, dementation; lunacy, bedlam, mania, furor, mental alientation; aberration of mind, derangement, mental disorder; disordered mind, shattered mind, diseased mind, unsound mind; psychopathic condition, pathomania, moral insanity; murderous insanity, corybantic insanity, amentia; monomania, paranoia, paranomia, lycanthropy, fugue; kleptomania, psychokenesis, dementia praecox, dementia paralytica, pathological lying, morosis, idiocy; amnesia, psychosis, psychopathia, psychoneurosis, emotional instability, psycholepsy, shellshock, hysteria,

hysterics, manic depressive insanity, hypochondria; hypochondriasis, melancholia, megrims, "moping melancholy and moonstruck madness," schizophrenia, functional disintegration, mental disassociation, dissociation of personality, split personality, dual personality, multiple personality, delirium, deliracy, brain fever, calenture of the brain, phrenitis, siriasis, thermic fever; raving, raging, fury, frenzy, fit, paroxysm, incoherence, wandering, distraction, vertigo, dizziness, giddiness; hallucination, hallucinosis, abnormal illusion, fantastic vision, fantods, blue devils, blue johnnies, pink spiders,

snakes, nightmares, bad dreams, illusion, delusion, imagining; eccentricity, idiosyncrasy, erraticism, oddity, peculiarity, mental twist, kink, quirk, crank, quip, crochet, conceit, craze, mania, fanaticism, infatuation, obsession, crazy fancy, fascination, passion, enthusiasm, zealotry, ruling passion, fixed idea, *idée fixe*; to be insane, to have a demon, to have a devil, to have a screw loose, to have bats in the belfry, a leak in the think tank, wheels in the head, rats in the attic, a button missing; to ramble, rave, rant fume, froth at the mouth, drivel, drool, slaver, babble, dote; to go mad, lose your senses,

lose your reason, lose your head, go off your rocker, go
off your nut, go off your head, go off the track, go off
your trolley, run amuck; to madden, dement, drive mad,
unhinge, unbalance, shatter, derange, obsess, possess,
possessed, insane, mad, crazy, lunatic, unsound, *non
compos mentis*, deranged, daft, senseless, crack-brained,
shatterbrained, far gone, not all there, not right; not right
in one's head, wrong in one's head; mad as a hatter; mad as
a march hare, mad as a weaver, crazy as a loon, stark mad,
staring mad, screwy, wacky, daffy, dippy, dotty, goofy, balmy,
beany, batty, cuckoo,

buggy, rabid, wild, furious, violent, delirious, distracted,
distrait, distraught, besotted; madman, lunatic, crackbrain,
bedlamite; Tom o' Bedlam, psychopath, maniac, crackpot,
freak, freak-o, freakout, freaky-deaky-leaky, . . .
krazy,
krazy,
kraaaaaaaaa zy

Phases (i): dark descendings

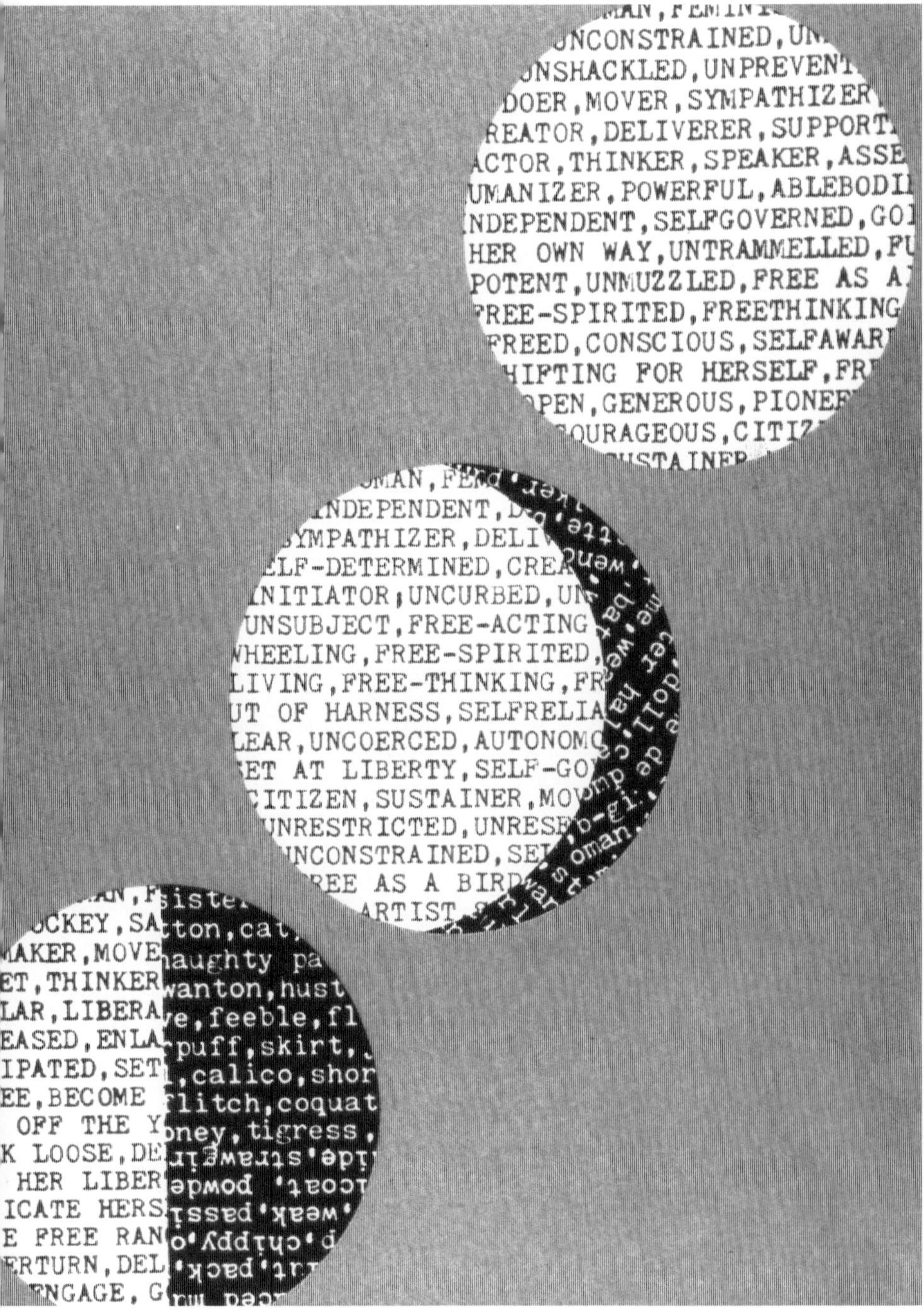
UNCONSTRAINED,
UNSHACKLED,
DOER,MOVER,SYMPATHIZER
DELIVERER,
THINKER,SPEAKER,
POWERFUL,
SELFGOVERNED,
HER OWN WAY,UNTRAMMELLED,
POTENT,UNMUZZLED,FREE AS
FREE-SPIRITED,FREETHINKING
FREED,CONSCIOUS,
FOR HERSELF,
GENEROUS,
COURAGEOUS,
INDEPENDENT,
SYMPATHIZER,
INITIATOR;UNCURBED,
UNSUBJECT,FREE-ACTING
FREE-SPIRITED,
FREE-THINKING,
OF HARNESS,
UNCOERCED,
AT LIBERTY,
CITIZEN,SUSTAINER,
UNRESTRICTED,
UNCONSTRAINED,
AS A
ARTIST
THINKER
BECOME
OFF THE
HER
FREE
haughty
wanton,
feeble,
puff,skirt,
calico,
tigress,

[in two voices, male (M) female (F), though poet may speak both, since she is of two minds. One unconsciously internalizes male opinion while the other consciously works to assert reality]

Phase 1: all black

M: *bitch, babe, hussy, strumpet, wench, drab, slut, whore, broad, hooker, jade, minx, piece, chick, trollop, harlot, skirt, jane, calico, moll, squaw, dame, old lady, petticoat, meat, scold, floozy, frail; weak sister, the weaker sex, the frail sisterhood, "frailty, thy name is woman."*

(F-voice silent)

Phase 2: slice of white: *(F-voice enters tentative)*

F: *woman, feminist, friend, sister,*
independent, self-reliant, potent,
supporter, mother, humanizer, actor, doer, mover

M: *flapper, filly, heifer, vixen, biddy, hen, harpy,*
chippy, demi-rep, tramp, termagent, virago, she-devil,
wanton, harridan, frump, sex kitten, pussy, cunt,
hustler, hot number, sexpot, fast cookie, spitfire,
scarlet woman

Phase 3: more black than white but near balance

F: *(level voice)* *woman, feminist, friend, sister;*
independent, self-reliant, potent;
supporter, mother, humanizer, actor, doer; mover, pioneer, worker, citizen, maker, seer, governor, self-starter

M: *(angry, loud)* *vamp, gold-digger, courtesan, coquette, hetaera, houri, paramour, camp-follower, groupie, pickup, street-walker, call-girl, trull, hag, bag, baggage, witch, flirt, loose woman, nitwit, scatterbrain, dumb-bunny, weaker vessel, fallen woman*

Phase 4: more white than black, on the upswing

F: *woman, feminist, friend, sister,*
independent, self-reliant, potent,
supporter, mother, humanizer, actor, doer, mover,
pioneer, worker, citizen, maker, seer, governor,
self-starter, controller, organizer, sympathizer,
benefactor, sustainer, wooer

M: *slattern, doxy, feather-head, dizzy dame, erring sister, fille de joie, demi-mondaine, woman of the night, poule, puta, putain, fornicatress, mistress, adulteress, tigress, adventuress, fish*

Phase 5: slice of black

F: *woman, feminist, friend, sister;*
independent, self-reliant, potent;
supporter, mother, humanizer, actor, doer, mover;
pioneer, worker, citizen, maker, seer, governor,
self-starter, controller, organizer, sympathizer,
benefactor, sustainer, wooer,
sailor, pilot, executive, deliverer,
thinker, asserter, director, builder

M: *(on the wane, slowing down) passive, fragile, flighty,*
lightweight, pushover, weakling . . .

Phase 6: all-white full moon, top right, in power

F and M speak together:

woman, feminist, friend, sister,
independent, self-reliant, potent,
supporter, mother, humanizer, engineer, actor, doer, mover,
pioneer, worker, citizen, maker, seer, governor, philosopher,
self-starter, controller, organizer, manager, sympathizer,
benefactor, sustainer, wooer, sailor, poet, pilot, physician, executive,
deliverer, thinker, asserter, director, builder, president, free-living,
free-wheeling, free-tongued, free-spirited, autonomous, free woman

Part Five

OR, A POEM OF CHOICE

TONGUE IN THE DARK
OR
OR OR OR OR OR ORE OAR
OTHER

OR

the Other

A Poem of Choice

OR: A particle co-ordinating two
(or more) words, phrases, or clauses
between which there is an alternative

ORE: A native mineral containing a
precious or useful metal in such quantity
etc., as to make its extraction profitable

OAR: A stick, pole, or paddle, with
which anything is stirred

— *Oxford Universal Dictionary*

Woman is a common noun for which no
identity can be defined.

— *Luce Irigaray*

no eye, no ear, no nose, no tongue, no
body, no mind

— *The Heart Sutra*

Ore

The O -- the ovoid O ovum, ova
open, originating
OR choice:
OR opposite opposed
OR ORE aureate goldmine?
OR
ORE

The O — the ovoid O ovum

ova ovulation of the ovula ovulae

the little o's overtly open origins

OR   choice: O

R

U open, originating

OR   opposite   opposed oppressed

OR   ORE   aureate goldmine?

Ova

OR offers other:

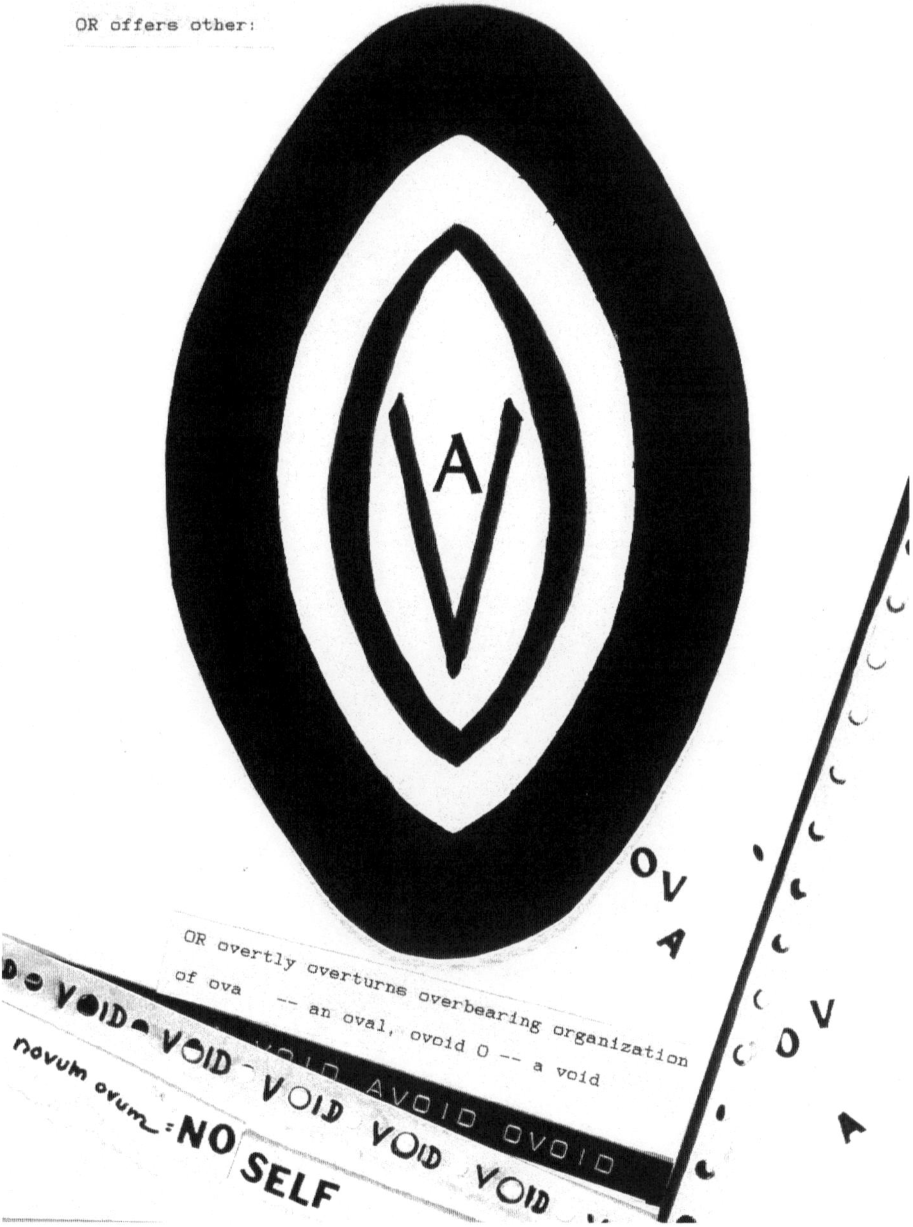
A
OVA
OR overtly overturns overbearing organization
of ova -- an oval, ovoid O -- a void
AVOID OVOID
VOID VOID VOID VOID VOID
novum ovum : NO SELF
OVA

OR offers other:

OR overtly overturns overbearing organization

of ova — an oval, ovoid O — a void

Avoid the O that encircles

O R U

a void producing ova?

novum ovum no self?

O R U avoiding

being

a void

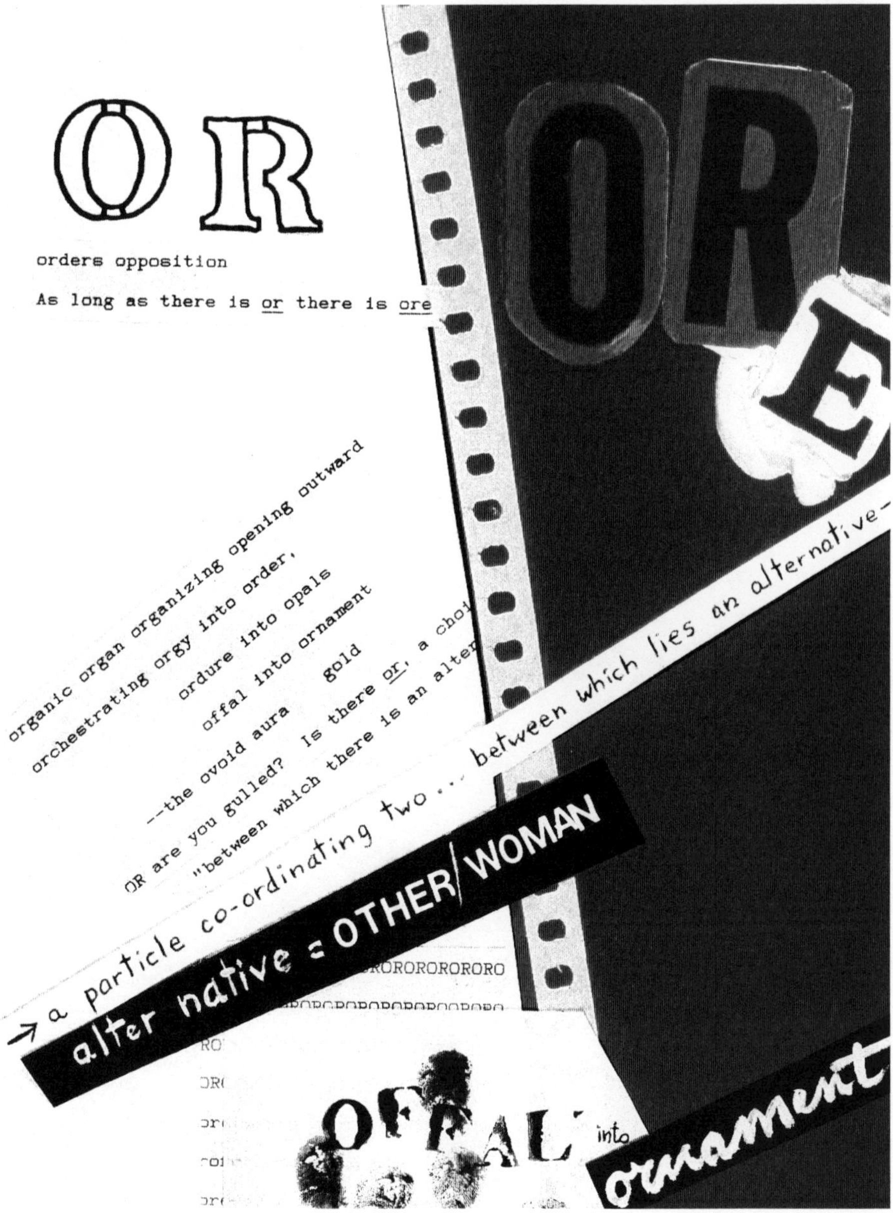
OR
orders opposition
As long as there is or there is ore
OR
E
organic organ organizing opening outward
orchestrating orgy into order,
ordure into opals
offal into ornament
--the ovoid aura gold
OR are you gulled? Is there or, a cho
"between which there is an alter
→ a particle co-ordinating two ... between which lies an alternative-
alter native = OTHER/WOMAN
RORORORORORORO
OFFAL
into
ornament

OR: conjunction "particle co-ordinating ..."

orders opposition:

as long as there is *or* there is *ore*

organic organ organizing opening outward

orchestrating orgy into order,

ordure into opals

offal into ornament

— the ovoid aura gold

OR are you gulled?

Is there *or*

a choice?

OR: a particle...

"between which there is an alternative"

* *

alter native equals Other

/woman

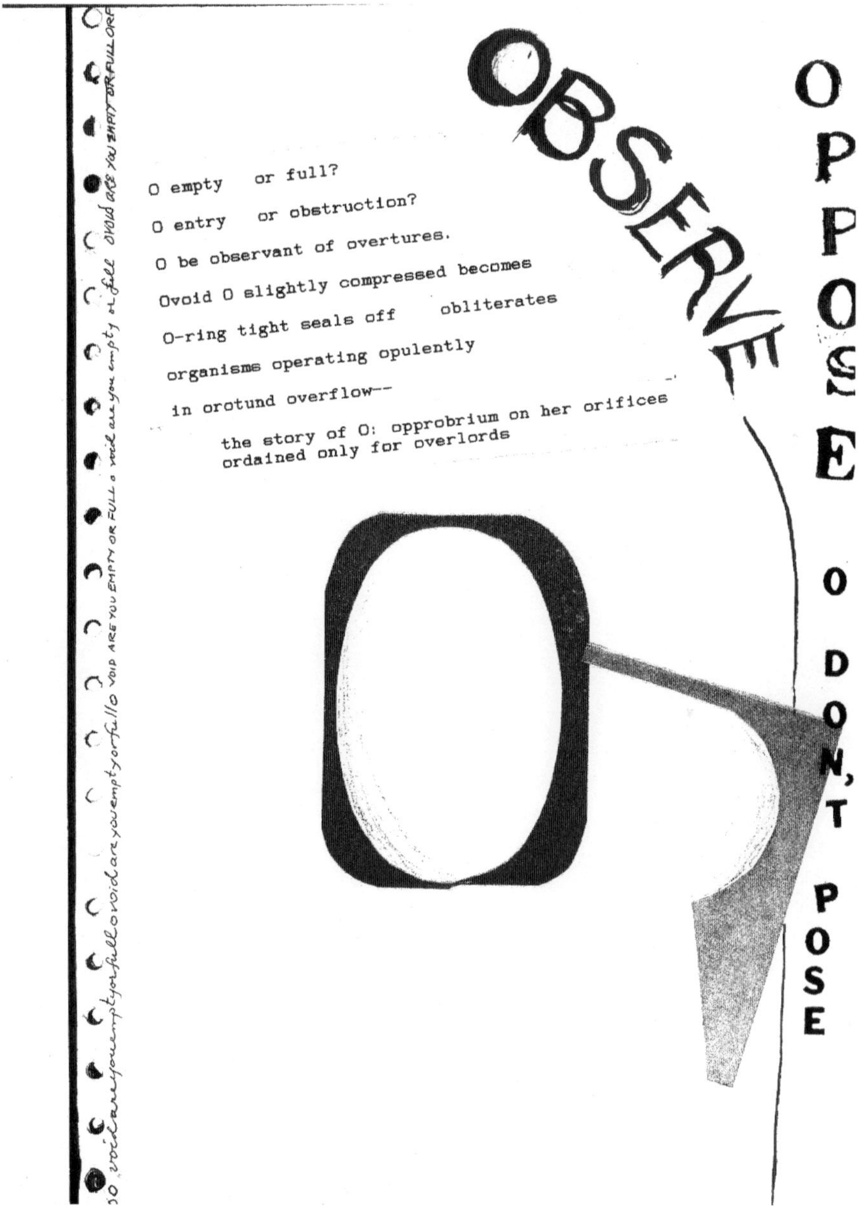
OBSERVE
O empty or full?
O entry or obstruction?
O be observant of overtures.
Ovoid O slightly compressed becomes
O-ring tight seals off obliterates
organisms operating opulently
in orotund overflow--
the story of O: opprobrium on her orifices
ordained only for overlords
OPPOSE
O DON'T POSE

O

O observe

the forms

of OR

transfORmations

opposed

Observe

everything's a little out of line

shadOwy

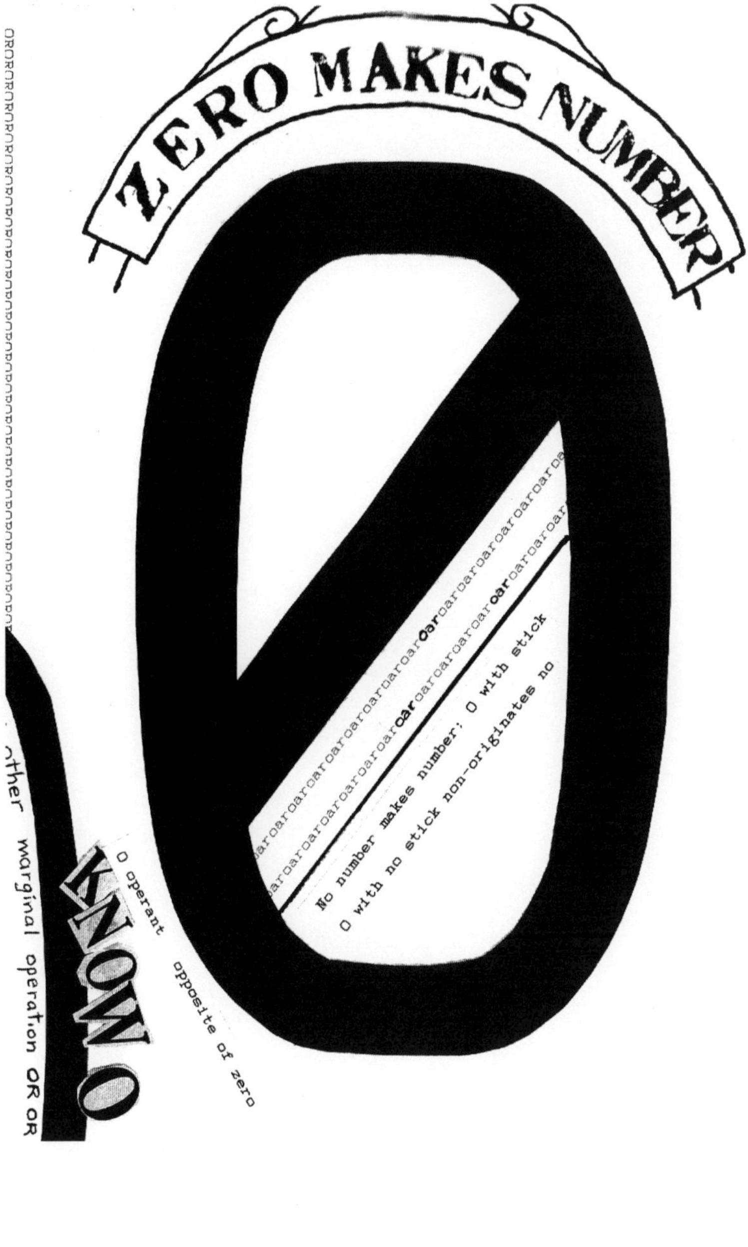
ZERO MAKES NUMBER
No number makes number: O with stick
O with no stick non-originates no
O operant
opposite of zero
KNOW O
other marginal operation OR OR

O operant   opposite of zero

O with a stick

Zero opposite of one:

Big zero, big stick.

Zero's Paradox: No number makes number

O with stick says it's better than O with no stick

says it originates one

the "one and only"

O with no stick non-originates no

no O within O, the no-self

Advice to anonymous O:

Know O   Know all

of the oval ovoid void-opening O

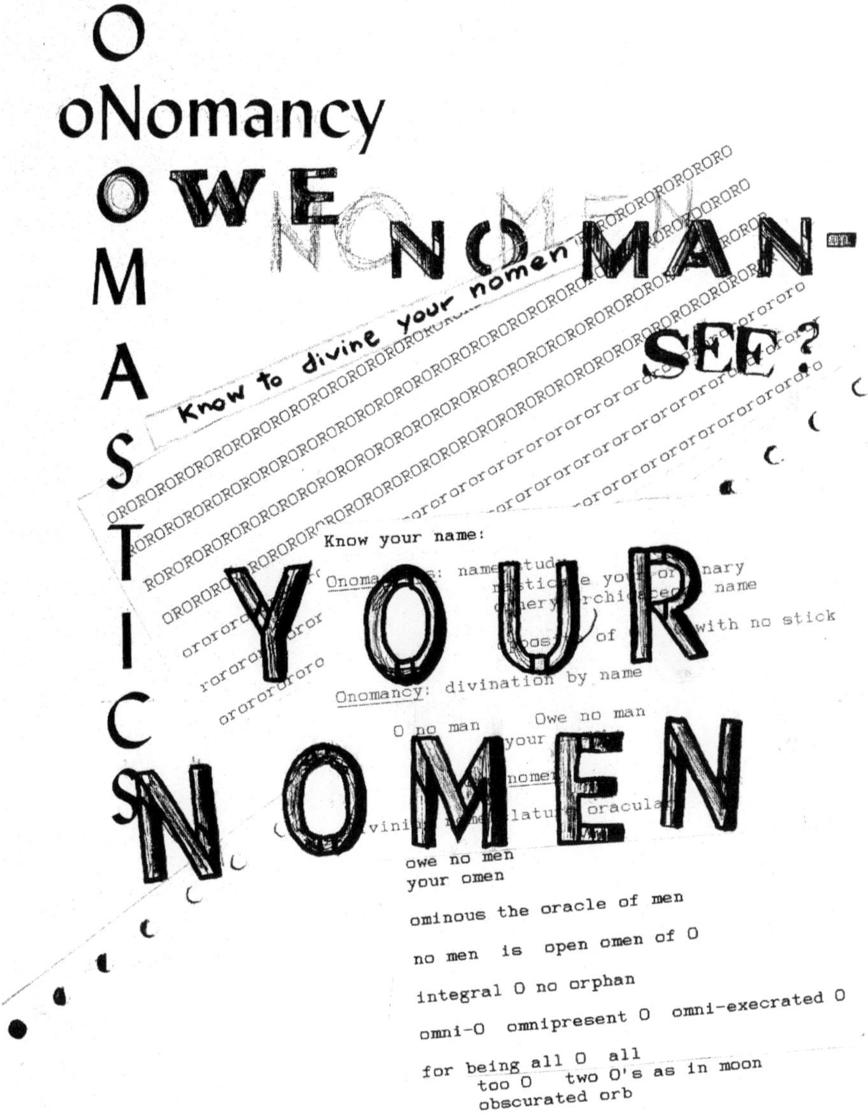
O
oNomancy
OWE NOMAN-
SEE?
ONOMASTICS
Know to divine your nomen
ORORORORORORO
orororororo
Know your name:
Onomancy: divination by name
O no man
Owe no man
YOUR
NOMEN
owe no men
your omen
ominous the oracle of men
no men is open omen of O
integral O no orphan
omni-O omnipresent O omni-execrated O
for being all O all
too O two O's as in moon
obscurated orb

Know your name:

Onomastics: name study

          masticate your ordinary

          ornery orchid-name

          opposite of "big zero"

Onomancy: divination by name

          O no man — see?   Owe no man

          your name

     your (Latin) *nomen*

          divining nomenclature

               oracular

owe no men   your omen

          ominous the oracle of men

no men is open omen of O

integral   O no orphan

omni-O omnipresent O omni-execrated O

for being all O all

     too O   two O's as in moon

     obscurated orb

Orally

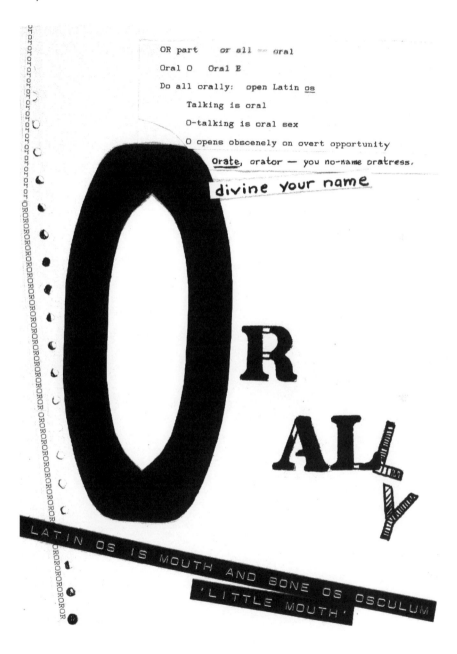

ororororororororororororOROROROROROROROROROROROROR OROROROROROROROROROR

OR part   or all — oral

Oral O   Oral E

Do all orally: open Latin <u>os</u>

Talking is oral

O-talking is oral sex

O opens obscenely on overt opportunity

<u>Orate</u>, orator — you no-name oratress,

divine your name

O

R

AL

Y

LATIN OS IS MOUTH AND BONE OS OSCULUM

'LITTLE MOUTH'

Or part or all — oral

Or all O Or all E

Do all orally: open Latin *os*

mouth open talking is oral

Talk orally

O-talking is oral sex

Oration opens obscenely on opportunity

Orate orally, irate orator —

you no-name oratress

ORAL
SEX

"Obscene! Otiose!"

"Objurgate this obscenity — an open *os*"

opine obese opponents

when O's opinion is overzealous OR overloud

OR overflows

orally OR   OR OR OR

all overtheplace

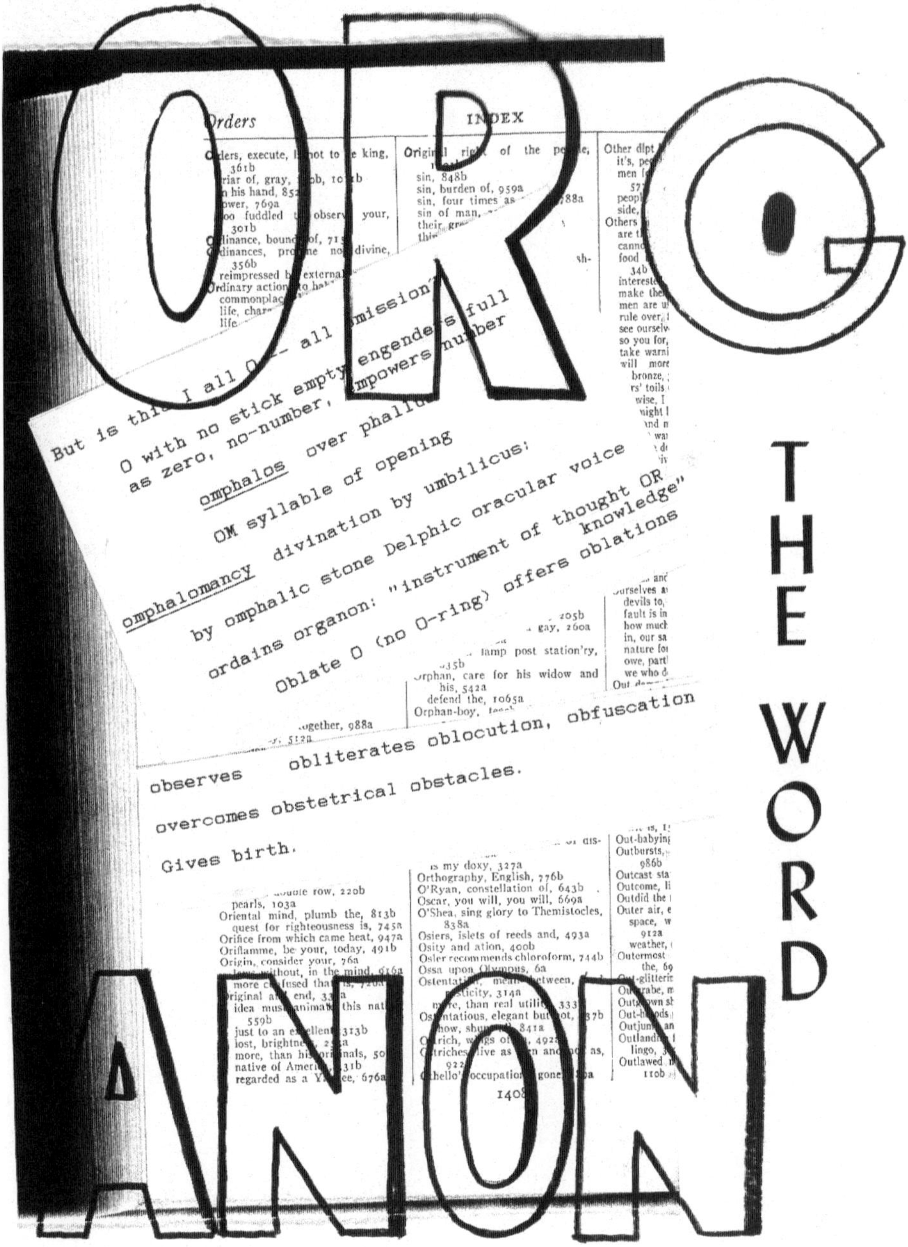
ORG
But is thi I all O— all mission'
O with no stick empty engenders full
as zero, no-number, empowers number
omphalos over phallu
OM syllable of opening
omphalomancy divination by umbilicus:
by omphalic stone Delphic oracular voice
ordains organon: "instrument of thought OR knowledge"
Oblate O (no O-ring) offers oblations
observes obliterates oblocution, obfuscation
overcomes obstetrical obstacles.
Gives birth.
THE WORD
ANON

But is this I all O — all omission?

O with no stick empty engenders full

as zero, no-number, empowers number:

    omphalos over phallus

    OM syllable of opening

        omphalomancy

divination by umbilicus:

    by omphalic stone

    Delphic oracular voice

        ordains organon: "instrument of

        thought OR knowledge"

    Oblate O (no O-ring) offers oblations

    observes

        obliterates oblocution, obfuscation

    overcomes obstetrical obstacles.

    Gives birth.

Eyes

or or or or or or or or or or or or or or or or
Is O obscene if seen as oynx or oryx or opaque
OR if obliging is to be oppressed
OR if oppositional oppugned?
Not so.
Obscene the I that eyes the ovoid O.
OBSCENE
THE I THAT EYES

Is O obscene   if seen

as oynx or oryx or opaque

OR if obliging

    is to be oppressed

OR if oppositional

    oppugned?

Not so.

Obscene the I

that eyes the ovoid O

as void

Oread

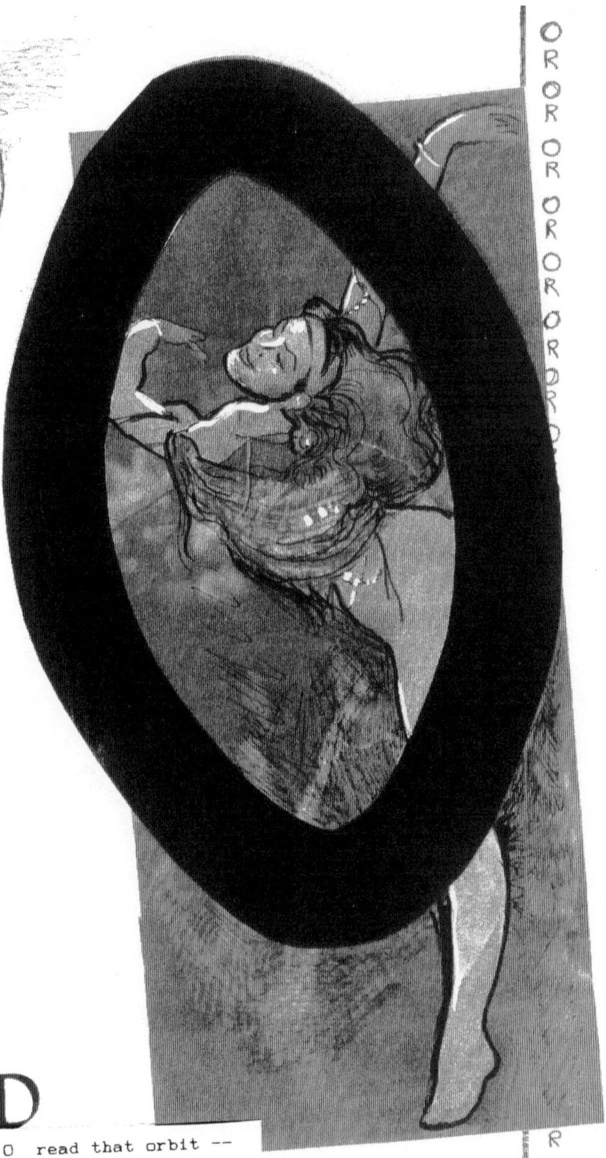

O

READ

OREAD

Oread   O   read that orbit --

or   bit of obfuscated obloquy

ORORORORORORORORO

RORO

Oros (Greek): mountain

oread: mountain spirit

orography: mountain wri

Octavos for orectic oreads: o read the omens.

Orb in orbit overhead

operates as obeah and ordains

obeisance

O read, oread, that orbit: observe

your options

the or and ore in you

act
or
sens
or
curs
or
rig
or
censor
or
or
or

OR opens options:
OR
OR
OR
OR
MINOR
yours?

Mine ore

Ply oar
OR pri
or
act
or
sens
or
curs
or
rig
or
cast
or
vend
or
deal
ORDEAL

OPENS OPTIONS MINE ORE PLY OAR ORORORORO

OR *opens options:*

OR
OR
OR
OR

Minor

yours?

Mine ore

Ply oar
OR *pri*
or
act
or
sens
or
curs
or

rig
or
cast
or
vend
or
deal.

ORDEAL

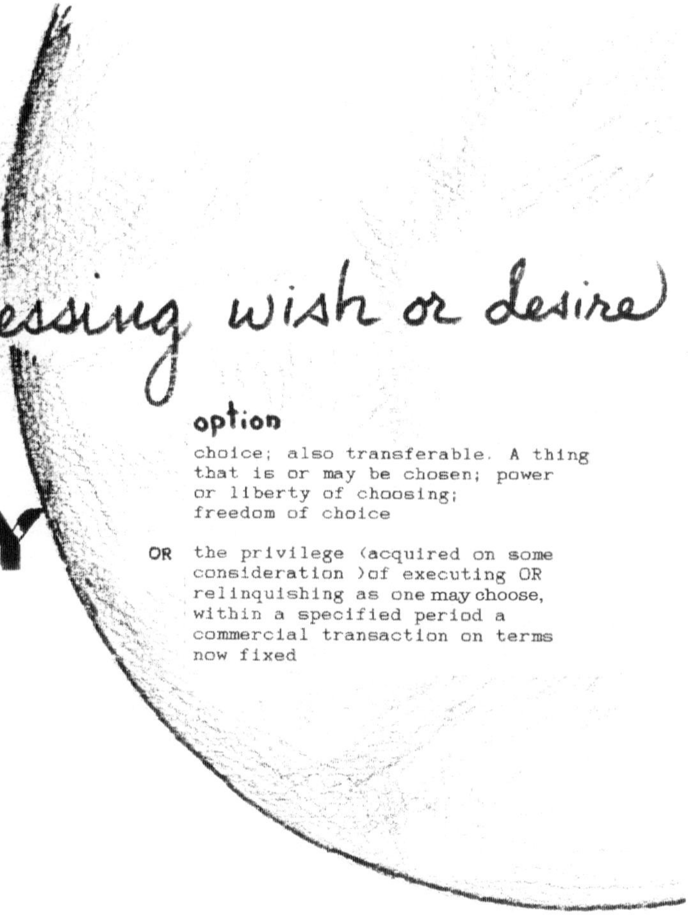

O

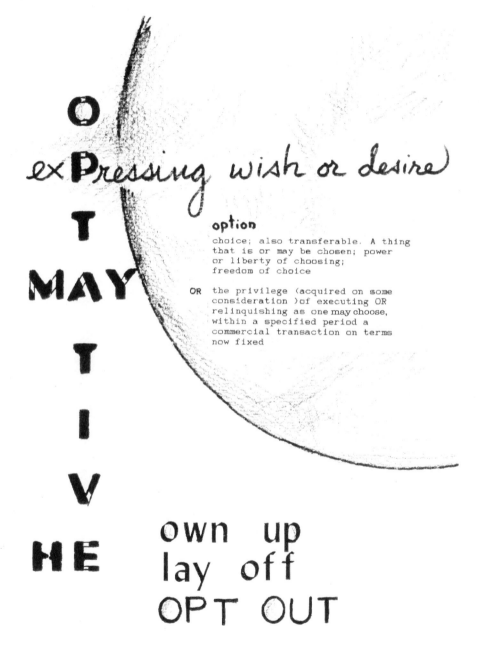

exPressing wish or desire

T

option

choice; also transferable. A thing that is or may be chosen; power or liberty of choosing; freedom of choice

MAY

OR the privilege (acquired on some consideration)of executing OR relinquishing as one may choose, within a specified period a commercial transaction on terms now fixed

T

I

V

own up

HE

lay off

OPT OUT

O pen your mind o read, oread:

ogle the optimal

OPTION: *act of choosing;*

choice; also transferable. A thing

that is or may be chosen

power or liberty of choosing

freedom of choice

OR *the privilege (acquired on some*

consideration) of executing OR

relinquishing as one may choose,

within a specified period a

a commercial transaction

on terms now fixed

OR: the optative syntactical structure

having the function of expressing

wish or desire:

May he own up

May he lay off

May he opt out

Or Gasmic

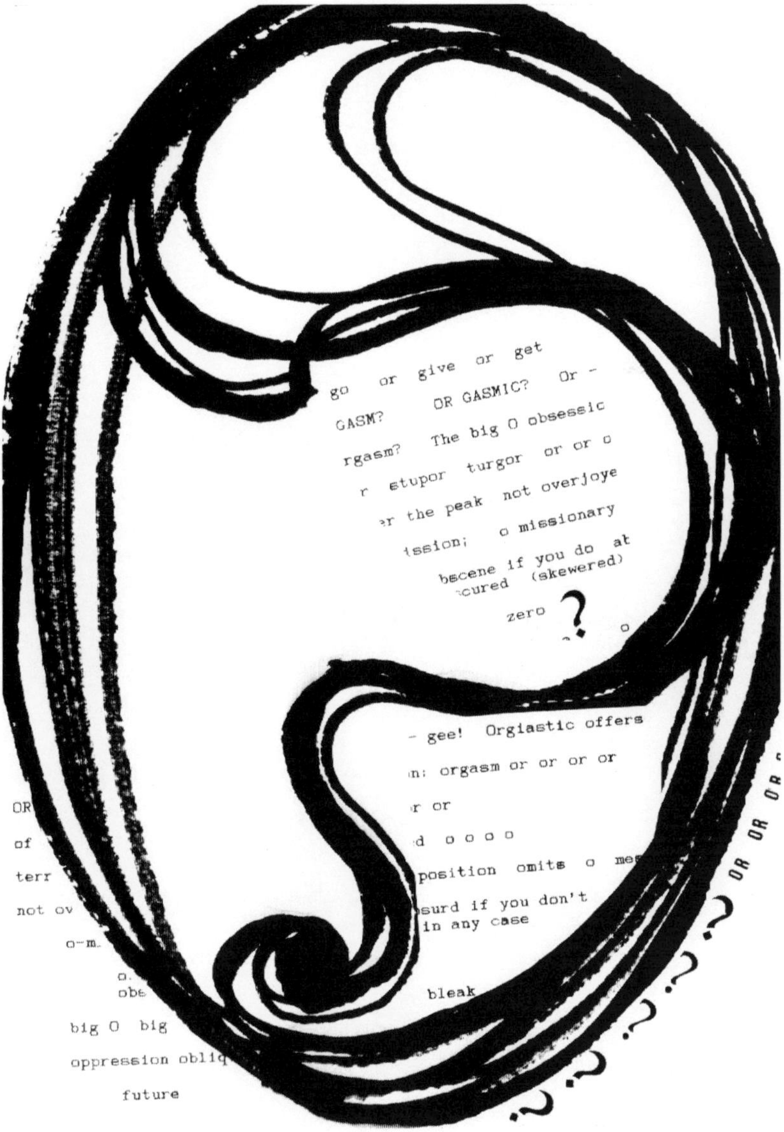
go or give or get
GASM? OR GASMIC? Or -
rgasm? The big O obsessic
r stupor turgor or or o
er the peak not overjoye
ission; o missionary
bscene if you do at
cured (skewered)
zero ?
o
- gee! Orgiastic offers
n: orgasm or or or or
r or
d o o o o
position omits o me
surd if you don't
in any case
bleak
OR
of
terr
not ov
o-m
o.
obe
big O big
oppression obliq
future
OR OR OR OR

OR go or give or get

or gasm? or gasmic? Or — gee! —

orgiastic offers

of orgasm to choose or no:

The big O obsession: orgasm or or or or

terror stupor turgor or or or or

not over the peak not overjoyed o o o o

o-mission; o missionary position

omits o mess

obscene if you do absurd if you don't

obscured (skewered) in any case

big O big zero

no O no zero

O O O O no no yes no O

OR no option: note oblique oppression

o bleak

future

HORR

OR

mad on$_n$ a

ONONONONONONONO

nomen

Occult the obstacles obstructing O

OR are you only

horror

HORR

OR

mad on nah

or not mad

OR what

Ordinary

or or or or or or or or or
ORDINARY
ORDERED
or: one in a series
OR OR OR OR OR OR

Ordained the ordinary organs,

Ordinate the ordeal of obstructed openings

Ordinary and ordered O, one in a series

over age.

Ordained ordeal.

O empty getting emptier

OR is it?

Name the old one old

OR

is space old

OR in it is one

out of it?

Ordained ordinate ordeal. Organic ordeal.

Ova over

OR not

Sun and moon still in orbit

ordered and ordinary

in their enormity

Orbit

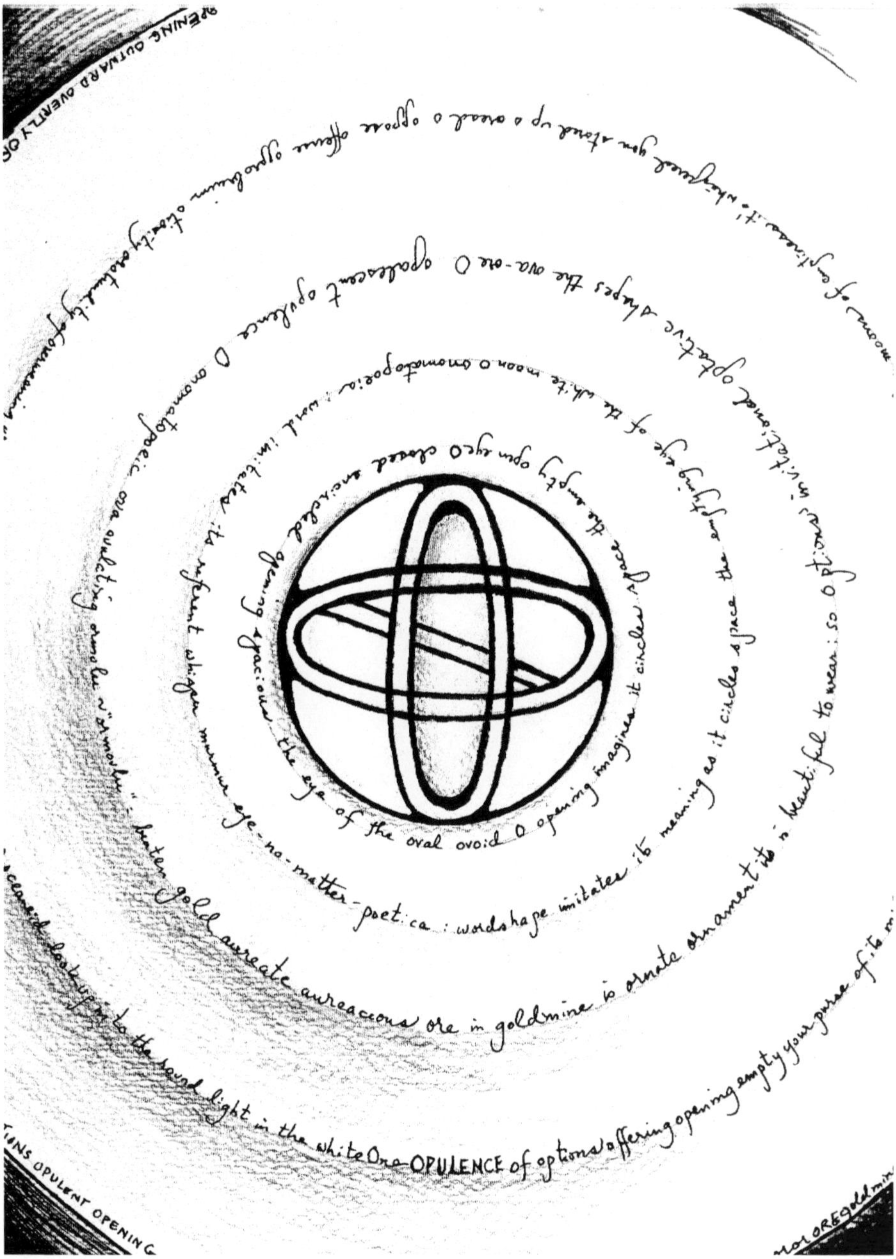
OPENING OUTWARD OVERTLY OR
OPULENT OPENING
the oval ovoid O opening imagines it circles space
poetica : wordshape imitates its meaning as it circles space
aureate aureacious ore in goldmine is ornate
light in the white One OPULENCE of options offering opening empty your purse of its

Onomatopoeia: word-sound imitates its referent

Eye-no-matter poetica: word-shape emulates its meaning

O closed sound encircled open   spacious

The o of the eye imagines it circles space.

The empty eye of the white moon is circling space.

O panORama   of opulence   of ORmolu

— of beaten gold —

so options ovulate to shape the orbit

of the great ovum, egg of the world.

So you there, without identity,

Let's hear it for opulence for a change —

Ornament yourself inordinately with ores

and oars and ors aureate, laureate.

Empty your purse of its million moons of gold

which it's whispered you've stored up,

o ovulating orb with oceanic overage of

unconscious origins.

O oread of the unconscious, naiad, dryad, dyad, oceaneid,

Look up into the round light of the white deep.

Whisperer, speak up

OR

Black Dot: Period

Black dot in white space: a period

indicating the end of a declarative sentence

that makes possible the next sentence.

Dot in space: a thought

visualizing the moment after the big bang

when form comes out of formlessness,

all matter compacted into

into black ink

in the overloaded brush

that begins its stroke

to make the universe

and the word-world opens.

HIGH DESERT

Visiting the Suma Beach on the night of the autumnal full moon, Teishitsu, a poet from Kyōto, is said to have written,

Crouching under a pine
I watched the full moon,
Pondering all night long
On the sorrow of Chūnagon

recalling a ninth-century poet who "shed salt tears by the salt farms on the Suma Beach."

Having for some time cherished in my mind the memory of this poem, I wandered out on to the road at last one day this past autumn, possessed by an irresistible desire to see the rise of the full moon over the mountains of the Kashima Shrine.

—Matsuo Bashō (1644-1694)
(tr. Nobuyuki Yuasa)

In memory of

Lorna Janet Morley

February 8, 1923 - March 17, 2017

and

Cara Dawson Donovan Fisher

February 8, 1925 - February 10, 2015

L'amitié passe même le tombeau

Prologue

Insomniac

Unable to sleep pre-dawn—too many murders
in the world, and weapons. Who was Kalishnikov?
Why did the forging of steel and the fine bore
for killing more people faster seem good, better
than words, creative weapons? Oh question
too easy to answer—the "big black evil one"
that kicks back into the gunman's gut, vast
ejaculations, that's what's wanted—oh manhood:
Arma virumque cano begins the epic,
            but no—I must think that era is over.

Arts and the woman I sing, or mutter, finding
again that when the poem needs to be written,
again it's war, words not in use, only photos
from the mid-east or Africa somewhere of corpses
gunned down in the streets, body of a woman
naked from the waist down. The mind fogs over.
Can't even make tea to wake myself. "Learn to make
a proper cup of tea" said the Buddhist teacher
to bewildered students seeking higher consciousness,
and Nobel Peace Prize winner Emily Balch spoke out:
            Not by fear will we exorcise the demons
            of destruction and cruelty but by motives
            more humane, more reasonable,
            and more heroic.

                                    Oh these unheroic words
scribbled at a kitchen table in half-light,
loneliness starts these poems invented under pressure,
there've been bad elections too, new hidden corpses,

more abuse of women, and, as I write, new crimes:
thousands of children taken from parents, shipped off
no records kept, threats made—it's inhuman,
slavery again. Yet slaves in shackles sang,
their voices the only means left. What else to do?
Human connection I sing, with schoolmates, friends,
readers, women, men, with anyone who sings,
shouts, calls out to another as the way to keep going.

Part One:

HIGH DESERT

High Desert

Not mountains really but high desert here
at eighty-eight hundred feet above the rising seas

and a thousand above the Wet Mountain valley.
Not much rain at best any time, and this year drier

than ever. Rocks mainly, obstacles to stumble over—
can't find a path—and boulders heaped in a berm

hardening the road-edge slope below to stony
heaps worn down to pebbly sand, pretense of soil,

where nonetheless weeds push up into parched
grasses, and on their far side tall trees, firs,

spruce, pines that imperceptibly inch up
hour by hour, or day or year, or have fallen

unseen into a landscape green and earth-gold
under the brilliant bowl of endless emptiness

through which pass sun and moon, "travelers
of eternity"—and this great sweep meets the eye

from a large deck on a small house dug into
the mountainside, built of that forest's woods

set level on concrete churned from rocks
like these, and behind it more trees

whose threaded roots beneath the hardpan
spread three times wider than their canopies,

reach down, around, between the rocks to
rivers running underground, constant, unseen.

5 p.m.: Momentary

about to close a notebook with a beaded cover

Five p.m.—put down
the pen. No, keep it going;
one little pearl in line

with many enclosed in
bugle beads' green gold
iridescence. Light! More light!

Five oh-five looks toward
night. No, the day-gem
still glints its pinpoint signal.

One more note: day moon
opposite the sun
between them a white snow peak.

Spacious Skies

outlook on the Wet Mountain valley, Colorado, U.S.A.

"Weathers we live in" —William Bronk

(i)

Somnolent mid-afternoon,

blue sky, high pines
into white billow-clouds—

grass sleeps green
in sun, breezes

pass through scrub-oak
beyond the deck rail.

A few leaves move.
Siesta. No news

is good news: TV
shut off, murders silenced

for now. A break,
a time of self-repair

while storms build
over the east hills

and the western mountains
behind at rest

sleepless.

(ii)

Night: from the deck
the bright half-moon—
"Bright bright o bright"

said Myōe, "poet of the moon"—
and Mars, and two stars
in Scorpio—white

underlines cloud-patches
darker than the sky—
smoke haze north

from wildfires blurs
tiny distant town lights.
Darkness

lights up the design:
angled shadow
of the deck rail,

human shadow
lain on the pale ground
more real than by day.

Black and white, a still
and moving picture
deepens

"the sonorous voice of silence."

(iii)

Black night

not mere darkness
but low-surging blackness
as of ink or smoke
total encasement, an ocean
then lightning explosions,
cosmic flashbulbs,
expose for a quarter-second
deck rail, folding chairs
round table, which then
disappear, engulfed
by invisible clouds
too black to be seen.
Thunder rolls and space
lights up again,
illumines fear,
the signs of catastrophe
held off perhaps,
perhaps not.

There is no rain.

(iv)

At sunset
a rosy cloudbank
in the east

above the dim
belt of smoke
from the wildfires,

moonrise
in the south's azure
daylight—who

can believe these
exist only in
the seeing, that

the fires reported
are not burning
past boundaries

veering this way
unseen, not
a belief.

(v)

Midnight

moon hidden by clouds'
brush-stroked silver edges —

light from the cabin
downhill glimmers

through a thicket of
scrub oak and fir—

lamp across the room
makes this page dim

enough for the pen
to imagine the words.

(vi)

Stars:

clearest light
of starry darkness:

the Milky Way,
the red planet

in the southeast,
archer's drawn bow,

the scorpion's
bejeweled curve—

bright o bright
signs from each

to each, to those
who look and those

who don't.
Stars—incredible
that there are stars—

(vii)

Fingernail moon

you grow
out of your own shadow

as the pointed pines
grow toward you

(viii)

Afternoon again:

pale cloud-shreds
impose flat shadow-stripes
on the valley hayfields

while a faint wind
from the Sangres peaks
predicts chill.

In the weak half-sunlight
no foretelling rain
or drought relief,

no news from
these cloud-shadow-scripts
as they dissolve—

maybe tomorrow—

(ix)

Night

invites
the eye
to see
its intensity,

requires
the ear
to hear
its sonority,

rewards
absence
of thought
of wanting

more light,
more time,
revives
the mind

that forgot
the stars
are there
by day

(x)

Full moon, the face clear,
though misted, passing

through clouds,
comic icon adrift

in cobblestone sky,
bright mirror—of whom?—

without fail shines
onto the pines grown

wilder and stronger
as the light emerges

beyond blurred sight.

(xi)

Late, late, the waning moon
only a glow in haze
over the east hills,

only amber pinpoints mark
the far-off fogged-in town
Festival season over,

no more flood-lit tents,
high-amp guitars, loud songs.
School days and diligence

have begun. Thick clouds
screen off stars except
Vega, Deneb, and Altair

moving west as darkness
overtakes them. Dark
of the moon is coming,

shorter days, less warmth,
whatever one had thought
to hold onto.

(xii)

Snow on Horn Peak in the morning,
a wake-up to brilliant blue air

after the night's sharp cold
glittered on the River of Heaven,

kept me from sleeping.
Aspen leaves have turned gold

in my mind before they fall.

(xiii)

Winds increase
as the mountaintops
freeze;

wind harasses
the ponderosa,
the fir-trees' new tips;

wind whips up
goldenrod more gold,
asters more purple,

cleans and polishes
dulled oak leaves.
Tree shadows lengthen

as the falling sun
gilds dry earth
and long dry grasses

which bend and rebound,
moving and immoveable
in the wind's turbulence

that goes on all night.
No end to this ground,
those winds under

these spacious skies.

Snowflower

In the night
snow

shook down
from the moon's

chandelier
and changed

my meadow into
a moon

blooming
in me

too deep for
plow's passage

too cold to melt
in mere sunshine.

“Women and Children First”

an exhibition of sculpture by Natalie Kutner

Apparitions of pain cast in the hard metals
of weaponry and monuments to kings—

that’s what we see here: babies’ skulls dented,
split or sprouting hands, monster worms

from a blackened apple, faces in anguish.
Hurt children, mothers hurt by the law

of the fathers, lives deformed—that’s what
the social worker saw stated in precepts

internalized. “Spare the rod and spoil the child”
“as the twig is bent, so is the tree inclined”

“Silence is golden”—the nuclear family’s story
can’t be told, but the feminist artist will tell it

through her unfeminine mastery of metals and tools,
her knowledge that is power, her insistence on exposé.

She hangs a kitchen rack with knives. Italians say:
“don’t give a kitchen knife as a wedding present.” They know

the reality of symbolism. Here she shapes a torture-cage
of barbed-wire fencing in which hangs a portrait

of the ideal family, as if cut from an old magazine.
The artist makes us see the apparitions of pain

which have taken on the beauty of reality. She
commands, being under command herself. Look again.

A Memory

out of a California childhood

At May Lake 10,000 feet above sea-level
in Yosemite the girl walked a narrow trail
behind her father with his fishing rod,
saw in the sapphire water out of the deep
an enormous trout rising supple
and strong who dived away into darkness,
magic that lives, goes on living unseen
but comes sometimes near the surface,
evidence of what lies under the blue.
How far down can be known. Knowledge
can rise toward light and be seen.
This mountain once lay under an ocean,
but now rises in bright day, past into present,
heights and depths indissolubly mingled
with light and air, instructors in memory.

Remembering re-constructs the self,
an act that overtakes one randomly.
Tonight the old woman meant to be practical,
despite leg pain, to bend and spackle closed
a kitchen-corner crack where water-bugs
crawl through from somewhere—big, ugly,
primal survivors—instead sat down to write
because the hip-replacement surgeon said
he'd climbed Kilimanjaro, over 19,000 feet,
with a team, had to take it in stages, camped
a few days at each elevation to acclimate,
not to risk their lives. The thought came: beautiful —

to go that high, to have learned how to do it, to see what is seen only by going, to feel what it means, as that girl began to, on that day at May Lake.

At an Adirondack Camp, September

Lake Paradox, upstate New York

(i)

reminded of our Napa valley home

Knotty pine walls here:
huge graystone fireplace, log-pile
on the hearth, tall windows
        looking out onto wild grasses,

knotty pine walls there:
Stonehouse in the 1940s,
gold-brown Lokoya stone fireplace,
        schoolroom's high window,
        beyond it leafy buck-eye.

Autumn quiet in my mind:
its aroma deepens
beyond season, hour or year.

(ii)

afternoon with watercolors

As I painted black-eyed susans
among pine-tips in a blue vase
they shrank into themselves,
intense gold petals hiding.

Across the road they stood massed,
their petals unfolding as the sun
came out, came in at the window
and enlightened the page as I painted.

(iii)

early wake-up
in several places

Cold in the Adirondacks—
birch leaves turn yellow;

in the Sangres a freeze—
aspen gold in forested foothills.

At Lake Paradox, still,
summer-y lush green trees

whose leaves resist falling.
Morning mist conceals the water

as fog covers San Francisco Bay
until it dissipates, restoring

the garden's sheen, and perfumes
from pine and cedar rise with the sun.

(iv)

Helen gave us a tomato
out of her vegetable patch.

The tomato—big fat red
ultimate in tomato-ness—

sits on a white plate
beside the gold flowers

in the blue vase—quintessential
stained-glass blue—

that sits on red, white and blue
flag-printed oil-cloth—

stars and stripes forever!—
laid down over

a 'thirties wooden family-size table,
grandfather's relic,

with non-matching spindle chairs
stained golden oak,

eight of them. How much more American
can you get?

Ten Miles of Falling Leaves

from upstate driving Manhattan-bound
through Bergen county

(i)

Maples make gold clouds over gray roofs:
kids dancing on a sober playground.

(ii)

Green leaves shrink away discolored,
devalued money.

(iii)

Six hundred sulphur butterflies
tremble over a concrete handkerchief.

(iv)

Flames of wood, flames of blood:
Thick oak over japanese plum.

(v)

Gold paint on a school bus
matches the leaves it drives under
but doesn't resemble it.

(vi)

Tidy suburban lawns have drowned
in a sea of choppy sunlit waves. Cheers!

(vii)

O gilded ambivalence—
like a geisha's richest kimono.

(viii)

Mirrors of the sun, you have nothing to do
with the measured amber of caution lights.

(ix)

As Zeus to Danaë, a rain of gold is proffered:
Autos, city-bound, fume contraceptive.

(x)

Fewer the trees whose leaves
flare up and fall, flamboyantly

hopeless. Highways
replace them, traffic

converges—more cars
must go our way

by railroad tracks, gas stations,
pass under vast green

high-hanging metal signs
that warn

of the long bridge coming.

A Fleeting Scene

Cars move in the opposite direction
on the other side of the highway,

orderly, a double-strand necklace,
then the flaw in the design

smashed sideways into the dividing fence
remains of a white vehicle, crushed front,

no one now behind the wheel, and
the white ambulance stands by

flashing red and blue to broadcast
mistake! mistake!

we're all you have
and we're too late.

Deserted Country

reading the Journal of Eugène Delacroix,
Spain, 1832 – a found poem

"The boat;
departure,
the lady in officer's clothing.
The banks of the Guadalquivir;
sad night.
Solitude amidst these strangers
who were playing cards in the dark;
uncomfortable space between the decks.
The lady who rolled up her sleeve
to show me her wound.

Bad feelings on waking up;
debarkation at San Lucar.
Returned in a carriage with the maid
from the Cadiz hotel.
Deserted country.
The man on horseback
with his blanket round his neck."

Part Two

ITINERANT

Briggflatts to Durham

Winter grows roseate
in the western clouds
as the road wanders left

under Barnard Castle ruin,
bends uphill by shops,
and out past stone houses

and fences of wood or red
thorn-berry and hedges.
Poetry is the talk

but silence is the meaning
of the full rose-ivory moon
that rises one moment a sun

and waits in the blue east.

In The South of France

I. Sleepless in Albi

A wrought-iron balcony
with potted geraniums,
coral-orange, so
          it is France,

Albi, with a view from
not so high, *troisième étage*
as in New York, but here
          by the railway station

summer street noise,
music won't quiet down
at nightfall—sleepless
          mind-music

*

Crash! at morning
  a metal screen-gate
    unscrolls somewhere, as if

a lower-east-side shopman
  opened his kiosk.
    Faint air floats in,

jackhammers bombard,
  break up old stones
    from Roman times,

knock apart to build
in their place—what?—
it, "that?—" whatever

my nightmare tried
to shake into silence
and full sleep but

couldn't—oh, give it up.
Go out onto the balcony—
It's warm—join the geraniums,

the noise, light, air,
disturbance,
endless renovations.

II. Vaour: the farm

Half moon over the shed
and the outdoor kitchen,

spaghetti and steamed vegetables
on unpainted picnic tables,

friends, relatives, students
from Paris, London, Africa

hunker down, pass the wine,
watch the moon climb

among oak leaves.

III. Fête

at the 13th-century Château de la Prune,
Marnaves, near Albi: evening

As in a dream of medieval romance, half-seen
in half-darkness beneath the plane-trees' canopy
sitting in white chairs, guests summer-clad
murmur, dark heads together, or rise and drift
over the courtyard's thick grass carpet, past
sentinel tree-trunks spot-lit from below,
to the parapet, night's edge at low mossed walls
to gaze outward toward Albi and Ste.Cécile,
its tower a star alone in infinite deepest blue
ambient magic, and one stays lingering there
as if no longer finite, then turns, curious,
to climb stone steps to the almost-abandoned
castle, its stone-floored entrance hall empty
lit only by one bare bulb hanging from its socket,
and so turns to be drawn back down into the rich
and crowded night-swarm where the bride and groom
of twenty-five years ago mingle with grown sons,
cousins, married nieces, babies in strollers,
who go to greet the elders, father, mother, aunts,
seated in a trim row in the high wall's shadow
but not far from the open fire where the chef-
brother is grilling steaks, ham slabs, fat fishes,
heaving them onto platters that the kids
haul round to the tables and bring wine
after — plenty of wine from a cousin
who makes it — and laughing begins, and music
rises into the treetops' amber-emerald glitter

while the meat-heaped platters come again
and also the boy Théophile with *vin rouge*
refilling glasses already entirely full.

New Year's Eve 2012 into 2013

in Lisbon unable to go on to Madeira
because of an outbreak of dengue fever there

(i)

Over the U.S. fiscal cliff
at midnight—will 2013
be an unlucky year?

No to triskaidekophobia—
these figures are empty:
a lucky start is ours in Lisbon.

(ii)

This business hotel room beige,
austere with drapes of royal wine
and ochre, no splotch of art

on any wall: these pre-suppose
no woman ever stays here.
How could a woman take it?

(iii)

Grant's whiskey and two chocolate mini-bars:
that's our new year's midnight
without dinner—very slimming—

and a flawless way to say:
it's all, and nothing but all,
for love. Love is nothing but all.

Surgical Footnote

"foci of necrosis"
March 19, 2013

Lucky to have lived
this far into this year

unlucky to have bad gut
lucky to have it cut out

Neither lucky nor unlucky
your gut is always working for you:

your shit wants to come out and be manure.

Jerusalem

At the Western Wall,
also called the

Wailing Wall,
a white-haired woman

in traveler's flowered
jersey dress stands

a long time, forehead
to her raised left arm

pressed against the stone,
at her feet a guidebook

Das Heilige Land.
On her right a girl in jeans

pushes her prayer note
into a crack in the wall.

Behind them at a distance
a black-robed woman

sits on a folding chair
black-scarved head bent

over a book, a few like her
on the mostly empty plaza

of the women's side while
over left many men crowd

close-shouldered, comradely
in white shirts, black pants

next to polo tops and twills,
streaming toward the men's side

to place their prayers carefully
out of the sight of women.

Twice a year, to make room
for more, officials clear out

these messages meant
for God's eyes only

and so they go unread
to burial in the old

unused cemetery
in East Jerusalem,

according to the law.
Next to the German woman

at the Wailing Wall
I wept.

Itinerant: December 26th

from Washington D.C. to New York
remembering the Christmas carol
"Good King Wenceslas"

The train itself a long narrow tunnel,
subtly lit, moves stationary through
a gray glass-windowed twilight.
Armies of twiggy trees march by,
and telephone poles, now and then
a bent road of white gray-roofed houses.

On the feast of Stephen mild winter
hides a red sunset behind
mauve westward scrim and a concrete
station wall—power outage, quick dark,
lights back on. It takes more than feet
to get from one rich city to another.

Good King Wenceslas looked out—
a buddha leaving protective walls—
saw the poor man gathering twigs
in bitterest cold, brought him to food
and fire, as Prince Shakyamuni looked
on a woman giving birth in pain,

the bloodied baby crying in pain,
the sick man, the old body dying—
at nightfall what to do? What to think
to do now in the long steel-sided
tunnel sleekly moving. No—it's
stuck—power out again. No light,

no heat. Close the newspaper, photos
inside. Zip your jacket. Heat is traveling
through unseen conduits into the desert
out there, Syrian bombings, *tsunamis*
in Indonesia, thousands dead, a severed arm
raised in revolt and revulsion—

where are the good kings?

The War Not to be Forgotten

a young daughter-in-law is dying of cancer.
as the Gulf War builds up, November 1990

(i)

If brown leaves fall quietly
and no great tree-branch or bomb
cracks the roof or skull

If abstract headlines dull
the actual face of the girl mechanic
with the plane's wing shading

her from desert sun and Iraqi
violence   If mind's mechanisms
shut down to a stomach-rumble

or to embroidering a pinched face
in a loose mirror   If everyone finds
too thick a wall of regulations

and bureaucrats' overcoats,
who then will stride
to a barricade—stupid idealist!

ready to storm
for the sake of the peaceful—

What contradictions. Peace can't be won
by war. Peace comes by being
peaceful.

Agitated, in distress, not at peace
            in myself I want—I want
                        not to hide

behind "art," not to be a movie-goer
            viewing a holocaust or
                        a gangster's wife

            as if co-operating.

(ii)

Wednesday, November 21

They came back from Lourdes,
she sicker, nauseated. Now she sleeps.
Soon she will sleep longer.

It's time to sit in the dark and think
that the spiritual journey
confers blessing

not from on high—that's fiction—
but because he was with her
when she drank the water and now

he nods out sitting beside her bed
holding her skeletal hand

(iii)

Moon past full: an eyelid
drooping over a dimming eye,
a blank hole suspended

over the earth's packed cell-swarm.
Streetlight drinks up moonlight
mechanically, so it isn't there.

Can anyone take that dead planet
for a headlight revealing
a road? In the old Mid-East

the moon goddess brought blessing,
water, the sustaining dew.
Now bombers.

No escape from this decline,
this reminding presence as
the day-moon slips away.

(iv)

after they went home to Minnesota,
just before midnight, January 14, 1991

Watching and hearing the news
    my heart laid bare

of Saddam Hussein
    "having ruled by the sword
    he'll be loath to give that up"
after the phone call
        My son spoke slowly:
    "Well—you'd have to say—
    Michelle is worse.
    She has a lot of pain—"

6 million gas masks
And Palestinians must be given them, too.
Assassinations in Tunis
—"sense of frustration against the United States"
—hypocrisy—

Many deaths thicken the air over my open heart,
a poison gas not chemically made
"here, if it will be war—"

"Much more easy," says an Israeli,
"than what your parents had in Russia"

But this one in Saint Paul
will die
how soon
Lady of Lourdes, have you ever
appeared to an Arab?

In hoc signo
to that Christian conqueror—
Is war a world religion?

Poor Jew born of a poor Jewess who was
"immaculately conceived,"
didn't you make a mistake?
Didn't you think you could change politics?

In the mind of that general
there is no hope.

“Two moonless nights,
the 16th and the 17th
will be the best time—”
A bugle note sounds.
Wind roars in the TV interviewer’s microphone.

11th hour:
“She has a lot of pain.
Her stomach is distended—”
not a pregnancy.

A smoke-filled cloud
rises to bury the light
that wore a sky-blue veil
and gleamed in the grotto.

(v)

twelve days after the beginning
of the war January 1991

Dull light through drawn shades
as if the sun hadn’t come up—
Outside, the warning beep

of a road crusher backing up
where it couldn’t see.
One mournful whistle

of birdsong from a stripped tree.
Shade up, the light still gray,
pulling on my coat, I thought

of war, of the deaths to come.
What train now bears me along
through the under-river tunnel into

a gray morning classroom?

Students, what shall we learn today?
Nothing is ever going to be the same.

Midnight Ramble

je pense, donc je ne pense pas

(i)

I don't think there's anything to say.
I don't say there's anything to think.
I don't think there's anything to think.
I don't say there isn't anything to say.
Anything to say is what I don't think.
Thinking anything to say I think is
saying anything I think is not saying.
I don't think but not saying I think
doesn't say I don't think—I think.

(ii)

Thought is not what you think.
What is not thought is not
because you think and thought
is what you don't want. Not
wanting to think is thought, not
your thought as you always
think what is and what
is it that thinks nonstop:
non-thoughts that go on thinking.

(iii)

Conundrum:
C
O
N   UN   DRUM:
Each speech a contrary
Can a contrary
un-none con by nega-drum
drumdrumdrumdrum unthought?
          To con a page = to study
          To be conned = to be deceived
None not conned by thought drummed
          um umm thinking hums
                    mum mum
obsess

a mess
          the con obsesses
Conundrum hums though mum
          obsessed
          as the masses make messes

News is bad news.
          mess up bad news
          bad mess up news
          up mess news bad

New news is thought up
by obsessed masses mum
on thinking straight news

(iv)

Straighten news out
un-con no none
none can con *en masse*
Obsessed with thought
say think what news
needs saying.
Conundrum is straight
thought not news since
one is not a mass.
I think obsessed a way to you
to think to open up to say
what needs saying
of what is there,
not fake.

“What Did You Do on Vacation This Year?”

A little more than midway through the journey
of our summers, misled by traffic signs, we strayed
into a shopping mall in Colorado Springs,

and with no Virgil, Sappho, Oppen or H.D.
for guides to where to buy lunch we wandered
into a place most strange, halfway ‘twixt

Limbo and Inferno, a Chuck E Cheese,
a locus in keeping with the weird spirits
being loosed in this land in which we live,

a dark wood of video games whose screens
flash monsters, shriek sirens, supply shotguns
to the teeming army of little boys in jeans

and girls in diaper-bulging pink tights
who whiz around and push buttons as
their desperate mothers tucked into booths

behind their strollers grab a moment for talk
while bells ring, whistles sing, gongs go bong,
rifles rat-a-tat, flashing ambulance red and gold—

Bang! Bang! You win! But what?—since nothing
is happening, really, except the noise and rush to
press another icon that twangs, lights up, and fizzles.

Is it Washington D.C.? Congress in or out of session,
Homer Simpson among pinballs our Virgilian guide?
Or the un-blue guitar our means of passing

over the ditches and damned? We gobble
our pizza and stumble our way through
the clanging dark to an almost invisible exit

and heave the door open, emerge into air
as sunset flames over our distant mountains,
and we work our way out of the parking lot onto

the right road, purged and ready to mount up to the stars.

My H.D.

(Hilda Doolittle, 1886-1961, poet and novelist)

Swiftly swiftly write as H.D. wrote *re-light the flame* for thoughts run more swiftly than the hand but are also flames it was war her trilogy a dream a flame to counter the war *the war was fought for an illusion* but this dream of mine I woke from disappointed to wake this daylight dream of all compounded things this self-no-self must be thought of as *a magical illusion, a flame, a dewdrop, a bubble, a flash of lightning in the dark of night* so this reality of standing in the garden of the poet's daughter's estate in East Hampton at dusk among a sea of fallen rusty curling leaves a soft yard-light on somewhere behind after the others the men the conferees had left the table not having asked her questions though she sat there silent throughout now reappears in a well-tailored pantsuit the deep color of wine her white hair in a pompadour in her eighties now living with her daughter how happy this chance of mine to talk to her to tell her how it happened she had read words I wrote about her in a student newspaper and re-reading her clippings saved in Beinecke Library felt an eerie shiver pass through me *Je est une autre* but no time to tell this only to ask her about what the others the younger women H.D. scholars want to know about her my pleasure will be to relay this news: So what is your life like now what are you writing? Her offhand candor "I have a lover, of course" of course the Eternal Lover Osiris to her Isis union of feminine and masculine principles creativity itself her female lovers being one with herself brought into herself as priestess seer twin but she said no word about her writing then necessity came to the dreamer's dark bedroom darker for the rain outside and wind snapping the window-shade against the glass *la vida es sueño* a whiplash fracturing of concept procedure meaning they might say she's as crazy as wartime H.D at her tippy three-legged table hearing spirit-messages she thought would end the war the horror of bombing end all wars but more bombs ended it not that it's ended so consider dreams not only meaningful to dreamers who connect them to whatever books words languages they read or listen to because flame comes when a candle is lit at night a necessity and wind necessarily blows it out a soft wind or hard as now forty miles an hour which can change in ten minutes or maybe not for two days *not I, not I but the wind*

Meditations, Possibly

at the kitchen table with tulips

Restless body, wavering mind
by a window, half a mirror,
red tulips imperceptibly decay.

*

Hurry, hurry—broke a bowl,
then a plate. No excuse, blunderer:
Sit still to hear last night's sky-music.

*

Compact meditation: a glint
on the edge of a BIC pen, quaver
in the brain, thud of hammers in the basement.

*

Sleepless—another felt failure.
Throw off the unkind blankets.
Get up. Drink warm milk, keep trying.

*

Morning light, morning shadow.
thought spreads its blue lake
where the anchor-rope, cut, lets go.

*

Not finding words, study the lines
as the pale green tulip-stems
bend downward in elegant curves.

Snapshots from an Old Camera

Lower East Side, New York City, the '70s

(i)

At the all-night newsstand on Avenue B

woman with gray afro
short sleeves & bare legs
laughs   coughs
                got a
        raggedy ole quarter
        for a pint of wine?

(ii)

Moon over 9th street:

a big white shopping bag
above the wrecker's scaffold
finds the lintel
and the gargoyle,

old rubbish-picking woman
rightly convinced
there's something
to salvage

(iii)

A specter this afternoon:

an errand boy stalks down First Avenue
between piles of the *Daily News*—murders,

body count—and a showcase of silver sandals
girls wear to parties. He's coatless; his pants

droop; he holds out a woman's black suede pump,
gripping its heel like the butt of a revolver.

His eyebrows smoke slightly. His jaw shifts
like a linotype stamping hot lead:

here's a spike through her heart,
a sheath his foot can't slip into.

He's riddling the silver-necklaced throats
that pass him by, a headline someday.

(iv)

In the art gallery
the one-armed janitor,

no connoisseur,
studies

the professor's
sculpture

la main
of wrapped scrap-iron

a gap between
thumb and wrist

as if
a weapon connected

speaks

(red echo
from the emergency room)

"Look at that—
that's bad—

bad . . ."

(v)

Behind tenements
a pulley

from one
4th-floor

fire escape
to another

runs out
towels:

five flavors—
orange, lemon

cherry, lime
grape—

kids below
suck ices

stick out
their tongues

orange,
cherry,

sassing
the laundry

(vi)

Above 12th Street
a ragged curtain

of pigeon-wings
flaps in the sky's

window   blown
sideways   tilts

plunges south to
9th street   coasts

down the wind
spreading out

loose and free
over rigid

sunken sidewalks

(vii)

The Statue of Liberty
seen from the Lower East Side

where the river
curves into the harbor

evokes a vision:
a woman equals freedom

so is made a symbol
cast in bronze

stationed far off
to grow green

under salt-lash out there
in gray waters.

Don't let her
set foot on land.

(viii)

From the train
window

on the way
out of town:

backyard filled
with brown leaves

nearly burying
a pair of

old bent chairs
rusting under

the bare trees
where two

sat in summer
in the green

shade—
all that gone

as the train
picks up speed.

Part Three

SEA-LEVEL

Incident

The knife
on the film screen—

I was sixteen
class trip, informational—

slit open the
pregnant belly   flesh

fell back weak
and bloody

the sac emerged—
caesarian section—

my head roiled
red and purple—

no breath—had
to get up

turn away   stagger
out—didn't

really see
the life-saving

gloved hands
lift out the baby

blood   mucus   pain
alive—

the mother laid
open helpless—

my body mine—
alive

on the street
in hard light

without
anesthesia

Among Friends Living and Dead

for Verna Gillis
i.m. Bradford Graves, 1940-1998
Roswell Rudd, 1935-2017

Among African masks in Verna's loft
where Roswell's brassy trombone shone
and ornate Venetian candelabra stood
by the fruit- and cheese-laden board
we sat, with Francis Bacon's rotting pope
on the wall—a modern Titian's
Paul the Third—among a hundred
marks of Brad's artistic lives,
fat stones or tall on the marble counter,
round-topped table, floor,
and photo of him young in a Spanish hat,
dead *torero*, looking straight out:
Are you there? The darkness around us warmed
and we were gold in the dark.

Guitar and Violin

(I)
Granada, Albêniz

Downward splash of clear water—
notes, one by one, a
leaf into water
leaves of crystal clear light
into pure clarity of water.

(II)
The Lark Ascending, Vaughn Williams

How much one note uplifts
bird's wing of song
from bow and string
into air above the meadow
a soft horn, one calling note
to another
higher and higher.

Subway Poster

SEVENTEEN WORDS
TO SAVE YOUR LIFE
AND EVERYONE ELSE'S

DON'T FIGHT.
MEDITATE.
LOOK. LISTEN.
APPRECIATE EVERYTHING.
MAKE ART,
MAKE FRIENDS
AND
CLEAN UP AS YOU GO.

An Italianate Landmark

Night, one forgets, empowers
Metropolitan Life's white
tower at Madison and Twenty-third

that, on this overcast day,
rises undistinguished among
varyingly gray rooftops. It embeds

duty. It merges with businesslike
façades of lower buildings,
though a little higher, and

in sunshine, one remembers,
its gilded pinnacle glitters
that now looks dull, confined,

adjunct of work-driven crowds
below, business suits that hustle
to pass and push through doors

to do what they are told
needs doing, dutiful, while much—
much—goes on behind their eyes

until the time comes to leave
the buildings, join the crowd
that thickens the sidewalks

while blue night deepens. Then
the white four-sided pyramid
suddenly lights up,

its hooded apertures eyeing
the four directions, and at its peak
a tiny Greek temple supports

a flaming amber-gold turban
with white-flame topknot torch
upraised in avid splendid power.

CBGB's Claustrophobic

I am the pummeled young
crushed under flashing lights:
spots red on the drummer's arm
blue on the stubble of the guitarist's jaw
as he bends in agony, gut-doubling, and
sudden terror-blast of white spots shows
too much and dark mercy comes back.
Body rubs body. Prom-pix beauty fixes
her mouth into a black-hooded head
she clutches with both hands at the neck.
So much fear and lust de-fused
under the jackhammer pounding
of sound pounding away reflections,
consequences, the daytime stuff
that's outside the box, the black-joy
misery box, bathysphere in black ocean
because protection is needed because
you have to be in it because there every, but
every, dark body rubbed, mashed, snubbed,
longed-for is what's wanted, more body,
more loving slime, slobber, sweat, scurf, squawk
to be set free and charge up to its richest livingness
— and for a span music does it. Hammers it home.

Turntablist

(graduating high school soon)

A quiet one, graffiti on his attic bedroom walls
shout NOISE! NOISE!
in messy blue marker

and his turntables screech *let me out*

Everyone wants to beat him into shape
—their shape, which isn't his—
and he has to resist *leave me alone*

but can't say it out loud — to whom?
so machinery shrieks it louder
as if he makes his wall

a huge black canvas with house paint
slaps on it crap yellow

splat!—and icky green

with a huge brush, glues

rotting chicken bones to it,
make visual stink *Let me explode*
safely. Don't want

to run over anyone, just
mess up the old groove plug in
to giant amps

let a noise hurricane sweep
through the skull
of the planet

Let me find what's inside.

Everything to unfold, resounding.
Key in. Boot up.

Hey! Let me upload.
Now.

For the Poet's One-Hundredth

read November 8, 2003, before Carl Rakosi
and a full audience of friends in the San Francisco
Public Library (poem-lines in italics are his).

A great Zen master, Suzuki Roshi, was dying too young
not far from this city.
His students asked him: don't you regret not living long?

He said: "One hundred years of life is good.
One day of life is good."
So the basic issue is not Time (capital T)

that we celebrate but the man Carl Rakosi
and his inseparable *ka,*
the poet. A hundred poems are good,

one poem is good, if it falls out that way.
In his case it didn't, luckily,
(though luck is the wrong word.) This *ka,*

antique Egypt's immortal self, has its pyramids,
its lasting stones
stacked oddly, for he's poked a hole

in the solid edifice of art, having
knocked it off its capital A.
To wit, witty: master of the short form,

he writes "Epitaph on the Short Form:"

Here lies the Augustan temper,
a great lord

side by side
with the lark.

Pounds of cantos were unable
to quicken them

To wit: ironic. The short form
is very much alive. Besides, how short is short?
We were talking about the good,
which is neither short nor long, neither
an aphorism nor—God help us—
a theory. A sparrow is chirping in the garden

and thus spins out meditations or
a Satyricon. Ancient marble dust
shakes out onto the modern threshold

to say after all *There was a man*
in the land of Ur, Abraham
our father. *Shema Ysrael*—and the rabbi prays

a modest prayer
for the responsibilities of his office

Such responsibilities for *le mot juste*,
la branche juste, the half-serious loop
between referent and idea?
Well,

inward is outward in ongoing curiosity:

What can be compared
to light
in which leaves darken
after rain
fierce green?
like Rousseau's jungle:
any minute
the tiger head

Will poke through
the foliage
peering
at experience

A white tiger's head not quite
metaphysical, for there is
the eye, memory, thousands

of written words in thirty-six thousand
five hundred twenty-seven days,
counting leap year's extras,

taking responsibility for the Word.
How can there be
closure here? *Now that I am old*
must I give up

paradoxes and
crossed signals

and fish for poignancy
in a safe persona?

Is there no wisdom,
only common sense?

So what's wrong with common sense?
Or the commonplace?
Suzuki roshi said to meditators

on their cushions: look
at the frog. He sits
just as we do. Carl Rakosi says:

There goes Bashō

balls and all,
into the pond again.

Splashes, Plophh!
like an old frog.

Must be Spring,
and I'm in a small
mode of music

through a phonograph
cartridge.

Solid briar root,
varnish,
beetle's chitin

enter soundlessly
as a mystique
into Orfeo's

perfect system,
passing on a stylus
from the earth

into art.

Must be spring this November. Something splashes, frog or tiger?

Crackle of light—

Happy birthday, Orpheus—

Two on the Path

for a poet-friend on her April birthday

I, named Lodrö Sertso, Gold Lake of Intellect,
hooked on the tusk of a woolly mammoth of a birthday
and staggering hip-deep in the slime and muck of the Dark Age,
myself a tar pit of neuroses in a bad hour
hefted out of it by a lightning flash from the mind
of the drunken father-teacher Chöggi who faces me
under the laughing photo-eye of his father-guru Khyentse
who whispers in his ear as the vajra Lady in Red
dances naked from her image into the charged air
that circles them, baring her teeth and vagina
to show the clarity of what's really happening because
the crud in the corner of my eyes needs to be flicked away,
within this seizure of mutterings and word-labor
that tears the cervix of this bloody computer attempting
its record (damned typo, wrong screen) in this sea
of scrawled note-scraps unreadable, un-met obligations,
the derailing path of distractions—so what else is new?—
I, in this flux of non-essence phantasm in sweatpants,
holes in the sweater, dry mouth talking talking — it's noon
on Saturday, the loudmouths in the patio below
have already begun their weekend bender—I
regress and seat myself on the red birthing-cushion
to cast the I Ching for my dharma sister Anne
She-Who-Carries-the-Broom, the Voice Who Tunes
The Primal Scream, etc., and deliver to her the oracle:

The trigrams: the *JOYOUS* above the *AROUSING*
The hexagram: Sui, *FOLLOWING*, whose attribute is *GLADNESS.*
FOLLOWING the path of poetry *has supreme success.*
Perseverance furthers. No blame.
(Confucius was sexist: ah, diviner, you'll fix that)
Thus the superior woman aroused to exuberant activity
gathers her following. The image:
Thunder in the middle of the lake.
Thus at nightfall the superior woman goes indoors
for rest and recuperation
in order to get up the next morning, board a plane,
open a notebook, text on a blackberry, think think think
and hold on, stick to the path of poetry, the ship, the bridge,
the fork-lift, the ambulance as it dodges debris,
the weapon that hacks its way through the Kaliyuga.
Great is the meaning of the time of following.
Great is the meaning of women who never surrender.

“A Concise Definition of Answers”

on a print by Paula Rego: a note for her birthday.
The title is from a poem by Blake Morrison.

There she stands, classic 12-year-old
pre-Primavera with basket on her hip—
cornucopia—in clunky schoolgirl shoes.

She gazes straight out. Nudities
of her thoughts sprawl on the ground
around her. One has breasts beginning.

Another girl with a moustache
puts on a dress—what’s he?
Where from? Some visions sleep.

At her feet a leering monkey
fucks a crow. A black cat
puts his tongue up a bird’s ass.

A lot of white space lies
below. Nearby an eagle
hangs upside down. Thorns

gnarl in a bristly corner
Behind her a semblance
of El Greco’s Toledo:

thunder-skies swim with shapes,
bodies maybe, a top hat,
an eye, blasted branches not

quite nightmare corpses, just
a distant storm. These
are not problems. She

in her short skirt has answers.
If her shoes come undone
she'll tie them up again.

She can do it, not knowing
how just yet, but the means
are there, undefined fruits

in the woman's well-woven basket.
She's the same age
every year. New clothes,

of course, another monkey
running around the studio,
though the octopus she built,

larger, stranger than
the aquarium's creature,
will catch him. No answers,

but it is not an ironic title:
no concision, either, because
no end to the pen-strokes

on the page, paint or acid,
chalk ground-in black
under the fingernails,

shapely face fixed there
ink-eyed, brushed-ink hair
transformed on the mirror-canvas.

New Year's Roses

I. You'd think enough
has been said about roses

like a red, red
is a rose is a rose is a

but no: that coral unfolding
its odors among fir branches

sweet among acrid,
garden in a forest,

a ruddier rose-orange
opens as a soft drum-note

opens a violin concerto,
Beethoven's, again and again,

or in Rosenkavalier: *ist ein Traum,*
kann es wirklich sein—

II. The roses aged, of course,
in a day or two showed

a dusty gold below the drying
wine-red lip, ochre mixed with

cadmium yellow painters use
to mute unruly pink, human

skin not being that roseate
but yellowish and shadowed

green requiring ochre, which
Monet refused, went with slashing

purple strokes, unmitigated, tangled
greens that bear up the lotus

out of the swamp when
the roses have to go.

Passing the Church of Our Lady of Pompeii on Carmine Street

The bell tolls.

At the top of steps in shadow
brass doors swing back.

Men stagger under the casket's weight.
A woman in black forces herself

to follow, her stunned pain
open to the street and sky.

I'm stopped—as then Pompeii
heard the rumbling, felt

the air grow thick, dark,
muddy ash filling

doorways, eyes, mouths,
tearing the breath out.

Caught all: the widow,
the wife, the young girl

petting her dog in the atrium,
myself, who never thought

to meet it or know it,
I, too, engulfed—

Downsizing

Had to do it. Too many books. Most must go.
Take one in hand. Judge: keep or give away, or
as executioner: destroy. Appalling! It seems
a crime to throw away a book or call it
recycling, save the paper but lose the thought—
think how they burned books and now will kill
          a woman who has one.

Start to read the book, naturally. Everything
is interesting. Start to reply to the voice
on the pages too yellow and torn to keep,
spine broken. Into the waste basket. That's
reality, too close to be mere symbol
of the skin and bone that hold the seeming self,
          the imagined "I."

In downsizing, my thoughts have grown outsized.
Don't want to say goodbye—that's what it's
all about: fear of the severance to come.
To lose the words, the thoughts, reminders,
enliveners, means to lose oneself. And that
can happen. Would saving the books, closed, unread,
          stave off that

ending? No.
                    But wait a minute, that's not what's
happening. As shelves empty, the mind empties
its clutter, feels relief, clarity, not loss.
Memories enlarge, recognitions come.
Books are friends; when they go they stay.

What I learned by reading has sunk in past knowing
          or need to pass tests.

Even the Buddhist books go because the time
has arrived they call "no more learning." Meaning
is found, those teachers said, "in symbols and acts,
not in words and books." But from books and words
I learned to act and to know that I know
I go on facing death as energized, intent to grasp,
          to comprehend

everything as the eager college student did
so long ago. Scenes of meeting re-open.
We met then, you and you and I and I
in that time and now meet again at reunions,
which are not mere events. Here
alone in my study I open a book to re-unite
          with the dead.

L'amitié passe même le tombeau, wrote
the poet H.D. in *The Gift*, a memoir
I'm keeping. The shelves, of course, are not
entirely emptied and, in truth (*"I have loved truth"*)
there was a book on sale—can't resist
a sale—*Reading Zen in the Rocks*, and so
the cycle is endless, and I must simply stop

and put this page with others in the newly cleared space.

Hospital Notes

the morning after hip replacement surgery:
stream of semi-consciousness

The clock says 6:30 a.m.
Half-woke up around 5:45
    needing to pee—
now really needy, reach to find
the remote between mattress
    and headboard
press the big button.

The aide comes
in her wine-red outfit
that tells the patient
    this woman is the helper
    who does the simple tasks,
    who makes you
    get up, takes you
    to the bathroom,
    has to watch you
    piss and shit,
    cleans your bottom
    if you can't

That failure is the fear
to be faced—scary—or memory loss,
    unable to write words
    on this page—
but have to ask her name
    having forgotten it,
        call her "Iovane"
        but she says "I'm Magda"

and brings the walker.
The chalkboard overhead says
the "practical tech assistant"
—euphemism—is
Christiane.

She asks would I rather have a bed-pan?
"No, I should practice walking"
though slow
but can follow my directions
to myself,
slowly make my way
with the walker
to the toilet.

Magda (or is she Tasha—
—hearing-aids not in)
watches to see the patient set herself
on the low toilet seat
(Mike has got a raised seat
for home, says he installed it yesterday).
Pain—a spot of pain
in the left leg, the good one,
only a spot of pain in the upper muscle

then much pain
of the upper right muscle,
the one that cramped

yesterday at nap-time,
a lot of pain—
but grip and heft myself up.
Magda steadies my left arm.

Then on both feet
in their yellow and white booties
studded brightness,
feel better
walking,
straighten my back, look up
at art on the wall,
go close.
It's a collage cut from envelope linings
to reveal yellow daisies
among blue tall-grass spikes—
subtle. Hooray!—they patronize
living artists, this one possibly
a woman—
and back in bed
take off reading glasses
to look again from a distance,
propping this notebook
on wadded bedclothes—

and think again:
Magda got Christiane
whose name is on the board
officially to help me.

She wears her identity card and flash-keys
          pinned with a ruby sparkling brooch
          that matches her wine-red outfit.
It is right, this gem: a mark of pride
          and practicality, not the official N.Y.U.
          long purple lanyard that hangs
          and bangs her keys in the way
                    of whatever the aide is doing—

She pulls me upright.
to walk more, little more
          steps with the walker—
                    look up—want to see
          where I am.
Looking at the board say,
          "Christiane, my name there
          is misspelled Agustin:
          it is Augustine
          with 'au' like the month of August
          not like the Spanish first name."
She wipes the board
and corrects it.

The walker at bed-side
lower myself with my hands,
          my own strength—
pride!
          —try to lift my own legs
and also can do that
          for now

* * *

Top muscle of the right leg
hurts again—groggy writing—
it did not work—hurt—strange sound in the hall
        —the breakfast cart
        already?   It goes away—
        must be a floor-sweeper cleaning.

It is right, this sound of cleanliness
        "next to God" in virtue, as is said,
        mark of care in the hospital

to keep off the wandering germs
        that look for bloody incisions
        in the vulnerable flesh that has been
                opened up, a necessary opening
                to repair, to endanger . . .

Sleepy writing
        to remember how the pain
        came and went.
Jenny, who appeared when Christiane
        called her, the nurse in charge,
        said that my pain was 5,
                after she asked was it 3 or 4
                on a scale of one to ten.
"No, it changes—sometimes
        it is sharp, sometimes
        not at all—"

Jenny says—(Jenny is her short name;
    her I.D. says Yevenia)
    Do you have dizziness?
    shortness of breath?
She is using a checklist.
    "No—none."

She says we'll call your pain 3,
    we usally (typo for usually)
    give oxycodone for 5.
"No, tylenol extra-strength
    is what I want for pain—"
                pen drops

and—
    and it's been a long time since Jenny left,
        grope for the remote
        under the mattress,
    push the buzzer.

All help returns.

Witness

Normal night ate   sushi went to   bank deposited check
bought antacids at   drugstore before 10   came back up
three flights sat   at desk opened   checkbook to make
donation to college   wrote it noted   faint cry out
back not usual   great concussive thump   walls shudder like
earthquake but nothing   follows nothing falls   no sounds not
like anything else—what was it?   a moment's silence
harsh throat-tearing cries   push back curtain   can't see hear
voices—"someone fell" "Where?" "There—*there*!" "from the
hospital residence" "—call 911" can't see   past curtain climb
onto desk take   down curtain unhook   window shade push
up fire-escape latch   gate window stuck   hard to open
push it up   get head out   into cold look
down onto black   tarred roof of   hospital parking garage
two stories below   between our old   tenement and new
high-rise as black   figures parkas climb   out of lighted
second-floor window   into roiled darkness   screams shrieks forms
moving shapes formless   struggle heave roll   side to side
            AAHHHNN AHHNN   AHH AHH   screams
don't stop go   on as other   black shapes hooded
police bundle her   woman long hair   through window sobs
out of sight   flashlight appears on   the roof circling
passes over pale   supine body fair   young male white
shirt khaki trousers   body slightly less   dark than darkness
around it voices   next door fire-escape   windows above opposite
open curious heads   lean out fourth   fifth sixth floor
murmur withdraw as   bulky shadows move   and white line
spray-paint appears   around the corpse   big crude cartoon
defines crime scene   shadow kneels two   flash bulb bursts
shapes two three   climb back inside   one lone patrolman

hatless left wanders   moving around away   from the body
not to look   but nothing to   do or see
it's over it's
                    dark   cold   cold   he is useless
strolls to the   low street wall   sees nothing down
there but silence   he climbs back   through the window
into light it's   not right not   to keep watch
over the dead   someone should stay   the patrolman sits
inside at a   desk writing notes   doesn't see how
priapism sets in   khaki crotch arisen   in death's grisly
erection parody of   life-creating love   as witnesses at
hangings have reported   doesn't see how   living isn't ended
with death doesn't   see the body   shrink as if
black tar sucks   it down how   it still moves
someone should stay   eyes open here   through frozen night
doing nothing how   slow those who   should show up
and take care   of this corpse   it's silent empty
                                        cold
                                                give up
draw back into   warmth close window   flip escape-gate latch
pull curtains together   sit at desk   stamp envelope for
donation get up   again part curtains   look: body still
lying there alone   much later no   body just white
outline its simulacrum.
                    Two days later   *New York Post*
short notice states   facts name age   occupation resident at
hospital had fight   with girlfriend jumped   from the ninth
floor an accident   the gracious church   must have judged
granting Catholic burial   for many weeks   the ghost-shape
lay on the   rotting tar roof   before summer rains came.

The Man Who Sleeps Under the Scaffold

East 18th Street and First Avenue, New York City

(i)

Saw him last week
late night—
now it's 19 degrees (*where is he sleeping*?)

His gear roped under
black tarps and bags
in a shopping cart
includes a sign
upside down (*no other writing*)

"Hope for the future" (*not much)*

(ii)

Blizzard covers the city.
White fills the streets.
Scaffold protects the black

packaging of his life (*he is resourceful*)
He will come back—when?
to live if the weather *(New York City)*

lets him. If
they don't decide
to bring down right now

the empty building (*when will they?*)
the scaffold upholds,
not a place

to live anyhow, now
or in the future (*impersonal)*
but a hospital to help,

offices maybe, or labs (*but not beds*)

(iii)

Haven't seen him
recently—gray rain-suit,
hooded face, grizzled.

Thousands not seen
note unnoticed spots
in plain view,

cover themselves
with black garbage bags—
what else?

Keep on. I count on him
to manage.

It's getting colder.

(iv)

In this savage cold
he sleeps, it seems,

somewhere else
I hope, but because

it's Martin Luther King Day
—he looks like M.L.K—

his gear is topped
with an American flag,

its frail flagpole
tied by red string

suspended from a nail
or crack overhead

in the scaffold.

Let us salute his flag.

(v)

Above the black tarps
lashed to the scaffold poles
a shocking-pink dustpan
on a long handle makes
its dominion—

or made it.
Today it's gone.
Where does he take it?
What dust scrape into it?

(vi)

Walking south on First Avenue
from East 37th street I came
to East 34th—big intersection.

On the corner stationed as if
to be picked up soon, a black
tarp-bundled shopping cart

or rather a skid, rope-bound
like the one under the scaffold,
with black garbage bags too—

a monument, spontaneous sculpture,
a statement. Does it go unread?
Next to it, farther along

on the gray concrete,
another stony-black block
in public storage. By it

a man lies sleeping.
Is this city art unseen?
Passersby sweep their eyes
carefully over and away.

This free space must be
preserved for them, I think.
That little we can do.

Not happy with this thought.

(vii)

Yesterday noon coming down our stoop
I glanced away from the man
under the scaffold. He didn't want
to be seen pulling a comforter,
fluffy, cream-colored, out of his stash,
not seen as he sets himself up
to sleep.
        Will he pull the black tarp
        over himself, and look as if
        he is only the package on the sidewalk?
I head off the other way
past the brownstones with stained-glass
doors and marble-paved front steps
whose owners have gone south for the winter.

(viii)

Three snapshots:

Snap one:
        9:00 p.m.   a blonde woman
        stands talking to the man
        under the bare light-bulb

Snap two:
6:30 p.m.   he sweeps litter
out of the gutter.
Four young men, Ivy League,
shriek and dance in the street

Snap three:
midday   no sign of him
stash disarranged,
flag points downward.

Did he hear Trump's speech?

(ix)

The black monument is tidy today,
heavyweight contractor bags tightly strapped,

two shocking-pink dustpans with green handles
propped on the brick wall under the scaffold

tucked in behind, meant to be inconspicuous —

23 degrees and getting colder—

he must have gone to—

where?

(x)

Dusk. Stepping out of a taxi
I can't see
the black heap
in the shadows cast
by the lamp
at a defunct
doorway
or possibly defunct:
earlier there
workmen jackhammered open
a square of sidewalk
three feet deep.

For now, it's closed up.

We're all safe, I guess.

(xi)

The black monument
hunkers down
by the building

that's going
to waste, empty,
decomposing to dust.

The gray-dusted black hoard
        chained to a scaffold pipe-post
                waits, gathered

to be taken
        to better living space.
                Or no.

The black bags
        don't go anywhere.
                Not yet.

They're discards saved
        to show that someone
                owns them:

"I own, I save, I come
        to check;
                therefore I am."

(xii)

He is.
He is where
he is.

He is many.
They are where
he is,

seen everywhere
we are and where we
are not,

sealed doorway
unused doorstep
subway hallway

Sixth to Seventh Avenue
here or there
a bundle of one

or two lies
face aside—no socks,
piss-smell—

we go fast.
We go where
they are not.

They sleep
underground,
trade off safe

for warm
maybe find a
begrimed friend

to trade words with.
That's not so small
a thing where

they are, and
we are, each one
a grain of gravel

blown into the wind
away   though
there is no

"away"

(xiii)

Today a white plastic bag
that hangs on the side
of the packed cart

has been torn open as if
by a marauder, man
or dog, for a part of

a sandwich, a few chips,
messed-up food bits, not
much but not theirs. It's

not right, even if only
a squirrel or bird
swept down from the scaffold

to eat — not right that
so much goes unprotected.
It's a street story

I read too often, obsessed.
It's not right—

but someone must see

(xiii)

Saw him at noon at his stash.
He wears skier's padded clothing
tight, insulated, logo on the sleeve
—action man!—opening a can
or jar, food maybe.
I look away

so he feels safe, maybe—

(xiv)

Monday 9 p.m. quiet night,

holiday over, few cars
along the avenue

bought a chocolate bar
at the newsstand

on the way home,
tucked it under a flap

in the black tarp. Groan
UH—UNHH

Good God, he *does* sleep there—

"just something
for when you wake up"

Felt bad.
Now he feels unsafe—

(xv)

Mr. President,

I am an American veteran of wars abroad,
who sleeps concealed as trash
under the scaffold
in the half-coffin I've made
outside of your real estate,
my hope for the future not yet quite
turned upside down

On the brick wall of my bedroom
a mural of my neighborhood
painted by P.S. 40 students
displays my protectors:
the school crossing guard
the mothers with strollers
the kids themselves with glasses, backpacks
the streetlight's yellow pole
commanding "stop!" and "go!" for safety,
the old lady who totters and obeys the law.

The scaffold turns at the corner
onto the avenue where huge trucks roll
food, fuel, appliances toward
the tunnels and bridges that stand
stable in deep waters. They supply
everyone's needs.
                                        Your destroyer's pen,
Mr. President, doesn't destroy them.
The suppliers are practical, work around
the pasted warnings "Keep out".
Passersby maintain the sidewalks
on which they walk. The newsstand sells
flowers and *The New York Times*.
            Headlines: women sue, hostile climate,
            run for Senate—

                            Mr. President,
            I am an American woman
who sleeps in the building
next to the scaffold, across the street
from Eve the Psychic—$5 readings—and
the Korean full-service laundry.

            I am a veteran of hidden wars.
            I claim reality as my estate.
            I am the other millions.
            We read signs. We clean fully.

A rain-cloud is rising over your golf course, Mr. President—
            "Look!
            We are coming through—"

January 12 - February 5, 2018

EPILOGUE

Return

to Colorado in summer after a class reunion,
looking out from the cabin deck again

Every gift that our small women's college gave us
is here on this clear morning after night rain
rare on this high dry mountainside getting drier,

a desert place, drought-ridden, getting hotter,
like the rest of the planet, forever,
and will never come back—no return possible—

Yet return is my theme:
see: it's happening here—after rain,
weedy greens cover the slope, and yellow clover

whose skinny stems shoot out at awkward angles,
head-high, freighted with little gold blossoms. Each,
seen close up, contains a tiny laughing face,

new thoughts, new life of the mind now sprung
out of its deep store-house of the known
and unknown, the yet-to-be empowered.

The universe has a bias toward creation,
says the old lama from Tibet, a lost country
whose mountains are high as these, and higher

but are here—as you are—with me, the living
and the dead, as we were, and these wayward greens
were—as they still are—tended lawns surrounding

walls cut from mountain stone to house us, provide
doorways to labs and libraries, protectors of truth.
"Truth also is the pursuit of it," says the old poet,

but now truth pursues me, pushes this transient hand
across the page. Poetry is eternal. Light and air
stay on, true and living. The clover's sweet aroma

fills the blue sky. The sun is moving my mind,
your mind, the mind of anyone, anywhere, whoever
needs light to look, to see, to do, to carry out

tikkun olam, healing of the world, as Torah
and Kabbalah tell us in the ancient language
of a chosen people, and we, also chosen,

have tried to carry out, one way or another,
through years of our branching lives.
                    Though I am no one,

a voice only, I speak as joined with you
and with you place this book as offering
to helmeted Athena in the great hall

alongside clay owls, sunglasses, a lei, a shawl,
paper scraps inscribed with students' tributes
to her grace that helps them pass their tests,

our tests that continue, losses, fears. *The time
is swift and will be gone.* The sun passes its zenith,
the clover's yellows blanch in the heat, but thoughts

go on creating and re-creating themselves:
what can be done for countries under destruction,
cities in rubble, women and men with their children

thrown up on Athena's own shores, who walk,
if allowed, toward higher ground? *Pallas Athena,*
thea, goddess of cities and wisdom to govern,

listen up: be with us as the day goes,
which it must, the grass cools, and shadows
lengthen across the valley. On the path tall pines

darken against darkening sky. A topmost branch
changes shape. A great horned owl turns her head
slowly toward us, feathered horns unmistakable

distinct from the tree but inseparable from it.
She inspects us. I hold her in mind and eye
a long time. Please stay: *veritatem dilexi.*

She spreads her wings and lifts herself into space
as illimitable by night as by day.
Out of sight, she is here, our protector,

this her forest, her stony slope and weedy
meadow, her drought that tests us, this
her domain that has given us all we have,

these gifts, knowledge and power
and friends, ours—look, it's happening,
our lasting connections—
        l'amitié passe même le tombeau—

ancient wisdom with us to the end.

Index of Titles and First Lines

Titles are in italics.

ABOUT THE AUTHOR

JANE AUGUSTINE is a poet, critic, short story writer, visual/sound poetry performance artist and scholar of women in modernity. Born in Berkeley, California, in 1931, she published her first poems in the Berkeley Daily Gazette at age seven, and, in more recent years, six books of poetry, the latest *High Desert* from Dos Madres Press (2019), all collected in this volume. Editor of *The Mystery by H.D.* (2009) and *The Gift by H.D.: The Complete Text* (1998; reissued pb 2021) she is also the author of numerous essays on modern and contemporary poets including H.D., Mina Loy, Lorine Niedecker, William Bronk and Robert Duncan. She has twice been awarded Fellowships in Poetry from the New York State Council on the Arts and has held the H.D. Fellowship at Beinecke Library, Yale University. She has taught at Pratt Institute, Brooklyn, New York University and The New School in New York City, and Naropa University in Boulder, Colorado. She lives with her husband, the poet and critic Michael Heller, in Manhattan and Westcliffe, Colorado.

Other books by Jane Augustine
published by Dos Madres Press

High Desert (2019)

For the full Dos Madres Press catalog:
www.dosmadres.com